Debt, Deficits and Exchange Rates

Debt, Deficits and Exchange Rates

Essays on Financial Interdependence
and Development

Helmut Reisen

OECD Development Centre, Paris

Edward Elgar

Published by
Edward Elgar Publishing Limited
Gower House
Croft Road
Aldershot
Hants GU11 3HR
England

Edward Elgar Publishing Company
Old Post Road
Brookfield
Vermont 05036
USA

British Library Cataloguing in Publication Data
Reisen, Helmut
  Debt, Deficits and Exchange Rates: Essays
  on Financial Interdependence and
  Development
  I. Title
  332.4

Library of Congress Cataloguing in Publication Data
Reisen, Helmut.
    Debts, deficits, and exchange rates: essays on financial
  interdependence and development/Helmut Reisen.
      p. cm.
    Includes index.
    1. Foreign exchange rates—Developing countries 2. Debts,
  Public—Developing countries. 3. Finance, Public—Developing
  countries. I. Title.
  HG3877.R44 1994
  332.4'56'091724—dc20

ISBN 1 85278 930 1

Printed in Great Britain at the University Press, Cambridge

Contents

Figures and Tables

Figures

Tables

Preface

Within the Organisation for Economic Co-operation and Development (OECD), the Development Centre is a focal point for the study of developing countries' problems and of the interdependence between OECD Member and non-member countries. Operating on the basis of three-year programme cycles, the selection of research themes is guided by two major criteria. First, research should deal with emerging issues that will become increasingly important over the next three to five years and, second, it should have immediate policy relevance for both OECD and non-OECD countries. The essays brought together in this volume, written over the past five years, satisfy both these criteria. They have a common theme: policy analyses of current international monetary problems in the Pacific area and in Latin America, and will appeal, more particularly, to policy-makers in central banks and finance ministries and to economists in international organisations, academia and commercial banks.

These essays provide innovative approaches to unsolved policy questions. They are firmly rooted in economic theory and solidly backed by empirical evidence. Their author, Helmut Reisen, who heads a major project on financial issues at the OECD Development Centre, has been active in helping to shift the focus of ongoing policy debates: from foreign exchange constraint to fiscal constraint in heavily indebted countries, from foreign to domestic public debt, from debt overhang to liquidity constraint, from interest rate to foreign exchange risk in debt management, from 'extravagant' exchange rate regimes to the possibilities for judicious exchange rate management. The essays selected for this volume present a design for financial reform to foster development without compromising stability.

Jean Bonvin
OECD Development Centre

Part 1

Public Finance, Exchange Rates and Incentives

Public Finance, Exchange Rates and Incentives

The first part of the collection brings together a number of essays dealing with various aspects of the developing country debt crisis of the 1980s. Most analyses of sovereign external debt had assumed that the capacity to raise foreign exchange revenue was the binding constraint in the repayment decision. By contrast, my prior work in that area had focused on the fiscal constraint since the repayment of foreign debt — most of which was owned by the government — had to be financed by the internal transfer of resources from the private to the public sector.* Today, most observers agree that the binding constraint was fiscal, not external.

The first essay was presented at a World Bank symposium in January 1989, just two months (accidentally?) before the Brady Plan of debt reduction was unveiled. My essay calls attention to the growth of domestic public debt in developing countries with a high level of external debt and to the implications of high domestic debt burdens for stabilization policies. I first ask why there was a debt crisis in developing countries, but not in OECD countries which at times have much higher debt-to-GDP ratios. My answer, vividly rejected by my discussant Vito Tanzi (IMF) at the conference but confirmed later in an IMF Occasional Paper on public debt, focuses on external transfers coupled with fiscal rigidities, high domestic interest rates and massive devaluation of the real exchange rates. For a realistic remedy to contain the rise in government debt, I finally discuss how fiscal adjustment can foster growth at the same time that it minimizes real depreciation of the exchange rate and reduces the cost of domestic public debt.

The second essay has been motivated by an important flaw in the currency pool of the World Bank from which it has lent money to its developing country clients. In the past, lending by the World Bank has tended to increase foreign exchange risk exposure for the benefit of a very question-

---

*   For an extensive analysis of the fiscal constraint see Reisen, Helmut and Axel van Trotsenburg (1988), *Developing Country Debt: The Budgetary and Transfer Problem*, OECD Development Centre Studies, Paris, and Reisen, Helmut (1989), *Public Debt, External Competitiveness, and Fiscal Discipline*, Princeton Studies in International Finance, no. 66, Princeton University, Princeton, N.J.

able reduction in the pure interest cost of the Bank's lending. Calculations for Indonesia (which is mostly indebted in the Japanese yen but earns mostly in US dollar-denominated export markets) show how it can best hedge its debt portfolio against the risks of exchange rate changes among key currencies. The hedge could have saved Indonesia's government 10 billion dollars during 1985-88, but had it followed the World Bank's debt management practices, it would have lost 6 billion dollars compared with its actual debt structure.

The debt overhang proposition, first outlined by Jeffrey Sachs of Harvard University, had established that the existence of a heavy debt burden would reduce the incentive for debtor countries to adjust. This widely held proposition had given an important rationale for the 1989 switch in international debt management from the Baker to the Brady plan, emphasizing debt relief rather than new money for problem debtors. An alternative hypothesis blames the lack of investment on a scarcity of financial resources as a country's savings are drained off by a net transfer. The third essay, written jointly with Bert Hofman, provides empirical evidence which rejects the debt overhang hypothesis but is in line with the credit constraint hypothesis. This finding was bad news for the Brady Plan as cutting the size of the debt would not by itself be enough to raise investment and growth.

The fourth essay, originally presented at the 1990 annual meeting of the *Verein für Socialpolitik* (the German economic association), gives an early evaluation of the Brady Plan as the plan has been applied to Mexico. Based on the sovereign risk approach, the essay first establishes that adjustment incentives derive from the government's comparison of savings from default with surpluses they can obtain from the Brady Plan. A calculation of the Brady Plan effects on Mexico finds that the direct effects of the plan on the external transfer has been weak, but it improved confidence and thus lowered the cost of Mexico's domestic debt. The essay predicts that Mexico is quite special and that the Brady Plan will be less successful in other countries.

The final essay of Part 1 leaves the developing debt issue behind. Written for a symposium organized by the OECD and the IMF, the paper explores under-researched interactions between public finance and foreign direct investment (FDI). The essay finds supply rather than demand factors to be relevant for the global allocation of direct investment. Unfortunately, however, the variation of global FDI activity (rather than the existence of FDI *per se*) has been left quite unexplained by the literature. I also suggest exploring tax avoidance strategies, both by resident and foreign investors, rather than an analysis based on statutory taxes to arrive at hard conclusions about the impact of taxation to FDI flows towards the South.

1. Public Debt, North and South*

1. Introduction

Economic theory provides little, if any, guidance on whether there is a debt ratio critical for solvency. In the forefront of high-debt OECD countries — Belgium, Ireland, and Italy — public debt relative to GDP is considerably higher than in prominent developing debtor countries. Yet for these OECD countries, insolvency has not developed, although the high debt generates considerable macroeconomic problems there also. Based on the recent experience of Brazil, Mexico, the Republic of Korea, Indonesia, and the three high-debt OECD countries, this essay will provide a somewhat eclectic and anecdotal discussion on some relevant aspects of high public debt. First, why has public debt as a fraction of GDP still risen in spite of rationed foreign lending and efforts at fiscal consolidation? Major debt determinants are: fiscal rigidities because of failure to broaden tax bases and to cut government consumption; high interest rates and low GDP growth, both largely explained by the nature of fiscal adjustment; massive real exchange rate devaluation (to generate the external transfer); and high swings in key currencies' value. Second, how can the rise in government debt be contained in a time consistent way and how can fiscal adjustment foster growth while minimizing real exchange rate depreciation and reducing the cost of domestic public debt? 'Easy' alternatives to growth-oriented fiscal adjustment — inflationary blow-out of domestic debt, unilateral default taxation of bond returns, and certain foreign debt reduction schemes — are dismissed as effective instruments for a sustainable reduction of total public debt.

2. Why Government Debt Is Still Rising

Because of different definitions of the public sector, comparisons of public debt ratios are very precarious. A comparison of changes in debt ratios is less arbitrary. Table 1.1 demonstrates for the 1980s the sharp rise in government debt as a fraction of GDP in all countries except the Republic of

*   Originally published in Husain, I. and I. Diwan (eds), *Dealing with the Debt Crisis*, The World Bank, Washington, D.C., 1989, pp. 116-127.

5

Korea. Except for Indonesia, where domestic debt is nonexistent and Italy, which has almost no foreign debt, the structure of public debt is now quite similar for such countries as Brazil, Mexico, Belgium, and Ireland. At first sight the picture is puzzling: the highest debt ratio is in Belgium and Ireland, where there is no 'debt crisis'. In Brazil, Mexico, and Indonesia, the reduction in foreign borrowing has accompanied a rapidly rising foreign debt ratio. External transfers have done nothing to reduce government indebtedness when they were prematurely imposed from abroad.

Table 1.1   Net public debt, 1981 and 1987 (percentage of GDP)

	Changes, 1981 to 1986-87			Levels, 1986-87		
Country	Domestic	Foreign	Total	Domestic	Foreign	Total
Brazil	12.2	12.1	24.3	20.5	26.1	46.6
Mexico	28.5	31.1	59.6	40.4	53.4	93.8
Indonesia	n.a	42.7	42.7	n.a.	53.0	53.0
Korea, Rep. of	1.2	-0.8	0.4	6.1	8.3	14.4
Belgium	21.5	11.1	32.6	92.6	21.3	113.9
Ireland	21.1	19.9	41.0	78.3	51.0	129.3
Italy	32.0	1.1	33.1	74.8	2.0	76.8

Note: Foreign public debt is net of official foreign exchange reserves. Domestic debt is net of money base. For Brazil and Mexico, debt stocks at year-end have been deflated by the consumer price index (1980=100) at the end of each respective year. They have then been divided by real GDP in 1980 prices. Data for Italy are based on new national accounts.

Sources: Banco Central do Brasil, *Brazil Economic Program*; Banco de Mexico, *Indicadores Económicos*; World Bank data; IMF, *International Financial Statistics* (for the Republic of Korea); OECD, Economic Surveys for Belgium, Ireland and Italy.

The link between the external transfer of foreign exchange from debtor countries' governments to foreign creditors and the internal transfer of resources from the private to the public sectors can be well understood by regrouping the government budget identity, which shows the link between the public borrowing requirement (fiscal deficit) and external and internal sources of finance.[1]

(1) $\qquad (r^*b^*-\dot{b}^*)e = (t-g) + (t^*-g^*)e - rb + M/P + b$

where:

r,r*=   the domestic and foreign interest rates respectively,
b,b*=   the domestic and foreign public net debt respectively,
$\dot{b},\dot{b}^*$= new additions to the domestic and foreign public net debt respectively,
g,g*=   noninterest public spending in the traded and nontraded goods sectors respectively,
t,t*=   tax revenues on traded and nontraded goods respectively,
e=   the exchange rate (relative price of traded goods in terms of nontraded goods), and
M/P=   the increase in real base money.

The left-hand side in equation (1) represents the external public transfer, which is given by the difference between interest payments on net foreign debt (gross debt minus foreign exchange reserves) and net new foreign lending. This quantity must equal the domestic public balance — on the right-hand side of equation (1) — which is composed of (i) sources of funds: taxes on traded and nontraded goods, money creation, and new domestic debt; (ii) uses of funds: interest on domestic debt and public spending on traded or nontraded goods.[2] To identify exactly where the debt problem lies, equation (1) must be transformed into a debt-dynamics equation:

(2) $\qquad x_t = x_{t-1}[(1-f)r + f(r^*+e) - n] - [(t-g) + (t^* - g^*)e] - (p+n)m$

where:

x=   the total public debt ratio to GDP,
f=   the percentage share of foreign debt in total public debt,
n=   the growth rate of GDP,
p=   the inflation rate,
m=   the ratio of base money to GDP,

and where the other variables introduced above are now expressed in percentages of GDP. Equation (2) reveals that the public debt ratio rises as long as the difference between the interest burden on public debt and GDP growth is not compensated by a surplus in the noninterest budget plus monetary finance.

Table 1.2   Debt determinants (average, end-1983 to end-1987)

Country	Primary deficit (percentage of GDP)[a]	Real interest less GDP growth (per cent)[b]	Real annual devaluation (per cent)[c]	Share of foreign debt in total debt	Seignorage and inflation tax, end-1987 (percentage of GNP)[d]
Brazil	0.7	2.3	2.0	0.56	1.8
Mexico	-3.9	9.7	6.6	0.57	1.5
Indonesia	1.2	2.1	18.2	0.99	0.7
Korea, Rep. of	0.9	-0.8	5.1	0.58	0.4
Ireland	1.0	2.5	-5.8	0.39	0.8
Italy	3.2	2.5	n.t.	0.02	1.8

n.t. Not taken.
[a] The primary deficit in Brazil excludes interest payments for foreign public debt from the operational public sector borrowing requirement. In all other cases, it excludes all interest payments from the nominal public deficit. A minus sign denotes a surplus.
[b] Real interest is the weighted average of the real domestic and foreign interest rate on public debt. For Brazil and Mexico, only foreign interest have been considered.
[c] Real annual devaluation is based on effective exchange rates (geometric averages based on moving currency debt weights), adjusted for domestic inflation.
[d] Seignorage and inflation tax are defined as changes in the inflation-adjusted money tax times the annual rate of inflation, as a percentage of GDP in 1980 prices.
Source: See Table 1.1.

Table 1.2 helps to explain why the debt-income ratio stopped growing in Korea and rose rapidly elsewhere during the 1980s. Korea could afford a primary deficit (albeit a moderate one) because extraordinary GDP growth moved ahead of interest rates. Mexico, in contrast was the only country to run a primary surplus (almost 4 per cent of GDP), but it did not offset the combined impact of negative growth, high interest rates, and (summing up the fluctuations of its real exchange rate) heavy debt-weighted devaluation. The foreign exchange rate is an important debt determinant with two components: local currency devaluation relative to the dollar to improve external competitiveness (to generate external transfers or cope with other external shocks), and movements in the dollar value of key currencies (like the yen or the deutsche mark). The foreign exchange rate was crucial in Indonesia, where most public debt is in hard currencies (such as the yen), and where all public debt is foreign. Before 1984 (when rationed lending forced debtor countries to switch their trade balances from deficit to surplus), the exchange rate also had a major impact on public debt ratios in all problem debtor countries. Monetary finance did not help in Brazil and Mexico (despite high inflation) to transfer more real resources from the private to the public sectors as it did in Italy, where inflation returned to single-digit levels. High inflation taxes were almost outpaced by negative seignorage since the demand for real base money fell rapidly.

3. Tax Collection, Noninterest Spending, and Inflation

When is there a public debt problem? The intertemporal budget identity provides no answer to that question because it is compatible with cases of ever increasing indebtedness. More binding is Spaventa's definition of feasibility: 'If there are perceived social and political limits to the government's ability to reduce expenditure and to increase taxation net of transfers. . . there are also limits to the level of the debt ratio which is compatible with a credible commitment on the part of the government to meet the intertemporal constraint' (1988, p. 16).

Spaventa's definition explains why public debt is more likely to turn pathologic in many developing countries than it does in richer countries. Tax ratios of developing countries tend to be much lower — less than half of the average tax ratio of industrial countries. There have been rare instances among developing countries (like Indonesia) where it has been raised by several percentage points of GDP, as has happened in some developed countries like Ireland and Italy (see Table 1.3).

Why has there been so little tax adjustment in problem debtor countries? There are at least three views on that question. First, supply-siders would relate disappointing tax collection to the microeconomic details of tax structures, in particular to marginal tax rates and the real income level to which these rates apply (Reynolds, 1985). Table 1.4 examines this claim, showing the top marginal rates for personal income taxes, the associated taxable income threshold (in thousands of dollars), the ratio of this income to per capita GDP (as a proxy for bracket creep), and the fiscal yield of personal income tax as a percentage of GDP. Tax pressures intensified (in the sense that top tax rates were applied to lower income) in Brazil, Belgium, and Ireland, but did not raise tax revenue in Brazil. Personal income tax is an important source of revenue in OECD countries, but it is a negligible revenue source in the South. Table 1.4 also shows that reduction of top rates (Korea, Indonesia) and of bracket creep (Indonesia) may produce more tax

Table 1.3   Nonoil tax receipts, 1981 and 1986-87 (percentage of GDP)

Country/average	1981	1986-87
Brazil	23.6	21.8
Mexico (nonoil)	10.6	10.5
Indonesia (nonoil)	5.9	8.1
Korea, Rep. of	18.2	18.2
Belgium	42.8	45.2
Ireland	38.8	44.3
Italy	32.9	38.9
OECD average	35.7	36.0

Sources: World Bank data; OECD for OECD countries.

revenues, even though the increase has been moderate. But the table does not explain why the fiscal yield on personal income tax has been almost nonexistent in Argentina and Brazil, or why there was no adjustment during the 1980s in contrast with other sample countries, including Korea and Indonesia.

A second view holds that depressed tax revenues have in part been the immediate consequence of the debt crisis. Lower consumption, profits, wages, per capita incomes, and imports, mostly unavoidable for effectively restraining overall demand, also meant shrinking tax bases. Moreover, the Tanzi effect — important losses of real tax revenues associated with inflation acceleration — was confirmed in problem debtor countries. Since progressive income taxes represent only a small share of total tax revenue in developing countries, fiscal drag is insignificant. Much of taxes levied with specific rates and the long lags in collection lead to inflation-induced losses for the governments (Tanzi, 1977). But automatic stabilizers do not tell the full story.

Low tax ratios and standard tax rates, bracket creeps and low fiscal yield suggest a third view: the failure to broaden the tax base is crucial in explaining persistent debt-servicing problems in many developing debtor countries. Administrative and technical bottlenecks in tax assessment, levying, and collection prevent tax revenues from rising, and powerful interest groups have

Table 1.4   *Personal income taxes: top rates and fiscal yield*

Country	Maximum individual tax rates[a]				Threshold ratio 1987[b]	Fiscal revenue[c]	
	1980		1987			1980	Latest
Argentina	45	(73.7)	45	(62.3)	26	0.0	0.0
Brazil	55	(76.4)	50	(15.6)	7	0.2	0.2
Mexico	55	(65.8)	60	(46.4)	27	2.4	2.0
Indonesia	50	(15.4)	35	(50.0)	86	0.4	0.7
Korea, Rep. of	89	(173.2)	55	(73.0)	25	2.0	2.4
Belgium		-	67	(140.4)	10	14.1	14.3
Ireland		-	58	(22.3)	3	10.9	13.1
Italy		-	62	(462.9)	35	7.5	11.4

[a] Maximum individual tax rates (percentages) and associated taxable income (in thousands of US dollars). Exchange rates used are period averages.
[b] Income at which the top rate applies divided by per capita GDP.
[c] Fiscal revenues from personal income tax as a percentage of GDP.
Sources: Coopers & Lybrand, *1988 International Tax Summaries*; IMF, *Government Finance Yearbook*.

often prevented tax reform to abolish tax holidays and exemptions. This became particularly apparent in Brazil in late 1987 when the finance minister resigned after trying unsuccessfully to enforce a tax reform to enlarge the tax base. The architect of Mexico's tax reform, Francisco Gil Diaz (1987), reports that 'considerable political resistance' has frustrated the elimination of tax shelters for truckers, agriculture, publishers and other groups-sectors to which profits are easily relocated. In Argentina, the cigarette tax alone collected 25 per cent more money than the profits, capital, and net-asset taxes combined. A mere 4.8 per cent of the companies that figure on the gains tax roll paid any tax at all in 1986.

Repeated failures of stabilization in Argentina and Brazil and interwar evidence from Europe suggest that thorough fiscal reform cannot be expected in countries in an 'unstable' political situation (Alesina 1988, pp. 34-79). In an "unstable" political situation, distributive disputes over which

taxes to increase (or which type of transfers to reduce) generate fiscal deadlocks which undermine the government's ability to increase explicit tax
revenues. This situation occurs if each group has enough power to 'block'
explicit taxes on itself but not enough political influence to impose explicit
taxes on others. This situation is to be contrasted with a 'stable' situation
where one political side controls economic policy decisions with a solid majority (say, Indonesia) or without polarization between political groups and is
thus able to impose the public debt burden on groups not represented in the
government. The degree of polarization between political groups is likely to
depend on the degree of income inequality, which tends to raise the pressure
for redistributive policies, to enhance the power of the elites because they
command more influence to resist taxes, and to reduce the size of the taxable
income classes. In Brazil, for example, the richest quintile of the population
earns 33 times more than the poorest quintile, while the respective ratio is
only 7 in Indonesia and Korea. For an interesting link between the probability of debt rescheduling and income inequality, see Berg and Sachs
(1988). Alesina's concept goes back to Keynes's Tract (1923) that was concerned with the distributional effects of a growing stock of public debt —
the domestic transfer from those who pay the taxes that service the debt
(workers, entrepreneurs) to those who hold the debt (rentiers).

The distributional impact of high public debt may well differ between
OECD countries and developing countries. To the extent that pension
schemes claim a significant part of domestic public liabilities, as is often the
case in developed countries, the taxed groups and the rentiers are identical
and the distributional concern is less warranted. This constellation is to be
contrasted with inflationary developing countries, where the poor in the informal sectors hold the noninterest part of the public debt (cash), which is
subject to considerable inflation tax, while the rich hold the high-interest part
of public debt or switch into foreign currency or real assets (for empirical
evidence on Mexico, see Gil Diaz 1987). Therefore, any external debt
strategy that relies on substituting high-interest domestic debt for foreign
debt may be short-lived, not only because the public sector runs into insolvency but also for its social implications.

In problem debtor countries, external transfers have encouraged growing
domestic public debt, and fiscal deadlocks have forced their monetization.
Inflation is the residual outcome. Clark (1945) observed that for several
European countries in the interwar period there seemed to be a limit to the
tax ratio. Every time this limit was reached (at about 25 per cent), inflation
increased. The political situation was 'unstable' in Argentina and Brazil but
was not so in Chile, Colombia, Indonesia, and Korea, where noninflationary
fiscal adjustment could be observed (see Table 1.5). Mexico was an in-be-

tween case. The year after tax ratios peaked in Argentina (1980, 1986), Brazil (1982), and Mexico (1986), again at about the level reached during interwar Europe (25 per cent), inflation accelerated by 50 per cent in all three countries and doubled two years after the tax ratios peaked.

Table 1.5   Tax ratios and inflation, 1980-87

Country	Year	Tax ratio		Inflation	Multiple of inflation to year when tax ratio peaked		
		Highest	Lowest	(percentage per annum)	Year 1	Year 2	Year 3
Argentina	1980	23.3	-	101	1.5	2.4	4.9
	1984	-	18.2	627	-	-	-
	1986	22.0	-	90	1.5	n.a.	n.a.
Brazil	1982	25.1	-	98	1.7	2.0	2.4
	1984	-	21.8	197	-	-	-
Mexico	1986	21.4	-	86	1.5	n.a.	n.a.
(nonoil)	1983	-	18.7	102	-	-	-
Chile	1985	43.5	-	31	0.6	0.6	n.a.
	1981	-	38.2	20	-	-	-
Colombia	1980	27.3	-	27	1.0	0.9	0.8
Indonesia	1986	10.1	-	6	1.5	n.a.	n.a.
(nonoil)	1984	-	6.2	10	-	-	-
Korea,	1983	19.0	-	3	0.7	0.7	0.8
Rep. of	1982	-	18.2	7	-	-	-

Sources: IMF, *International Financial Statistics*; World Bank data.

Table 1.5 also confirms the Tanzi effect for high-inflation countries: the lowest tax ratio is noted when inflation had risen to triple-digits. But as Table 1.2 shows, with the demand for base money falling, there were limits to the resources that governments could acquire through the inflation tax.

When interest rates exceed GDP growth, the need to pay growing interest outlays complicates cuts in overall spending (and tax burdens). This observation is widespread: it is true for the OECD (on average), particularly for the high-debt OECD countries, and there is thus little reason to believe that it should be different for developing debtor countries. But by comparing 1981 and 1987, Table 1.6 reveals that cross-country differences are important. In 'unstable' cases like Brazil and Italy, there were no cuts in current outlays (such as subsidies and public salaries), and the noninterest current account increased by 4 percentage points of GDP. The opposite was observed in Belgium and Korea, where current public spending was reduced by about 4 percentage points of GDP, and in Mexico (2.5 per cent). Even if cuts in noninterest public spending were important, they were rarely 'growth-oriented', since they often concentrated on capital expenditure. To the extent that these cuts affect infrastructure capital rather than 'white elephants', they lower the productivity of complementary private sector capital and future output growth.

Table 1.6 *Structure of public spending, 1981 and 1986-87 (percentage of GDP*

Country	1981			1986-87		
	Capital	Interest	Other	Capital	Interest	Other
Brazil	7.6	10.9	8.8	5.4	11.3	12.7
Mexico	12.9	5.0	21.8	5.5	19.5	19.2
Indonesia	6.4	0.7	7.3	8.4	3.3	9.4
Korea, Rep. of	10.9	1.4	18.5	9.0	1.3	14.4
Belgium	5.0	7.9	44.4	2.8	11.1	40.1
Ireland	15.2	7.6	23.2	9.6	11.3	23.5
Italy	5.9	3.4	34.2	5.2	8.7	38.6
OECD average	3.5	2.5	33.3	3.1	3.8	34.3

Sources: See Table 1.1. For OECD average, see OECD (1989b), ch. 5.

4. Interest Rates and GDP Growth

Much of the increase in public debt ratios has been unrelated to primary deficits in the government budgets. As Table 1.2 shows, since year-end 1983 the difference between real interest rates and real GDP growth accounts for one-third of the relative debt increase in the lowest case (Italy) and for two-thirds in the highest case (Mexico). So for a country like Mexico, one can easily imagine a disaster scenario in spite of its primary budget surpluses: foreign debt service crowds out investment and reduces output growth and the tax base; this process feeds on itself until no resource base is left from which to service the public debt. It is thus important to know to what extent public finance can contribute to higher growth and lower interest rates, and to what extent it cannot.

Pooled time-series-cross-section regression estimates reported in the 1988 OECD Survey of Belgium identify the budget deficit-private saving ratio as a significant determinant of real bond yields. The ratio explains a third of the increase in bond yields from 1979 to 1983 and a third of their subsequent decline. Another third is explained by the US bond yields, indicating that their determinants (like the US deficit-savings ratio) are important concerns for the OECD, and more so for developing countries where the foreign share in public debt is higher.

But in countries like Mexico, real bond yields have failed to decline with a falling operational deficit (which corrects for the inflation component in the government's interest outlays). Debt-income ratios have continued to increase, suggesting that debt stocks have affected interest rates more than the deficit. The savers have apparently considered the risks of imminent default and inflation by requiring correspondingly higher interest rates on domestic government debt. Since high interest rates feed public debt, they not only reflect inflationary expectations, but also determine the inflation rate. Whether the economy ends up in a situation with low interest rates and low default risk, or with high interest and high default risk, depends on the credibility of the government.[3] After a long experience of high and variable inflation, coupled with repeated periods of negative real returns on government bonds, the risk premium in domestic interest rates is unlikely to disappear rapidly. Finally, as long as a fixed exchange rate policy is not fully credible (like in Mexico's 1988 stabilization), in addition to default and inflation risks, interest rates incorporate expectations of forthcoming devaluations.

High inflation, excessive minimum reserve requirements, and forced sales of government bonds have enlarged the wedge between the interest yield for domestic savers and the interest costs for domestic borrowers. Returns on savings are often too low to mobilize saving for capital formation while credit costs are too high to finance profitable investment. The concomitant losses of efficiency and opportunities for growth are often exacerbated when rationed credit is extended to favoured (big or public) enterprises at preferential interest rates. When the public budget deficit exceeds the current account deficit, public sector borrowing must be matched by a surplus of private sector savings over investment. Public sectors then become net users of household and corporate saving, which are then unavailable for private investment. This explains why investment levels are so depressed in many problem debtor countries (like Mexico), and why they are up in Korea (in spite of massive external transfers).

Italy's experience reveals, however, that the negative effects of fiscal deficits can be offset to some extent. This is not because of 'tax discounting' (as embodied in the Ricardian Equivalence Theory) in the countries characterized above as 'unstable'. Taxpayers do not increase private savings to prepare for future taxes that governments will eventually have to levy to pay increased interest payments on their debt. Why should they, when they can easily evade taxation? Even in most OECD countries, the tax-discounting factor appears to be close to zero (Nicoletti, 1988). But fiscal deficits can displace private consumption and lure savers into purchasing public debt when high real rates of return, offered by near substitutes of Treasury bills, are taxed (Italy) or unhedged against high inflation (Brazil).

The output effect of a given fiscal deficit depends on the (incentive) structure of taxes and public spending. When countries like Argentina intensify tax pressure on export production, agriculture, and domestic financial intermediation, the disappointing performance in savings, exports, and output growth should come as no surprise (Reisen and van Trotsenburg, 1988). Output growth also depends on the composition of government expenditure. Only cuts in government consumption equal to the increases in debt service succeed in maintaining the growth rate without intensifying inflationary pressures. Instead, cuts in public capital formation lower the nation's overall investment and depress private investment's profitability, which translates into lower growth, lower savings, and lower taxes.

5. Real Devaluation and Cross-Currency Movements

Efforts to reduce foreign debt demand a real devaluation of the exchange rate below purchasing power parity to generate the real transfer (trade surplus) for foreign debt service. Here is one of the main differences between high-debt OECD countries and Latin American debtors. While Ireland, Italy, and Belgium belong to the European Monetary System, and hence have a de facto peg with the deutsche mark, Latin American debtors can no longer borrow abroad, calling for sharp depreciations of their currencies. A large shift in real exchange rates is called for when external borrowing (putting upward pressure on the exchange rate) and later external transfers increase in a short time period. Real effective exchange rates (trade-weighted) in major developing debtor countries are now often 40 per cent below their 1980-82 average. Add to this the major swings in the value among key currencies — for example, the yen has appreciated more than 100 per cent against the US dollar during 1985-87 — and it is obvious why changes in the foreign exchange rates have mattered so much for debt dynamics.

Problem debtor countries like Brazil and Mexico suffered the heaviest capital losses because of real devaluation during 1982-83, when their foreign public debt ratio doubled. Debt-weighted real annual devaluation also accounted for much of the rising public debt ratios during 1984-87. It explains 85 per cent of the rise in the public debt ratio in Indonesia that engineered massive devaluations, where all public debt is foreign and most of it is in yen. Debt-weighted real devaluation accounts for 27 per cent of the rise in the debt-income ratio during 1984-87 in Brazil and Mexico.

Devaluation also has an immediate effect on the government budget (Reisen, 1989). The impact will typically be negative in the (largely inward-oriented) problem debtor country. The rise in tax receipts and new inflow of foreign finance are too limited to make up for the rise in local currency costs of servicing foreign debt after a devaluation. While the immediate consequence of a sustained real devaluation is a proportionate rise in the real interest payments on foreign debt, its impact on the noninterest part of the government budget is much more difficult to determine. The budget is likely to be affected by devaluation because of changes in prices (price effect) or because of changes in various tax bases induced by shifts in wages, corporate income, or export and import volumes (output effect).

By definition, a sustained real devaluation raises the prices of tradable goods relative to nontradables. To analyze the price effect, it helps to break down the noninterest budget deficit (or surplus) into taxes and expenditures that depend on home prices — nontradables — and those that depend on world prices — tradables (see equation 1).

For example, expenditure on nontradables includes public sector salaries, and on tradables, imported capital goods, while tax receipts fall on nontradables like taxes on labour and on tradables like trade taxes. A government of an outward-oriented economy (like Korea) or with an important public mineral sector (like Nigeria) is more likely to profit from devaluation than a government of an inward-oriented economy without a large export-oriented public sector (Brazil, for example). In the last type of country, the dollar value of tax receipts that arises in part from taxes on nontradables will tend to fall, while the reduced dollar value of spending on nontradables does not fully offset the losses in tax receipts.

A real devaluation exerts a negative price effect on the public budget when the real interest on net external debt plus the noninterest budget deficit on tradables exceeds new net external debt. To put it differently, a real devaluation is likely to improve the fiscal situation only when the public budget on tradables is in an initial surplus or when the net foreign exchange flow (net debt minus interest) to the government is positive. In an open economy, real interest rates on domestic debt can fall, provided the exchange rate overshoots (Ize and Ortiz, 1987). If the exchange rate depreciates initially, expectations of future appreciation would create a wedge between returns in domestic and foreign currencies, which would allow debt servicing on local currency debt to fall. But a devaluation will still exert a negative impact on the fiscal deficit when the foreign currency portion of public debt plus the initial tradables deficit is higher than the savings made on domestic currency denominated debt.

Exchange rate adjustment may also worsen fiscal imbalances because of widespread multiple exchange rates. Multiple rates imply an implicit tax-subsidy structure (Dornbusch, 1986). Imports can be taxed by a high price of foreign exchange as can exports by a low exchange rate at which foreign exchange earnings must be surrendered. But government may also use the multiple-rate system to subsidize imports or exports with preferential rates. The net fiscal revenue from the multiple-rate structure depends on the excess proceeds from foreign exchange sales divided by the revenue from purchases.

Devaluation can reduce the differential between official and black market rates and can also be used to unify multiple rates. Eliminating the exchange rate differential leads to a sharp drop in the implicit export and import taxes when the affected government is a net seller of foreign exchange (Pinto, 1987).[4]

The second component of the debt-weighted exchange rate is currency swings. In the 1980s, the currency composition of foreign debt dwarfs cross-currency differences in interest rates as a determinant for foreign debt service costs. Because of institutional barriers or high transaction costs that prevent them from participating actively in futures markets, most developing nations are not hedged against the risks of exchange rate changes among key currencies. But they can minimize their exchange risk exposure by matching the currency mix of their debt with the currency mix of their cash flows with due consideration, if possible, of the pass-through effects of exchange rate changes on the different good markets, and of the covariance of key currencies.[5]

The World Bank is now the biggest net lender to highly indebted countries, but its currency pool seems particularly inadequate for almost all developing countries because it tends to increase their foreign exchange risk exposure for the benefit of a very questionable reduction in the pure interest cost of the Bank's lending.[6] Calculations for Indonesia show that if it had matched the currency mix of its foreign debt with the currency structure of its cash flows, it would have minimized the foreign exchange risk of cross-currency fluctuations and saved about $10 billion during 1985-88 against its actual currency composition. But if the Indonesian government followed the World Bank's debt-management practices, it would have lost about $6 billion during the same period compared with its actual debt structure (Reisen, 1988b).

6. How to Contain the Rise in Government Debt

(i) 'Easy' Alternatives
Easy alternatives to growth-oriented fiscal adjustment do not exist. Hyperinflation, unilateral default, taxation of domestic bond returns, and voluntary foreign debt reduction are often advocated to relieve the public budget of

Table 1.7   Money base and domestic public debt (percentage of GDP)

Country	Real money base (percentage of GDP)		Real money base (percentage of domestic public debt)	
	1981	1987	1981	1987
Brazil	3.5	2.2	42	11
Mexico	15.9	4.5	134	11
Indonesia	7.1	8.0	n.a.	n.a.
Korea, Rep. of	5.7	7.4	116	121
Belgium	10.3	7.8	14	11
Ireland	11.0	10.0	19	13
Italy	15.0	15.5	35	21

Note: Money bases at year-end have been deflated by the consumer price index (1980=100) at the end of each respective year and have then been divided by real GDP in 1980 prices.
Sources: Table 1.1; IMF, *International Financial Statistics*.

debtor countries. But recent evidence suggests that these devices do not work.

An unanticipated burst of inflation helped Argentina (1982) and Mexico (1983) reduce domestic public debt and the real cost of debt service. Such a strategy of 'surprise' capital losses for domestic bondholders has become increasingly ineffective as a way to alleviate the public debt. First, maturities of government bonds are now extremely short term. Moreover, public debt in problem debtor countries is often contracted on a floating rate basis or fully indexed to price inflation. Second, rapid monetization of government debt is not a solution since most problem debtor countries are by now extremely demonetized (see Table 1.7). The money base is now about 2 per cent of GDP in Brazil (down from 3.5 per cent in 1981) and 4.5 per cent of GDP in Mexico (down from 15.9 per cent in 1981). A policy that doubled the money base in a week (for example, through open market purchases) would reduce publicly held debt by a mere 11 per cent in Brazil and Mexico. Note that the respective figures are not significantly higher for Ireland, Belgium, and Italy. An inflationary erosion of domestic public debt does not work anymore in most countries with a long history of fiscal deficits and would not justify the subsequent inflation.

(ii) Default

Outright default on foreign or domestic debt cannot prevent the growth of public debt unless tax revenues exceed noninterest spending. This condition seems only satisfied in Chile and Mexico. But default also imposes a heavy financial burden on governments. Brazil's temporary interest moratorium (from February 1987 to February 1988) has cost the country from between $710 million (according to the government) and $1.5 billion (according to some Brazilian economists). These figures would include higher spreads on short-term trade loans ($140 million); the transfer of official reserves to the Bank for International Settlements (BIS) to avoid seizure ($20 million); delayed restructuring of debt so that Brazil has had to continue paying for higher interest margins over a longer period of time ($550 million); support for foreign affiliates of Brazilian banks that had been excluded from interbank business ($750 million); and substantial private capital flight because of reduced confidence from the moratorium.

Domestic default may generate similar problems. Often, loss of reputation because of repeated domestic default impedes domestic government finance and stimulates capital flight (Ize, 1987). But exceptional situations can develop when an old regime collapses and the new regime can credibly commit not to default again. Another difficulty is that domestic banks are often very important (captive) lenders to their government, and domestic default would severely deplete their capital and could drive them into bankruptcy. The government would then be compelled to support the domestic banking system to avoid economic chaos. Otherwise it would face negative consequences for domestic output.

Taxation of domestic bond returns would dampen debt dynamics only if the tax did not raise the bond yields required from the savers (OECD Survey of Ireland 1987). Under this unlikely condition, governments could increase the tax base by the amount of public interest outlays on domestic debt. But if there is perfect foresight and if assets are perfect substitutes, taxing interest payments has no effect on budget deficits. Changes in tax rates on any assets bring about an equal change in their equilibrium returns, and hence leave after-tax yields unaltered (Giovannini, 1988). But Italy may have succeeded in dampening the rise in bond yields with a total tax exemption of interest on public securities, allied to the withholding tax of near substitutes of Treasury bills like bank deposits (Spaventa, 1988). Directing savings toward government debt was helped by initially high financial savings in Italy and the decline in the price of real estate.

Even foreign debt-reduction schemes do not necessarily reduce total public debt and debt-service charges when domestic bond yields largely exceed the effective cost of foreign debt. Debt-equity swaps, for example, are usually financed by the debtor government (or the central bank). If this finance does not come from printing new money, and if the swap does not increase tax collections, the government must issue new domestic debt. Reduced foreign debt, translated into local currency through the real exchange rate, will then be offset by increased domestic debt, corrected for the redemption discount. So, the government budget is likely to benefit from a debt-equity swap only if the increased interest payment on domestic debt falls short of the interest saving on foreign debt. When there is real appreciation, as occurred last year in Mexico, the redemption discount has to be even higher to improve the government budget.

7. Possible Remedies

(i) How Much Fiscal Discipline Is Needed?
How much fiscal discipline is necessary to restore a government's creditworthiness and credibility? Because of changing market perceptions and unstable lending conventions, this question cannot be fully answered. A more modest approach is to determine the government budget needed to stabilize debt ratios and simultaneously meet other macroeconomic targets.[7]

Table 1.8   Brazil and Mexico: required public sector noninterest surplus

	Brazil		
	1983	1984-87	From 1988
Required noninterest surplus as percentage of GDP (=)	7.5	2.0	2.1
Real interest bill on domestic debt (+)	1.8	2.3	3.0
Real interest bill on foreign debt (+)	1.5	2.4	1.8
Monetary finance (-)	0.1	0.5	0.4
New domestic borrowing consistent with constant debt ratio (-)	-0.3	1.0	1.0
New foreign borrowing consistent with constant debt ratio (-)	-4.0	1.2	1.3
Memo: *Actual* noninterest balance (negative sign denotes deficit)	-0.9	-0.4	-1.0[a]
Assumptions			
Ratio of money base to GDP	4.4	4.4	4.4
Annual inflation rate	5.0	5.0	5.0
Real interest rate on domestic debt (net of taxes)	14.5	14.5	14.5
Observations[c]			
Real annual GDP growth	-2.5	6.3	5.0
Real annual devaluation	24.0	2.0	0.0
Real interest rate on foreign debt	10.1	8.6	7.0

[a] Refers to January-March 1988.
[b] Refers to April-June 1988.
[c] Data from 1988 are based on assumptions. Real interest rate on foreign debt refers to the effective rate net of inflation in the US consumer price index.
Sources: Banco Central do Brasil, *Brazil Economic Program*; Morgan Guaranty Trust Company, *World Financial Markets*; IMF, International Financial Statistics; Banco de Mexico, *Indicadores Económicos*; Dornbusch (1988).

Table 1.8   *Brazil and Mexico: required public sector noninterest surplus*

	Mexico		
	1983	1984-87	From 1988
Required noninterest surplus as percentage of GDP (=)	10.6	10.1	5.1
Real interest bill on domestic debt (+)	1.8	3.2	6.2
Real interest bill on foreign debt (+)	1.9	3.7	3.7
Monetary finance (-)	0.3	0.5	1.1
New domestic borrowing consistent with constant debt ratio (-)	-0.3	-0.2	1.6
New foreign borrowing consistent with constant debt ratio (-)	-6.9	3.4	2.1
Memo: *Actual* noninterest balance (negative sign denotes deficit)	-0.9	4.1	-6.9[b]
Assumptions			
Ratio of money base to GDP	12.0	12.0	12.0
Annual inflation rate	5.0	5.0	5.0
Real interest rate on domestic debt (net of taxes)	15.4	15.4	15.4
Observations[c]			
Real annual GDP growth	-2.9	-1.2	4.0
Real annual devaluation	31.4	6.6	0.0
Real interest rate on foreign debt	9.7	8.5	7.0

[a] Refers to January-March 1988.

[b] Refers to April-June 1988.

[c] Data from 1988 are based on assumptions. Real interest rate on foreign debt refers to the effective rate net of inflation in the US consumer price index.

Sources: Banco Central do Brasil, *Brazil Economic Program*; Morgan Guaranty Trust Company, *World Financial Markets*; IMF, International Financial Statistics; Banco de Mexico, *Indicadores Económicos*; Dornbusch (1988).

More fiscal discipline is needed to avoid inflation and rising debt ratios when the demand for base money is low, when GDP growth is low relative to real interest rates, when public debt is high relative to GDP, and when real depreciation raises the real value of net foreign debt. Only when real GDP growth exceeds real interest rates and accumulated debt is low relative to seignorage can the government run a primary deficit without raising the debt ratio.[8]

Table 1.8 contrasts the required noninterest surpluses in Brazil and Mexico that would be consistent with constant debt ratios, low inflation (5 per cent a year), and real interest rates high enough to make capital flight unprofitable. The last requirement would appear to be met in Brazil for early 1986, when real after-tax returns on Treasury bills were 14.5 per cent and net errors and omissions in the balance of payments were small (Cardoso and Fishlow, 1989). In Mexico, the same conditions seem to have applied in late 1986, when the tax-free real return on Treasury bills was 15.4 per cent (Dornbusch, 1988). With sustained fiscal discipline, real domestic interest rates would probably find a lower equilibrium level, as government debt could be sold at a lower risk premium, reflecting more credibility for future fiscal restraint. Finally, we require an assumption about the ratio of base money to GDP. The remonetization of the Brazilian economy after the Cruzado Plan (when inflation was zero) brought the ratio up to 4.4 per cent (from 2.3 per cent in 1985). In Mexico the 1986 ratio of base money to GDP was very high — at 15.9 per cent in 1981 — but has declined continuously, falling to 4.2 per cent in 1987. Without other evidence, it can be assumed that with inflation at 5 per cent and real interest rates at 15.4 per cent, the Mexican ratio of base money to GDP would have been 12 per cent.

Further assumptions are that the external positions of both Brazil and Mexico require no further real devaluations of their currencies, that the real effective foreign interest rate is 7 per cent, and that the real GDP growth rates are sustained at 5 per cent in Brazil and 4 per cent in Mexico. But private agents might deem the public debt ratios at end-1987 too high to inspire confidence in public finances, in which case the required fiscal discipline would be more harsh. Several results must be stressed:

–   First a higher noninterest surplus will be required for Mexico than for Brazil. This result is largely — but not exclusively — determined by the currently observed public debt ratio, which is approximately equal to GDP in Mexico, but only half as high in Brazil. In 1988 the Mexican authorities seem to have achieved the required fiscal adjustment (although it is too focused on cuts in public investment), while the fiscal disequilibrium in Brazil is estimated at about 3 per cent of GDP.

–   Second, the domestic public debt burden often matters more than the foreign debt burden, provided that further devaluation-induced increases in the real cost of servicing foreign debt can be avoided and that the interest cost of domestic debt continues to exceed the cost of foreign debt.

–   Third, bringing down inflation from current levels to those observed in stable debtor countries would yield an important one-time gain in seignorage and regular tax revenues, especially in Mexico. If this gain is used to amortize part of the high-cost domestic debt, the required noninterest budget surplus will be reduced.

Debt dynamics continue to impose restrictive fiscal policies on high-debt OECD countries (OECD, 1989b). Calculations on debt stability requirements, based on a somewhat simpler procedure than that described for Brazil and Mexico, show that Belgium, Ireland, and Italy still have a fiscal disequilibrium with rapidly rising debt ratios. The current public borrowing requirements still exceed the level that would stabilize debt ratios, by 3.5 per cent of GDP in Belgium, 2 per cent in Ireland, and 3.2 per cent in Italy (OECD, 1989b, Table 5.23).

(ii) Growth-Oriented Fiscal Adjustment

Running a certain noninterest surplus in the medium term is not enough to stabilize (then reduce) the public debt ratio. GDP growth must be fostered, real exchange rate depreciation contained, and real interest rates cut, for such a strategy to be sustainable. If fiscal adjustment is sought at the cost of lower output growth, it is more likely to be disrupted and less likely to reduce government indebtedness.

How can public finance in problem debtor countries contribute to savings, investment, and growth? More focus should go to increased tax collection and less on cuts in public spending than usually occurs. First, spending cuts have made more strides than increased taxes and cannot be expected to be further reduced, except in Brazil and Argentina. Second, effective tax ratios are low in most debtor countries, and there are nondistorting ways to increase them. Third, low effective tax rates and low import dependence suggest a high-income multiplier for government expenditure, so spending cuts have a considerable negative short-term effect on output.

The menu for tax reform would include (*World Development Report 1988*):

– Keep marginal tax rates low to strengthen incentives to work and save, but raise effective average tax rates. This means broadening tax bases and eliminating exemptions and special incentives.

– Choose a tax (like the value added tax) that is simple, enforceable, has low administrative costs, and raises substantial revenues. Successful performers, like Korea, Indonesia, Chile, and Turkey, have all successfully implemented the value added tax. But there is also room to increase revenues from personal income tax, especially by eliminating loopholes for top income levels.

– Raise compliance and enforcement through low tax rates, high penalties on outright avoidance, and abolition of discretionary elements in tax legislation.

– Introduce effective withholding schemes on wages, dividends, and interest, and strengthen tax administration to cross-check different tax sources.

– Stop taxing exports and financial savings.

– With raised tax revenues, public spending should be shifted back toward investment, and away from consumption, without reducing its real level.

– To encourage private investment and to limit devaluation-induced capital losses on foreign debt, the priority for public spending should be on infrastructure that favours foreign trade.

NOTES

1. For an extensive discussion of the link between external and internal transfers, see Reisen and van Trotsenburg (1988).
2. All variables are adjusted for domestic inflation
3. See Calvo (1988) concerning the responsibility of government debt for multiple equilibriums.
4. Similarly, financial losses in Mexico associated with exchange rate differentials between dollar assets and debts of nationalized banks after devaluation added 4 per cent of GDP to the consolidated public deficit in 1982.
5. For a discussion of optimal hedging rules for debt-service constrained countries, see Gawronski (1990).
6. The World Bank shifts exchange rate risks to debtor countries by lending the proceeds of the borrowings in the same currencies in which they were borrowed (Lonaeus, 1988). Since 1980, the currencies used for disbursements are pooled, and all borrowers owe the bank the currencies in the pool in the same proportions.

7. This has been a concern for both OECD Economic Surveys (see, in particular, OECD Economic Survey of Ireland 1987) and the World Bank (Anand and van Wijnbergen, 1989).
8. To see that, solve the debt-dynamics equation (6-2) for the required noninterest surplus needed to get the debt-income ratio to decline, yielding the stability condition:
    $[(t -g) + (t^* -g^*) e]$ x $[(1 - f)r + f(r^* + e) - n]$ - $(p + n)m]$.

REFERENCES

Alesina, A. (1988), 'The End of Large Public Debts' in F. Giavazzi and L. Spaventa, eds, *High Public Debt: The Italian Experience*, Cambridge, Cambridge University Press.

Anand, Ritu, and Sweder van Wijnbergen (1989), 'Inflation and the Financing of Government Expenditure: An Introductory Analysis with an Application to Turkey', *World Bank Economic Review* 3, (January), pp. 17-38.

Banco Central do Brasil, various issues, *Brazil Economic Report*, Brasilia.

Banco de Mexico, various issues, *Indicadores Económicos*, Mexico City.

Berg, Andrew, and Jeffrey Sachs (1988), 'The Debt Crisis: Structural Explanations of Country Performance,' NBER Working Paper 2607, Cambridge, Mass., National Bureau of Economic Research.

Calvo, Guillermo A. (1988), 'Servicing the Public Debt: The Role of Expectations', *American Economic Review* 78(4), pp. 647-61.

Cardoso, Eliana, and Albert Fishlow (1989), 'The Macroeconomics of the Brazilian External Debt' in Jeffrey Sachs, ed., *Developing Country Debt,* Cambridge, Mass., National Bureau of Economic Research.

Clark, C. (1945), 'Public Finance and Changes in the Value of Money', *Economic Journal* 55(220), pp. 371-98.

Coopers & Lybrand (1988), *International Tax Summaries*.

Dornbusch, Rudiger (1986), 'Special Exchange Rates for Capital Account Transactions', *World Bank Economic Review* 1, pp. 3-33.

— (1988), 'Mexico: Stabilization, Debt and Growth', *Economic Policy* 7 (October), pp. 231-83.

Gawronski, Pier Giorgio (1990), 'Optimal Currency Composition of Foreign Debt: The Case of Five Developing Countries', OECD Development Centre Technical Papers, no. 23, Paris.

Gil Diaz, F. (1987), 'Some Lessons from Mexico's Tax Reform' in D. Newbery and N. Stern, eds, *The Theory of Taxation for Developing Countries*, New York, Oxford University Press.

Giovannini, A. (1988), 'Capital Controls and Public Finance: The Experience of Italy' in F. Giavazzi and L. Spaventa, eds, *High Public Debt: The Italian Experience*, Cambridge, Cambridge University Press.

International Monetary Fund, various editions, *Government Finance Yearbook*, Washington, D.C.

— Various editions, *International Financial Statistics*, Washington, D.C.

Ize, Alain (1987), 'Fiscal Dominance, Debt and Exchange Rates', IMF, Fiscal Affairs Department, Washington, D.C.

Ize, Alain, and Guillermo Ortiz (1987), 'Fiscal Rigidities, Public Debt, and Capital Flight', *IMF Staff Papers* 34(2), pp. 311-32.

Keynes, John M. (1923), 'A Tract on Monetary Reform', reprinted in *The Collected Writings of John Maynard Keynes*, vol. IV, London, Macmillan, 1971.

Lonaeus, Hakan (1988), 'How the Bank Finances Its Operations', *Finance & Development* 25 (September), pp. 40-42.

Mansoor, Ahsan (1987), 'The Budgetary Impact of Privatization', IMF, Fiscal Affairs Department, Washington, D.C.

Morgan Guaranty Trust Company of New York, various issues, *World Financial Markets*, New York.

Nicoletti, G. (1988), 'A Cross-Country Analysis of Private Consumption, Inflation and the "Debt Neutrality Hypothesis"', *OECD Economic Studies* II, (autumn), pp. 43-87.

Organisation for Economic Co-operation and Development (1987), *Economic Survey: Ireland*, Paris.

— (1988), *Economic Survey: Belgium*, Paris.

— (1989a), *Economic Survey: Italy*, Paris.

— (1989b), *Economies in Transition*, Paris.

Pinto, B. (1987), 'Exchange Rate Unification and Budgetary Policy in Sub-Saharan Africa', World Bank, Washington, D.C.

Reisen, Helmut (1988a), 'Export Orientation, Public Debt, and Fiscal Rigidities: The Different Performance in Brazil, Korea, and Mexico', *Journal of International Economic Integration* 3(1), pp. 98-115.

— (1988b), 'Dollar, Yen and Interdependence: Cost of Different Currency Compositions of Indonesia's Debt 1985-1988', OECD Development Centre, Paris.

— (1989), *Public Developing Country Debt, External Competitiveness, and Required Fiscal Discipline*, Princeton Studies in International Finance no. 66, Princeton, NJ., Princeton University.

Reisen, Helmut, and Axel van Trotsenburg (1988), 'Developing Country Debt: The Budgetary and Transfer Problem', OECD Development Centre Studies, Paris.

Reynolds, A. (1985), 'Some International Comparisons of Supply-Side Tax Policy', *Cato Journal* 5(2); pp. 543-69.

Sjaastad, Larry (1983), 'The International Debt Quagmire: To Whom Do We Owe It?' *The World Economy* 6(3), pp. 305-24.

Spaventa, Luigi (1988), 'Introduction: Is There a Public Debt Problem in Italy?' in F. Giavazzi and L. Spaventa, eds, *High Public Debt: The Italian Experience*, Cambridge, Cambridge University Press.

Tanzi, Vito (1977), 'Inflation, Lags in Collection, and the Real Value of Tax Revenue', *IMF Staff Papers* 24(1), pp. 154-67.

Tanzi, Vito, and Mario I. Blejer (1988), 'Public Debt and Fiscal Policy in Developing Countries' in Kenneth J. Arrow, Michael Boskin, and International Economic Association, eds, *Economics of Public Debt*, New York, St. Martin's Press.

World Bank (1988), *World Development Report 1988*, New York, Oxford University Press.

2. Dollar, Yen and Interdependence: Costs of Different Currency Compositions of Indonesia's Debt

1. Introduction

Swings in key exchange rates (US dollar, yen, deutschmark, etc.) affect the level, the structure, and the economic cost of developing country debt. When these swings become as important as those experienced in the 1980s, the currency composition of foreign debt can be shown to dwarf the differences in interest rates as a determinant for debt service costs.

Most developing nations are unhedged against the risks of exchange rate changes between key currencies. They may face institutional barriers or too high transaction costs which prevent them from participating actively on the future markets. But they can minimize their exchange risk exposure by matching the currency mix of their debt with the currency mix of their cash flows (Mayer, 1987; Kroner, 1988).

This chapter sets out to compare the costs of Indonesia's actual currency structure of debt with two concepts of a hedging debt portfolio as well as with the World Bank's current currency pool. The calculation refers to the period 1985-88 which was characterized by a strong depreciation of the US dollar.

2. The Alternatives

The *reference currency mix* is Indonesia's foreign debt at end-1984 when it stood at $32.4 billion. It is assumed that there was no net lending after this date: changes in the total US dollar value and in the currency mix are determined solely by movements between key currencies. As becomes clear from Table 2.1, this is in fact very close to what actually happened: the hypothetical and the actual currency mix at end-1987 are very similar.

The *World Bank currency pool* is one of the three alternatives to the reference currency mix. The World Bank shifts exchange rate risks to the debtor countries by lending the proceeds of the borrowings in the same currencies

Debt, Deficits and Exchange Rates

in which they were borrowed (Lonaeus, 1988). Since 1980, the currencies used for disbursements are pooled, and all borrowers owe the Bank the currencies in the pool in the same proportions. Apparently misguided by the endeavour to reduce the average interest cost of borrowings, the Bank has even used currency swaps to concentrate its currency mix even more in 'hard' currency than before swaps. The data given in Table 2.1 refer to the 1988 composition.

Table 2.1   *Indonesia: currency mix of foreign debt*

	$	¥	DM	FF	SFr	£	S$
1. Reference mix:							
end-84	.54	.32	.07	.03	.01	.03	—
end-85	.48	.36	.08	.04	.01	.03	—
end-86	.43	.40	.09	.04	.01	.03	—
end-87	.37	.45	.10	.04	.01	.03	—
6-88	.38	.45	.09	.04	.01	.03	—
Memo: actual end-87	.36	.47	.09	.05	.01	.02	—
2. World Bank currency pool	.17	.28	.29	.01	.23	.02	—
3. Optimal debt portfolio (Max. correlation with tot — variance)	.87	.03	.13	-.10	—	.07	—
4. Optimal debt portfolio (net cash flows)	.85	—	—	—	—	.06	.09

Sources: World Bank and DCD for actual end-1984 data. Lonaeus, H., "How the Bank Finances Its Operations", *Finance and Development*, September 1988 (Netherlands guilders have been attributed to Deutschmark share). Kroner, K.F., *Optimal Currency Composition of External Debt — Applications to Indonesia and Turkey*, University of Arizona, mimeo, August 1988. United Nations, *Commodity Fund Statistics 1984*, Series D, vol. XXXIV, no. 1-23, New York, 1988.

The second alternative is based on Kroner's (1988) calculations of Indonesia's *optimal debt portfolio*, defined as a portfolio which has maximum correlation with the changes in the terms of trade. Kroner provides quarterly portfolios running from 1/1986 to 1/1988. Since these portfolios do not change much through time, their simple average is taken (scaled to add to one).

Quite a similar result is found with another concept of the *optimal debt portfolio*, which aims at matching the currency mix of debt with the currency structure of net exports. Estimates on the currency structure of Indonesian trade have been based on the trade matrices given in the UN Commodity Trade Statistics and on Magee-Rao's (1980) definition of vehicle and nonvehicle pricing in international trade. The currency invoicing of raw commodities follows the predominant currency on the respective world markets (see e.g., Far Eastern Economic Review), i.e. $ for petroleum, £ for coffee, and the Singapore dollar for rubber. The currency invoicing of trade in manufactures is allocated according to the following assumptions: the $ is the vehicle currency in trade with other developing and with non-market economies; trade with Japan, the UK, France, Switzerland, and Germany is dominated by their currencies; all other trade with Europe occurs in DM (that is to say, with a currency belonging to the DM-bloc). All other Pacific trade is in US dollars. It results that Indonesia has a positive cash flow in US dollar, pound sterling, and Singapore dollar which can be used to hedge against the exchange risks of foreign debt. It has an important negative cash flow in Japanese yen, and a minor negative cash flow in DM, French and Swiss francs. Thus, foreign exchange reserves, not foreign debt, should be constituted out of these currencies to hedge against import risks.

3. Exchange Rate Indices and Interest Rates

During 1985-1987, the US dollar depreciated strongly against all major currencies that are relevant for Indonesia's debt and trade (Table 2.2). Only the Singapore dollar kept close to the US dollar. In the first half of 1988, the US dollar appreciated.

The assignment of weights for the different debt portfolios (as given in Table 2.1) to the respective currencies yields the weighted exchange rates of each debt portfolio (Table 2.3). The considerable component of Indonesia's debt denominated in appreciating non-dollar currencies has blown up the dollar value of debt by 44 per cent at end 1987. But had Indonesia been indebted in the World Bank currency mix, its liabilities would have grown even more, by 83 per cent. Because the hedging debt portfolios contain a large component of US dollar (and currencies which were relatively weak during 1985-88), their dollar value would have grown only slightly in the course of cross-currency movements.

Table 2.2   *Nominal exchange rate indice vis-à-vis the US dollar*
                  End of period, 1984 = 1

	¥	DM	FF	SFr	£	S$
1985	1.25	1.28	1.27	1.24	1.25	.97
1986	1.58	1.62	1.49	1.59	1.27	.98
1987	2.03	1.99	1.80	2.02	1.62	1.01
June 1988	2.00	1.73	1.56	1.71	1.48	1.05

Source: IMF, *International Financial Statistics.*

Table 2.3   *Weighted exchange rate indices vis-à-vis the US dollar*
                  End of period, 1984 = 1

	1985	1986	1987	6/1988
1. Reference mix	1.12	1.26	1.44	1.41
2. World Bank currency pool	1.20	1.49	1.83	1.67
3. Optimal debt portfolio (max. correlation with tot-variance)	1.04	1.07	1.12	1.09
4. Optimal debt portfolio (net cash flows)	1.01	1.01	1.04	1.03

Source: Author's calculations.

To complete the picture on overall borrowing costs, average annual rates of interest are computed for each of the four currency baskets. For OECD currencies, the three-month Eurodollar LIBOR rates were used, for the Singapore dollar the three-month minimum lending rate (IFS line 60 p) was applied. Assigning the currency weights in Table 2.1 to these annual rates of interest yields the weighted average interest rate for each debt portfolio (Table 2.4). It is seen that the World Bank currency pool has the lowest average rates of interest because it is heavily dependent on low interest/hard currencies such as DM and SFr. The hedging portfolios carry higher average rates because interest rates on the US dollar and pound sterling have been relatively high throughout 1985-88.

Table 2.4   Average annual rates of interest (in per cent)

	1985	1986	1987	6/1988
1. Reference mix	7.47	6.25	5.78	6.33
2. World Bank currency pool	6.38	5.25	4.77	5.37
3. Optimal debt portfolio (max. correlation with tot-variance)	7.99	6.55	6.74	7.91
4. Optimal debt portfolio (net cash flows)	8.59	7.11	7.24	8.14

Source: IMF, *International Financial Statistics.*

4. Net Savings and Losses of Alternative Debt Portfolios

We are now equipped to answer the following question: How big would the savings (or losses) of foreign exchange have been during 1985-88, had Indonesia diversified the currency composition of its foreign debt at end-1984 to correspond with a) the currency mix of the World Bank currency pool, b) the variance of its terms of trade, and c) the net cash flows arising from its foreign trade earnings? In general, it should be expected that hedging against foreign exchange risks (alternatives b and c) has a price, i.e. that diversification towards a hedging debt portfolio would have meant net foreign exchange losses when compared to the actual currency mix. And the possibility to borrow along the strategy chosen by the World Bank should have meant net foreign exchange earnings when compared to the actual currency mix of Indonesia's debt. In fact, the opposite has occurred (Table 2.5).

The computations in Table 2.5 are based on two assumptions: a) maturing debt is rolled over and no net lending takes place; b) interest payments accrue at the end of the year and are not debt-financed.

Pure interest effects then measure the gain (loss) from borrowing at a lower (higher) interest rate using one of the alternative portfolios. The

Table 2.5   *Net exchange and interest savings (+) and losses (-) of alternative debt portfolios in US dollars (billions)*

	1985	1986	1987	6/1988
1. World Bank Currency Pool				
Pure interest effects	+.39	+.40	+.47	+.44
Interest effects of change in conversion value	—	-.16	-.18	-.28
Change in conversion value	-2.59	-3.76	-5.19	+4.21
Net savings (losses)	-2.20	-3.52	-4.90	+4.37
2. Optimal Debt Portfolio (max correlation with tot-variance)				
Pure interest effects	-.17	-.10	-.31	-.52
Interest effects of change in conversion value	—	+.16	+.21	+.27
Change in conversion value	+2.59	+3.56	+4.21	—
Net savings (losses)	+2.42	+3.62	+4.11	-.25
3. Optimal Debt Portfolio (net cash flows)				
Pure interest effects	-.36	-.28	-.47	-.59
Interest effects of change in conversion value	—	+.22	+.26	+.31
Change in conversion value	+3.56	+4.54	+4.86	-.65
Net savings	+3.20	+4.48	+4.65	-.93

Source: Author's calculations.

multiplication of 34.2 billion US dollars (debt at end-84) with the respective differences in interest rates yields the result. It springs from Table 2.5 that the World Bank mix generates pure interest rate savings while the hedging portfolios inflict pure interest rate losses. The maximum difference of interest rate burdens are observed in mid-1988 when pure interest losses of the debt portfolio aimed at matching cash flows ($590 million) and the pure interest savings of the World Bank pool ($440 million) add up to almost

$1 billion. However, the calculation on interest payments has to be corrected for exchange rate movements to tell the full story (Mohl/Sobol, 1983).

Interest effects of changes in conversion value do just that. They adjust the interest payments for last year's changes in the conversion value against the reference mix, by multiplying it with the current year's respective annual interest rate. It appears that some of the World Bank pool's interest savings are already absorbed by the interest effects of the inflated conversion value.

Changes in conversion value denote the foreign exchange savings and losses on the principal during a given year. They reflect the year-to-year difference in the weighted exchange rate index of the alternative debt portfolio *minus* the year-to-year difference in the weighted exchange rate of Indonesia's reference mix, multiplied by the end-1984 debt stock. Table 5 demonstrates that the strong downward (1985-87) and upward (1988) movement of the US dollar dwarfs the interest costs as a determinant of the overall debt burden. Had Indonesia matched the currency mix of its foreign debt with the currency structure of its cash flows, it would not only have minimized the foreign exchange risk of cross-currency fluctuations, but also would have saved around 10 billion US dollars during 1985-88. On the other hand, had the Indonesian government followed the World Bank's debt management practices, it would have lost about 6 billion US dollars during the same period in comparison to its actual debt structure.

5. Some Conclusions

This paper has been written with hindsight. It does not follow from the analysis that a hedging debt portfolio is cheaper than a low-interest debt portfolio such as Indonesia's actual mix or the World Bank's currency pool. As the figures for 1988 show (and those before 1985 could have shown), even the World Bank's pool can at times combine interest and exchange savings though uncovered interest parity makes it rather unlikely to hold for any lengthy period.

The following can be concluded, however:

1) Indonesia's actual currency composition of debt magnifies its foreign exchange risk exposure. Net exports are in US dollars, net imports mostly in yen and some European currencies; yet its foreign debt is only to a small part in US dollars. With such a currency mix in debt *and* trade, Indonesia suffers from a build-in destabilizer. With an appreciating yen, the yen weight in foreign debt increases and at the same time Indonesia suffers from a negative J-curve effect on its trade account.

2) With highly volatile key currency movements, annual interest cost on foreign debt have only a minor importance as a determinant for the overall cost of foreign borrowing. Changes in the conversion value of outstanding debt plus the interest effect of these changes outweigh the pure interest effects in the comparison of alternative debt portfolios as a function of a) the level of outstanding debt, the currency structure of that debt, c) the variance and covariance of key currency fluctuations and d) the differences in interest rates among different key currencies.

3) The World Bank's currency pool seems particularly inadequate for almost all developing countries because it tends to increase their foreign exchange risk exposure for the benefit of a very questionable reduction in the pure interest cost of the Bank's lending. Rather than using currency swaps to undiversify its lending into hard currency, the Bank should use the swaps to diversify its original currency structure in accordance with the cash flows of the given developing country.

REFERENCES

Kroner, Kenneth F. (1988), *Optimal Currency Composition of External Debt — Applications to Indonesia and Turkey*, University of Arizona, mimeo, August.

Lonaeus, Hakan (1988), 'How the Bank Finances Its Operations', *Finance & Development*, September, pp. 40-42.

Magee, Stephen P., and Ramesh K.S. Rao (1980), 'Vehicle and Nonvehicle Currencies in International Trade', *American Economic Review*, May, pp. 368-373.

Mayer, Helmut W. (1987), 'The Impact of Exchange Rate Changes Between Key Currencies on the Debt Structure and Debt Service Burden of Developing Countries', *SEACEN Occasional Papers* no. 5, December.

Mohl, Andrew and Dorothy Sobol (1983), 'Currency Diversification and LDC Debt', *FRBNY Quarterly Review*, Autumn, p. 19.

3. Some Evidence on Debt-Related Determinants of Investment and Consumption in Heavily Indebted Countries*

1. Introduction

Investment in most heavily indebted countries has been weak since 1982. Several papers (Krugman, 1988; Corden, 1988; Sachs, 1988) have subsequently established the debt overhang proposition: the existence of a heavy debt burden reduces the incentive to invest and to save.[1] This proposition has given an important rationale for the 1989 shift in international debt management, emphasizing debt relief rather than new money for problem debtors. Empirical research on the debt overhang proposition has either investigated the secondary market for developing country debt or, directly, explored the debtor countries' investment and savings behaviour.

The first approach measures the elasticity of the secondary market price of commercial bank debt with respect to its face value. The secondary market approach has systematically found a low estimate (see, notably, Cohen, 1989a). While these results cannot reject the existence of a debt overhang, they imply that debt relief cannot be Pareto improving. Thus 'across-the-board debt forgiveness... is not in the interest of the creditors for most highly indebted countries' (Claessens, 1990).

The second empirical approach to test for debt overhang looks directly at investment and savings (or consumption) behaviour. Some preliminary analysis by the IMF (1989) has concluded that the debt overhang plays a large part in explaining the slump in investment in problem debtor countries. Doubts about the method applied by the IMF analysis motivate this chapter. In particular, the IMF analysis does not consider other determinants of investment and savings besides debt levels. By contrast, we specify and test conventional investment and consumption functions in order to contrast the debt overhang proposition with competing explanations for investment and

*   Originally published in *Weltwirtschaftliches Archiv, vol. 127*, no. 2, 1991, pp. 281-297.

consumption behaviour. We find that the switch from positive to negative
net financial transfers to the debtor countries is a more important explanation for the investment drop than are levels of debt outstanding. Our finding
suggests that cutting the debt stock with no or little new lending is unlikely
to spur investment in heavily indebted countries.

The remainder of this chapter is structured as follows: Section 2 discusses
the debt overhang proposition and its implications for investment and consumption behaviour. This is contrasted with the behaviour of a debtor
country under liquidity constraints. The covariance tests performed in Section 3 reveal that savings and investment ratios did not significantly differ
between various country groups, rejecting the IMF (*ibid.*) analysis. Section 4 specifies and estimates investment and consumption functions in order
to test the conflicting hypotheses spelt out in Section 2 for the various credit
regimes. Section 5 draws conclusions for the international debt management.

2. Debt Overhang and Liquidity Constraints

The debt overhang proposition belongs to the group of moral hazard interpretations of the current debt crisis. Their advocates argue that a debt overhang provides a disincentive for adjustment. Both concepts have been put
into a specific context (see the presentation of Corden, 1988). 'Adjustment'
(which can be thought of as economic reform) refers to the debtor's decision
to invest or to consume in a two-period model. The economy 'inherits' a
given stock of debt in the first period, which must be serviced in the second
period. The decision in period one is to consume or to invest, the latter
yielding a return in period two, which serves to pay back the debt and to
consume. This decision is presumed to be biased towards consumption in
the presence of a debt overhang. 'Debt overhang' is defined as the difference between the face value of debt outstanding and its market value —
the expected present value of future resource transfers (debt service minus
new debt) from the borrower to the lender.[2] The debt overhang may act like
a tax on the debtor's consumption in period two. This is because for over-
indebted countries debt service does not depend on scheduled interest and
amortization any more, but is linked to their economic performance via arrears and involuntary lending. If a debtor is only servicing part of his debt,
the reduced consumption in period one is not offset by a higher consumption
in the future because the creditor would reap all or most of the benefits of
that adjustment effort. Consequently, it does not pay to invest. The country
will instead consume its resources in period one and will then (have to)
default upon its debt. Hence, the conclusion is that debt relief would in-

crease the incentive of a debtor country to make an adjustment effort (to invest) because a larger share of the investment benefits would be left to the debtor. Debt relief would be in the interest of both debtor and creditor, since then at least part of the debt is repaid. The provision of new money would instead, according to the debt overhang proposition, leave the problem of debt-stock related disincentives unresolved.

However, debt is not the only variable affecting investment and consumption behaviour of debtor countries. The credit regime the country is subject to is a crucial determinant of investment and consumption. If a country has unrestricted access to the international capital market, i.e. is only limited by its inter-temporal budget constraint, investment and consumption decisions are *separated*. The country invests until the marginal productivity of capital is equal to the world interest rate [see Hofman and Reisen (1990) for a formal exposition], and it borrows up to the point where marginal utility of consumption is equated in each period. The capital market is used to allocate wealth over time, and the country consumes according to its wealth constraint (see, for example, Sachs, 1984, pp. 6 ff). With unrestricted access to foreign capital markets, neither new money nor debt relief affects investment behaviour, which is only governed by the world interest rate and marginal productivity.

Unrestricted access to capital markets seems hardly a relevant case for most LDC borrowers and especially for the problem debtors over the 1980s. The inability to borrow as much as desired, or indeed the net lender position enforced upon these countries, affects the optimal investment-consumption choice, since these variables are then interrelated. With liquidity constraints, investment becomes less attractive, since this constraint reduces the possibility to consume in the same period. The opportunity costs of capital then exceed the world market interest rate and are additionally governed by the availability of new money and the marginal utility of consumption. Wealth can no longer be freely allocated between present and future consumption. Consumption in period one is lower than in the case of unconstrained borrowing. What is the impact of debt relief and new money under this credit regime? Debt relief will *reduce* investment because it increases the resources for consumption in period two without the need to invest for these resources in period one (Corden, 1988). New money instead will raise both consumption and investment in period one because the opportunity costs of capital are reduced towards the world interest rate.

Whether the debt overhang hypothesis or the hypothesis of liquidity constraints can better explain investment and consumption behaviour is basically an empirical question. Before we set out to present our evidence on these conflicting hypotheses, we will have a closer look at the empirical evidence provided by the IMF in favour of the debt overhang proposition.

3. A Rebuttal of the IMF Test

The IMF (1989) bases its support of the debt overhang proposition on two pieces of evidence. First, the savings ratio in the so-called Baker-15 countries[3] fell, rather than increased, when external finance dried up. The necessary squeeze in domestic demand relative to output was therefore more than fully reflected in lower investment. Second, a comparison of the country group of problem debtors with a group of other heavily indebted countries, which did not experience debt servicing problems shows that investment and savings ratios dropped in the former group but not in the latter. This evidence supposedly confirms the debt overhang hypothesis, which attributes disincentive effects to the fact that debt service is linked to economic performance in problem debtors, thus weakening the incentive to invest.

A closer inspection of the IMF analysis reveals several shortcomings, however.

–   First, the base period 1975-81 against which the IMF compares events after 1981 is highly exceptional because it includes the years when the build-up of foreign debt was overshooting at an unsustainable pace. Especially during 1978-81, foreign savings financed exceptional levels of investment in problem debtor countries. Expectations explain largely why investment ratios peaked in that period and dropped thereafter (Dornbusch, 1985). The increasing anticipation of a future depreciation of the real exchange rate acts as a temporary investment stimulus in developing countries, since imports are an important input in the production of investment goods. While anticipated depreciation means an immediate jump in the real price of assets, real capital costs start only to rise once real depreciation sets in. Then disinvestment takes place.

–   Second, the IMF analysis selects a control group of middle-income nonproblem debtors which is highly arbitrary. Nonproblem debtors are defined as indebted countries that are not confronted with serious debt-servicing difficulties. The IMF sample picks only high-investment countries (Indonesia, Korea, Malaysia, Thailand and Turkey). We have added Algeria, Greece, Israel, and Portugal, which also belong to the group of nonproblem debtors in order to extend the control group for a covariance test on investment and savings ratios.[4]

Table 3.1   A covariance test for savings ratios and investment ratios

		1971 -81	1982 -87	1982-87 vs 1971-81	1971 -81	1982 -87	1982-87 vs 1971-81
		Savings ratios			*Investment ratios*		
I.	Ratios						
	Problem debtors	19.4	14.5	-4.9	23.3	17.8	-5.5
	Non-problem debtors						
	IMF sample	22.7	23.5	0.8	25.1	26.4	1.3
	Extended sample	24.1	21.9	-2.3	27.9	25.8	-2.0
II.	Variance within country groups						
	Problem debtors	48.2	97.6	52.0	25.5	51.1	33.8
	Non-problem debtors						
	IMF sample	7.0	11.9	9.2	6.2	10.0	3.9
	Extended sample	40.9	48.1	24.6	28.7	21.8	17.7
III.	Variance among country groups						
	IMF sample	2.1	15.2	6.0	0.6	14.0	8.8
	Extended sample	5.3	12.9	1.6	4.8	15.1	2.9
IV.	F-statistics						
	IMF sample	1.0	3.6	2.4 (<4.4)	0.5	6.2	6.0 (>4.4)
	Extended sample	2.4	3.3	0.7 (<4.3)	3.6	7.6	2.1 (<4.3)

Note: Savings ratios are defined as gross national savings as a percentage of gross national product, at current prices. Investment ratios are defined as gross domestic investment as a percentage of gross domestic product, at current prices. For the definition of country groups, see text. Figures in parentheses for F-statistics show the critical values at the 95 per cent confidence level.
Source: World Bank, World Tables 1988-89, Tape Documentation.

A covariance test is presented in Table 3.1 for savings ratios and investment ratios. The test reveals that the change in savings ratios (comparing
the periods 1982-87 and 1971-81) was not significant at a 95 per cent confidence level, regardless of whether the IMF sample or the extended sample
was chosen as a control group. There was indeed an important drop in savings ratios and investment ratios in problem debtor countries during the
1980s. But the variance of national savings ratios within the country groups
of problem and nonproblem debtors was too big and the variance between
these two country groups too small to confirm the debt overhang proposition
along these lines. The only difference which is significant at a 95 per cent
confidence level is found for the changes in investment ratios between problem debtors and the IMF sample of nonproblem debtors.

The fact that investment behaviour changed more markedly than savings
behaviour between problem and nonproblem debtors suggests that net financial flows to the debtor countries are at least as important in explaining this
behaviour as are debt stock related disincentives. Table 3.2 illustrates this
point for the Latin American countries: investment/GDP ratios in the 1980s
fell on average by 6.8 percentage points compared with the 1970s, almost
exactly equal to the increase in the noninterest external surplus (which
roughly measures the reduction in liquidity).

While investment ratios in Latin America dropped immediately in 1983 to
accommodate the switch in net financial transfers (net new debt minus interest), they have stabilized thereafter on a modest upward trend (IDB, 1989,
Table 2-4). Table 3.2 shows also, contrary to what is often maintained, that

*Table 3.2   Latin America: investment and the noninterest current
            account (per cent of GDP)*

	1960-69	1970-82	1983-88
Investment	18.6	23.2	16.4
Noninterest current account	5.3	-0.4	6.1

	Change 1983-88 against	
	1960-69	1970-82
Investment	-1.8	-6.8
Noninterest current account	0.8	6.5

Source: IDB, Economic and Social Progress in Latin America, 1989 Report.

investment ratios in Latin America are not low by historical standards. Investment ratios and the noninterest current account are now as high as they were in the 1960s. Given this *prima facie* evidence, assessing debt incentives independent of the credit regime to which a country is subject, seems a serious flaw. We will rather assess the impact of both liquidity and debt on investment and consumption in problem debtor countries, and provide empirical evidence on the relative importance of these factors.

4. Debt-Related Determinants of Investment and Consumption

(i) Empirical Specification

To discriminate between the hypotheses discussed in Section 2, debt and liquidity constraints will be integrated into standard empirical specifications of consumption and investment.

To be sure, the liquidity constraint becomes a function of the level of indebtedness once creditworthiness has been lost. And, in turn, new money will add to the (absolute) debt level. Such interdependence may blur the discriminative power of the tests performed below, but only to a small extent. First, even if existing debt stocks determine the debtor's capacity to borrow new money, debt relief in turn is unlikely to relieve the liquidity constraint. Second, it still holds that debt stocks exert a negative effect on investment when a debt overhang prevails, while debt stocks exert a positive effect on investment when the liquidity constraint is more binding than the debt constraint.

The effect of debt-related determinants on investment is estimated in the context of an investment equation, containing the variables discussed in Section 2:

$$(1) \qquad I = \alpha_0 + \alpha_1 r + \alpha_2 S + \alpha_3 (dF/dK) + \alpha_4 NTR + \alpha_5 D + \mu,$$

where I = investment, r = real interest rate, S = domestic savings, dF/dK = marginal productivity of capital, NTR = net transfer to the debtor country, D = debt burden, and μ = error term.

As discussed in Section 2, the expected sign of the debt burden coefficient is negative under the debt overhang proposition, zero under the hypothesis of unrestricted borrowing, and positive under liquidity constraints. The net transfer coefficient is expected to be zero under (the extreme version of) the debt overhang proposition, zero also under the hypothesis of unrestricted borrowing, and positive under liquidity constraints. World interest rates are expected to have a negative impact on the level of investment, most strongly in the case of unconstrained borrowing.

The impact of interest rates weakens with tightening constraints on borrowing, and can even be expected to be zero under the debt overhang proposition. Domestic savings are expected to matter for investment only under the hypothesis of liquidity constraints, since liquidity constraints interrelate consumption and investment. Savings have no expected impact under the two competing hypotheses. Capital productivity is expected to have a weakened impact on investment under the debt overhang proposition, while productivity definitely matters under the two other credit regimes.

In order to estimate eq. (1), a number of proxies for the variables had to be taken of which the most important one is that of debt burden. The debt burden, D, can be measured in a number of ways. In the empirical research concerning the determinants of repayment problems, usually a measure of debt/exports, debt/GDP or debt service is used. Neither of these variables is a perfect measure of the real burden, and all of them are endogenous variables to a certain extent: rational creditors would only allow a country to build up a high debt or debt service level (compared with GDP or exports) if they ascribe a high creditworthiness to this country, or in other words, if the debt burden for the country is manageable. Besides, the correct measure for debt burden depends upon the nature of the problem: if the debt crisis is basically seen as an internal transfer problem, debt to GDP is a more accurate ratio than debt to exports or debt service to exports, whereas the latter is a more accurate indicator if the problem is the external transfer (Reisen, 1989). Debt service depends to a large extent on the maturity distribution of the debt and is rather a measure of liquidity than of debt burden. As such, it is already included in the transfer variable of eq. (1). Differences in timing of repayments and levels of interest for different countries would make the discounted present value of future debt service a better indicator, but if liquidity is constrained, not only present values count, but also the timing of debt service. Finally, without any change in debt, debt service, or any other conventional measure, the *real* burden may increase, e.g., due to terms of trade movements, a rise in interest rates, if the debt is a floating rate debt, etc.

Given these qualifications, one can expect to find the conventional measures to have only a weak relation with debt burden. However, this relationship may become stronger, if we add *a priori* information: *given* that a country has debt servicing problems, an increase in the debt GDP ratio will more likely indicate an increase in the debt burden than a reduction of it. A more direct measure of debt problems is equally tested as a proxy for debt burden: interest arrears. Again, this is not an undisputed measure of debt burden, but it does track the debt overhang proposition.

As a proxy for world market real interest rates, the US government bond yield deflated by the percentage change in the US GDP deflator was taken. Productivity of investments was proxied by GDP growth. For the savings variable, domestic savings as a percentage of GDP were taken. Net transfers were calculated as net long-term capital disbursements minus long-term interest payments. Short-term capital movements were excluded, due to lack of data over the 1970s.

As discussed in Section 2, the unconstrained borrower will divide his wealth between consumption now and in the future. Debt and credit constraints have an influence on the marginal propensity to consume, as well as on wealth itself. In order to distinguish empirically between these effects, we will test the hypotheses on consumption in the context of the Permanent Income Hypothesis, the specification of which has received the best empirical support in developing countries (see IDB, 1989). According to this hypothesis, permanent consumption C_p, is a function of permanent income Y_p:

(2) $\qquad C_p = kY_p,$

where k is the marginal propensity to consume out of permanent income. Assuming that adaptive expectations are a reasonable approximation of expectations formation in developing countries, (2) can be readily operationalized. Permanent income is then proxied by a weighted average of present and past income.[5] Taking into account a trend factor in income and using a Koyck transformation yields [see for a full derivation, König (1978)]:

(3) $\qquad C_t = k\,\beta\,Y_t + (1 + \alpha - \beta)\,C_{t-1}, + \mu_t,$

with C_t = consumption in period t, Y_t = income in period t, α = trend in income, β = coefficient of expectations adjustment, and μ_t = error term.

The term k can now be identified from the coefficients of C_{t-1} and Y_t if either α is neglected or estimated directly. In the case of a debt overhang, one would expect k to be higher than in the case of normal credit relations. If a country is constrained on the capital market, one would expect k to be lower than in the case of free access to the capital market, due to imperfect smoothing of consumption (see Section 2).

The problem with the hypotheses on k is, of course, to find the normal k. If we accept the IMF criterion of rescheduling as a sign of disrupted capital market relations, the 1970s can be considered as a reasonable counterfactual. We will therefore take the change in the marginal propensity to consume out of permanent income between 1971-81 and 1982-87 as an indicator for the presence or absence of debt overhang.

Table 3.3   *Investment in problem debtor countries, 1971-87*

	1971-81			1982-87		1971-87	
	(a)	(b)	(c)	(d)	(e)	(f)	(g)
Variables							
Constant	8.95	7.34	16.13	18.85	9.58	2.54	3.76
	(3.58)	(3.70)	(3.44)	(3.58)	(1.21)	(1.75)	(3.42)
Investment(-1)	0.70	0.75	0.5	0.55	0.59	0.80	0.81
	(8.66)	9.48	(5.28)	(5.03)	(4.85)	(12.89)	(13.32)
Investment(-2)	-0.28	-0.30	-0.35	-0.30	-0.43	-0.28	-0.28
	(3.34)	(3.67)	(3.24)	(2.56)	(3.56)	(4.72)	(4.68)
Real interest	-0.51	-0.48	-0.57	-0.56	-0.17	-0.43	-0.42
	(2.64)	(2.69)	(2.31)	(2.66)	(0.55)	(4.17)	(4.33)
Growth	0.11	0.10	0.16	0.23	0.09	0.12	0.12
	(1.56)	(1.33)	(2.29)	(2.96)	(1.00)	(2.44)	(2.54)
Savings	0.12	0.11	0.28	0.14	0.24	0.20	0.16
	(1.80)	(1.64)	(3.65)	(1.68)	(2.66)	(4.96)	4.64)
Net transfers	0.25	0.23	0.50	0.53	0.62	0.29	0.23
	(2.16)	(2.07)	(4.29)	(4.39)	(4.46)	(3.65)	(3.09)
Debt/GDP		-0.03		0.05		-0.00	
		(1.05)		(2.01)		(0.49)	
Debt/exports	-0.01		0.01		0.00		
	(1.92)		(2.92)		(0.87)		
Arrears				0.02			
				(0.97)			
Time	0.39	0.32	-0.60	-0.59	-0.06	0.21	0.21
	(3.88)	(3.75)	(2.80)	(2.40)	(0.20)	(3.08)	(3.65)

The consumption function was estimated with total per capita consumption and per capita gross national product, using 1980 prices. This assumes that government consumption is equally valued as private consumption, but avoids the problem of defining disposable income for each country.

	1971-81			1982-87		1971-87	
	(a)	(b)	(c)	(d)	(e)	(f)	(g)
Statistics							
R^2	0.84	0.83	0.91	0.91	0.90	0.87	0.87
F-statistic	35.4	37.4	41.0	38.3	30.2	73.7	76.4
Number of observations	147.0	147.0	87.0	87.0	72.0	234.0	247.0
Sum of squared residuals	601.4	674.2	158.0	168.5	120.7	949.2	1,000.3
ϕ	0.00 (0.03)	-0.04 (0.44)	-0.12 (1.03)	0.07 (0.59)	-0.12 (0.99)	0.03 (0.30)	0.01 (0.18)
$B(Chi^2_{23})$	12.5	9.8	7.9	2.4	7.4	7.9	7.9

Note: Estimation method is OSL; fixed effect model. The country group is defined in Section I. All variables, except the investment terms, are averages of period *t* and *(t-1)*. Absolute value of *t*-statistics in parentheses. The variables are defined as follows: *Investments* (-1): Fixed investment as a percentage of GDP, lagged one period. *Investments* (-2): Fixed investment as a percentage of GDP, lagged two periods. *Real interest rate*: Yield on US government bonds corrected for depreciation: REALRA=RUS-(INFLt) with RUS=Yield on US government bonds, INFL=percentage change in US GDP-deflator. *Savings*: Gross domestic savings as a percentage of GDP. *Growth*: Percentage growth in GDP measured as 100 x d log (constant GDP). *Net transfers*: Long-term capital disbursements minus long-term capital repayments minus long-term interest payments as a percentage of GDP. *Debt/GDP*: Public and private long-term external debt minus international reserves as a percentage of GDP. *Debt/exports*: Public and private long-term external debt minus international reserves as a percentage of exports and non-factor services. *Time*: Time variable, with 1968=1 . . . 1987=20. Arrears: Interest arrears outstanding as a percentage of total debt service due. The statistics denote: Φ : Estimated first-order correlation of the residuals. B: Breusch/Pagan test statistic for heteroscedasticity.
Sources: World Bank, World Tables, 1988-89, Tape Documentation; IMF, International Financial Statistics Yearbook 1988 (for yield on US government bonds and US inflation); Institute of International Finance (arrears data); own calculations.

(ii) Results

Equations (1) and (3) were estimated for the period 1971-87 and the two subperiods 1971-81 and 1982-87, using pooled time-series cross section data for problem debtor countries in order to gain the necessary degrees of freedom. For the consumption function, the Instrumental Variable method was used, since shocks on income are likely to affect consumption as well. Dummy variables allowed for different intercepts in both investment and consumption estimations. The results can thus only be interpreted for an

Debt, Deficits and Exchange Rates

Table 3.4   *Correlation coefficients between actual and predicted values*
of investments and consumption from reported regressions

	Investment			Consumption		
	(a)	(c)	(f)	(h)	(i)	(j)
Argentina	0.82	0.92	0.93	0.69	0.72	0.67
Bolivia	0.65	0.93	0.91	0.92	0.95	0.85
Brazil	0.01	0.92	0.88	0.98	0.97	0.98
Chile	0.69	0.84	0.81	0.89	0.39	0.86
Colombia	0.21	0.31	0.21	0.99	0.97	0.99
Ecuador	0.65	0.83	0.73	0.99	0.85	0.88
Ivory Coast	0.81	0.97	0.95	0.83	0.96	0.83
Mexico	0.82	0.82	0.87	0.99	0.93	0.97
Morocco	0.88	0.64	0.85	0.98	0.87	0.96
Nigeria	0.18	0.95	0.72	0.37	0.97	0.64
Peru	0.88	0.73	0.83	0.79	0.99	0.88
Philippines	0.96	0.96	0.95	0.98	0.94	0.95
Uruguay	0.98	0.89	0.96	0.97	0.97	0.88
Venezuela	0.80	0.94	0.88	0.93	0.69	0.91
Yugoslavia	0.87	0.97	0.93	0.92	0.92	0.91

Note: Equations refer to the estimations reported in Tables 3.3 and 3.5.

'average' problem debtor. This precludes detecting the presence or absence
of debt incentives for an individual country.

The estimated investment equations in Table 3.3 perform rather well in
terms of R^2 and F-statistics, but this is due to the lagged investment terms,
which were included to suppress autocorrelation of the residual. Inclusion
of a time trend suppressed heteroscedasticity.[6] Investment behaviour showed
a structural change between the two subperiods.[7]

The evidence on debt-related variables allows rejecting the debt overhang hypothesis for the average problem debtor in the sense that no negative correlation of debt and investments could be detected. On the contrary, in the 1982-87 period, both debt/GDP and debt/exports were significantly positive at the 5 per cent level. This is in line with the theoretical findings for a liquidity constrained country. Arrears did not seem to influence investment behaviour in the 1982-87 period, which would occur under the debt over-hang hypothesis. The coefficient for net transfers is significantly positive in both periods, and in each specification. Estimations were also performed with net transfers split up into long-term debt service and long-term capital disbursements, using further the specification of equations (a) and (c). In 1971-81, the values were respectively (t-values in parentheses) -0.39 (2.25) and 0.24 (2.12). For the 1982-87 period, the values were -0.52 (3.28) and 0.49 (3.66). For both periods, the null hypothesis that the absolute value of the coefficients were equal could not be rejected.[8] This indicates that debt service had no other effects than liquidity effects; possible negative effects, due to taxation for financing the debt service, cannot be detected in this way.

The domestic savings variable was only in the 1980s significantly posi-tive (equations c and e). A joint test of the significance of both the net transfers and the savings variable accepts the null hypothesis of no signifi-cant difference from zero in equation (a), but rejects the same hypothesis for equation (c).[9] This indicates that over the latter period the problem debtors became more constrained in their access to the international capital market.

The negative correlation between interest and investment in the 1982-87 period is compatible with the credit constraint hypothesis given that the problem debtors were net lenders over this period. Given the joint insigni-ficance of the net transfer and savings variables over the 1971-81 period, one might conclude that the negative correlation between interest and invest-ments indicates an unconstrained capital market access for this period.

Although more formal tests for the pooling procedure used in the estima-tions were rejected — or could not be performed due to a lack in the de-grees of freedom — the equations estimated for the whole sample performed quite well for individual countries, as can be seen in Table 3.4 [For a similar procedure of testing the pooling procedure, see Pastor (1989).]

The estimation results for the consumption function are presented in Table 3.5 The marginal propensity to consume out of permanent income, k, showed a fall in the 1980s as compared to the 1970s. This holds also for the marginal propensity to consume corrected for a trend factor, kg.[10] We con-clude, therefore, that it is more likely for the problem debtors that the margi-nal propensity to consume was lower in the 1980s in comparison with the 1970s than the reverse, thus contradicting the debt overhang proposition and

Debt, Deficits and Exchange Rates

the evidence quoted in IMF (1989). The fall in k is predicted by the credit constraint hypothesis as presented in Section 2. The results shown in Table 3.5 should, however, be interpreted with caution. Apart from the specification of the Permanent Income Hypothesis, the estimated coefficients are not very stable over time, and the observed heteroscedasticity indicates that there are omitted variables. An F-test for the subperiods refutes the hypothesis of no structural change between the 1970s and 1980s.[11] Moreover, the causes of the movement in k are not further analyzed, and there might be other than debt and liquidity variables. Integrating these in the Permanent Income set-up would be necessary to derive firmer conclusions.[12] This is left for further research.

Table 3.5   Consumption in problem debtor countries, 1971-87 (dependent variable: consumption)

	1971-81 (h)	1982-87 (i)	1971-87 (j)
Variables			
Lagged consumption	0.556 (8.34)	0.143 (2.93)	0.576 (11.05)
Income	0.328	0.553	0.257
k	0.74	0.64	0.60
kg	0.70	0.57	—
Statistics			
R^2	1.00	1.00	1.00
F-statistic	2,738	1,046	4,815
Sum of squared residuals	1.8×10^9	7.9×10^8	2.4×10^9
ϕ	0.06	-0.13	0.10
Number of observations	165	90	255
$B(Chi^2_{16})$	15.5	17.5	14.8

Note: Estimation method: Instrumental variables, fixed effect model. Instruments: Lagged consumption, lagged income and country intercept dummies. The constant term, in all but one case insignificant, is not reported. The variables used in the regressions are expressed in local currency per capita, using 1980 prices. Consumption is private plus government consumption. Lagged consumption is private plus government consumption lagged one period; income is gross national product. k is the marginal propensity to consume from permanent income (see text); kg is the marginal propensity to consume from permanent income, corrected for a trend

factor. Φ denotes estimates of first-order auto correlation. B is the Breusch/Pagan test statistic for heteroscedasticity. Population is calculated using 1968 data, and extrapolated using population growth rates from the World Development Report 1989. Absolute values of t-statistics are in parentheses.
Sources: World Bank, World Tables, 1988-89, Tape Documentation; World Bank, World Development Report, 1989; own calculations.

Although a formal F-test would again reject the method of pooling chosen, the correlation between the predicted values from the estimated equations and the actual values observed for the individual countries is generally high (see Table 3.4). Exceptions to this are Colombia, Brazil and Peru in the period 1971-81.

5. Conclusions

Whether the drop in problem debtors' investment is due to the debt overhang rather than to the switch in net transfers, has important implications for policy. If the debt overhang is to blame for weak investment, the provision of liquidity alone would leave the problem of debt-stock related disincentives unresolved. A debt reduction would give investment a bigger boost than new foreign money. On the other hand, countries that are constrained only by liquidity need new funds to take advantage of profitable investment opportunities. Cutting the debt stock without lending new money would not spur investment there.

This paper has developed hypotheses on the impact of debt-related variables on investment and consumption behaviour. The empirical evidence presented here allows rejecting the debt overhang proposition and is rather in line with the liquidity constraint hypothesis. These findings complement the results derived by the research on the secondary market for developing country debt. The findings of this paper are also in line with Borensztein's (1990) simulation results, which show even at high levels of debt the dominance of the credit constraint over the debt overhang in explaining investment behaviour, and add to Cohen's (1989b) results of estimating the influence of debt and liquidity variables on growth and investment.[13]

This is bad news for the new international debt strategy which relies on 'voluntary, market-based' debt reduction. For the available evidence, presented here and elsewhere, implies that it is unlikely that banks will gain (increase the market value of their claims) by granting debt reduction. Their claims could be better protected by the provision of new loans because new money is more likely than debt reduction to spur investment in heavily indebted countries.

NOTES

1. The concept of investment stands here for the broader concept of 'economic reform', like trade liberalization, privatization, or tax reform. Both investment and 'economic reform' are expected to increase future output and the capacity to service debt.
2. The debt overhang can be illustrated by the so-called debt relief Laffer curve. The curve relates the market value of debts to their book value. It starts with zero; it first rises at pari to the book value and then continues to rise, although at a slower rate; finally, it reaches a maximum after which the market value continually decreases towards zero, while the book value stretches to infinity. The debt overhang is "weak" when it is to the left of the curve maximum, and 'strong' when it is to the right.
3. Another term often used for the countries is 'problem debtors'. They include Argentina, Bolivia, Brazil, Chile, Colombia, Ecuador, Ivory Coast, Mexico, Morocco, Nigeria, Peru, Philippines, Uruguay, Venezuela, and Yugoslavia.
4. The sample of nonproblem countries could be further extended according to the selection criteria used by the IMF if some small island economies were added for which, however, investment and savings data were not readily available.
5. This concept of permanent income is valid if current and past income provide a reasonable indicator for future income streams. This concept is not undisputed (see, e.g., Hall, 1978).
6. This time trend may capture the effect of omitted variables equally trended, but candidates for this, such as the terms of trade and the real exchange rate, either showed insignificant signs or deteriorated the estimation results due to high correlation with other explanatory variables.
7. An F-test for structural changes in the investment equations (H_0,: no structural change) gave the following results:

Equation	F-value	Accepted/rejected at 95% level
(a) and (c)	$F_{23,188}= 2.04$	rejected
(b) and (d)	$F_{21,201}= 1.63$	rejected

8. It was tested whether there is a significant difference between the absolute values of the coefficients for debt service and long-term capital disbursements (H_0: no difference in absolute value). The unrestricted equation includes these variables separately; the restricted equations are (a) and (c) in Table 3.3. The results are:

Sum of squared residuals		F-value	Accepted/rejected at 95% level
Unrestricted equation	Restricted equation		
595.7	601.4	$F_{1,123}= 1.18$	accepted
157.9	158.0	$F_{1,63}= 0.06$	accepted

9. A test for the joint significance of the savings and net transfer variables (H_0,: not significantly different from zero) yields the following results:

Equation	F-value	Accepted/rejected at 95% level
(a)	$F_{2,124}=2.85$	accepted
(b)	$F_{2,64}-14.52$	rejected

10. The trend factor was found by regressing the logarithm of per capita GNP on time: *In (GNP/CAP) = a + bt + e* . The trends, α, for the debtor groups and the two periods are then found by [see World Bank (1988)]: α = antilog(*b*) - 1. The values found for α are 0.022 (1971-81) and -0.006 (1982-87). It should be noted that the time coefficient was not always significant. Furthermore, the value of -0.006 for the problem debtors is unlikely to be the expected trend. A higher value for α would imply a lower value for the problem debtors' trend-corrected marginal propensity to consume over the 1980s.
11. A test for a structural change in the consumption function (H_0: no structural change) shows that the hypothesis is rejected for equations (h) and (i) at the 95 per cent level ($F_{17,221} = 3.79$).
12. Adding debt and net transfer variables to the consumption equation in an ad-hoc manner yielded positive signs for both in the 1971-81 period, with only net transfers significantly different from zero. In the 1980s, both variables have a significantly negative sign.
13. Cohen (1989b) found a positive, significant relation between debt and growth; and a positive, but insignificant relation between debt and investments. He shows also that net transfers from the rescheduling debtors crowded out investments.

REFERENCES

Borensztein, Eduardo (1990), 'Debt Overhang, Credit Rationing and Investment' *Journal of Development Economics*, vol. 32, pp. 315-335.

Claessens, Stijn (1990), 'The Secondary Market and the International Debt Problem' *World Development*, vol. 18, pp. 1671-1677.

Cohen, Daniel (1989a), 'How to Cope with a Debt Overhang: Cut Flows Rather Than Stocks' in Ishrat Husain, Ishac Diwan (eds.), *Dealing with the Debt Crisis* , Washington, pp. 229-235.

— (1989b), *Slow Growth and Large LDC Debt in the Eighties: an Empirical Analysis*, Paris, mimeo.

Corden, W. Max (1988), 'Debt Relief and Adjustment Incentives' *IMF Staff Papers,* vol. 35, pp. 628-643.

Dornbusch, Rudiger (1985), 'External Debt. Budget Deficits, and Disequilibrium Exchange Rates' in Gordon W Smith, John T Coddington (eds.), *International Debt and the Developing Countries*, Washington, pp. 213-235.

Hall, Robert E. (1978), 'Stochastic Implications of the Life Cycle — Permanent Income Hypothesis: Theory and Evidence' *Journal of Political Economy*, vol. 86, pp. 71-87.

Hofman, Bert, Helmut Reisen (1990), *Debt Overhang, Liquidity Constraints and Adjustment Incentives*, OECD Development Centre Technical Papers no. 32, Paris.

Inter-American Development Bank (IDB) (1989), *Economic and Social Progress in Latin America, 1989 Report*, Washington.

International Monetary Fund (IMF) (1989), *IMF World Economic Outlook* Supplementary Note 1, Washington.

König, Heinz, 'Konsumfunktionen' (1978), in Willi Albers et al. (Hrsg.), *Handwörterbuch der Wirtschaftswissenschaft*, Bd. 4. Stuttgart, pp. 513-528.

Krugman, Paul R. (1988), *Market-Based Debt Reduction Schemes*, National Bureau of Economic Research, NBER Working Paper no. 2587, Cambridge, Mass.

Pastor, Manuel, Jr. (1989), 'Current Account Deficits and Debt Accumulation in Latin America' *Journal of Development Economics,* vol. 31, pp. 77-97.

Reisen, Helmut (1989), *Public Debt, External Competitiveness and Fiscal Discipline in Developing Countries*, Princeton University, Princeton Studies in International Finance no. 66, Princeton.

Sachs, Jeffrey D. (1984), *Theoretical Issues in International Borrowing*, Princeton University, Princeton Studies in International Finance no. 54, Princeton.

— (1988) 'Conditionality, Debt Relief, and the Developing Country Debt Crisis' in Jeffrey D. Sachs (ed.), *Developing Country Debt and Economic Performance, Vol. 1: The International Financial System*, Chicago, pp. 255-295.

The World Bank (1988), *World Development Report 1988*, Washington.

4. The Brady Plan and Adjustment Incentives*

Capital formation in highly indebted developing countries has been weak since 1982. The widely accepted debt overhang proposition[1] interprets the investment drop as a moral hazard problem: a heavy debt burden raises the incentive to consume[2], since the marginal return from investment would accrue to the creditors. The debt overhang hypothesis has provided theoretical support for the Brady Initiative of March 1989. International debt strategy no longer focuses on the provision of further credit — as under the 1985 Baker plan — in return for stabilization and structural reform in problem debtor countries, but on debt relief.[3]

During 1990, four debt-relief agreements were concluded under the Brady Plan — with Mexico, the Philippines, Costa Rica and Venezuela. The Brady Initiative's incentive effects on debtor countries have thus been put to a first test. The test produced widely divergent, if not inconsistent, views at the last IMF/World Bank annual meeting. While according to the Institute of International Finance, 'the strategy has encouraged some countries to consider debt reduction an entitlement and to run interest arrears to commercial banks', the World Bank writes in its Annual Report 1990 that the Brady Plan has 'strengthened the incentives for member governments to embark on, or sustain, growth-oriented adjustment programs'.

The following aims at clarifying that debate: first, by a short look at the nature of Latin America's recurrent debt problems; second, by a critical discussion of academic moral hazard interpretations (the debt overhang proposition and the sovereign risk approach); and third, by a closer look at the results of the most important debt agreement under the Brady Plan so far, which has been with Mexico.

Since 1982 Latin America has had to transfer abroad a net total (debt service minus new debt) of over $200 billion. There have been no voluntary bank loans since then, a situation which has also affected less indebted countries (Colombia) and those which have always paid up (Chile). High inflation, excessive real interest rates, depressed savings and investment as well

* Originally published in Intereconomics, March/April 1991, pp. 69-73.

as repeated currency crises are symptomatic of Latin America's unsolved budgetary problem.[4] The recurrent debt problems in Latin America are mainly caused by fiscal rigidities.[5]

It is scarcely possible to distinguish whether the fiscal rigidities reflect unwillingness or inability to pay. Mainly public investment has been curtailed on the expenditure side. This could be interpreted as willingness to pay, but Corden[6], for instance, interprets the cut in investment as 'endogenous' default, since the basis for resources concerning the future debt service is narrowed and default is accordingly 'objectively' enforced.

Fiscal rigidities were most pronounced on the revenue side. Tax ratios of developing countries tend to be much lower than those of industrial countries, less than half as large on average, but there has been no instance in which a developing country has been able to raise the ratio several percentage points of GDP over the medium term, as has happened in some developed countries.[7] The erosion of the taxes in the debtor countries again hardly provides any distinctive evidence of either inability or unwillingness to pay. The many explanations include administrative and technical bottlenecks in tax assessment and tax collection; the stabilization-induced contraction of important tax bases such as wages, consumption, corporate earnings and imports; the inflationary erosion of tax yields because of the small share of progressive income tax and delays in tax collection; as well as the prevention of tax reforms by pressure groups who fear the withdrawal of tax incentives and exemptions.

Fiscal rigidities have now resulted in demonetized economies with high public domestic debt on which governments often have to pay a higher real interest than on foreign debts,[8] since domestic bondholders demand high inflation and default premiums. In particular with respect to public finances, the compliance with and accordingly the credibility of IMF conditionality has also declined considerably compared with previous decades.[9]

A few conclusions can be drawn from these observations. First, the Brady Initiative cannot make up for creditors' natural lack of information about the debtors' intentions so that, as in the past, it will be possible to distinguish only to a limited extent between 'good' and 'bad' payment behaviour. This implies that geopolitical motives will be over-emphasized in the choice of beneficiary countries. Second, it is important, precisely since it is so difficult to disentangle the moral hazard problems implied by sovereign risk, to highlight the incentive effects of international debt initiatives. Third, this is only meaningful if government finances are adequately stressed.

The Debt Overhang Hypothesis

According to Sachs[10] and Krugman[11], a debt overhang reduces the incentive for a debtor country to undertake economic reform. Within a two-period model the debtor has to decide whether to invest or to consume. The economy 'inherits' in the first period a given debt which must be serviced in the second period. According to the hypothesis, this decision is distorted in favour of consumtion by the debt overhang, which is defined as the difference between the face value and the market value of debt, i.e. the expected present value of the future net transfer from the debtor to the creditor.[12] The debt overhang may act as a tax on the debtor's output in phase two if the debt service no longer depends on the scheduled interest and repayment plans, but on the debtor's economic performance (through payment arrears and involuntary new lending). In this case lower consumption in phase one (to the benefit of investment) is no longer rewarded by higher consumption in phase two since most or all of the investment yield goes to the creditor. Krugman and Sachs therefore conclude that debt reduction will enhance adjustment incentives since the debtor keeps a higher proportion of the return from investment.

The effect created by the debt overhang and therefore by debt reduction closely depends on assumptions about minimum consumption in phase two, below which the debtor would default.[13] If this minimum consumption threshold is set at zero, i.e. if the possibility of a moratorium is ruled out, the investment incentive is always strengthened by debt commitments and weakened by debt reductions. The debtor must then invest in order to generate resources for the transfer to creditors. Debt reduction removes the pressure on the debtor to sacrifice a part of present consumption for future debt service. Even if default is not ruled out (i.e. if minimum consumption in phase two is positive), the debt overhang must not weaken the adjustment incentive. This applies firstly to the debtor who sets his anticipated output in period two far below the minimum consumption level: the increase in investment in phase one is not followed by any debt service in phase two or by any marginal tax on his adjustment effort. Neither should we forget the debtor whose commitments encourage him to make a special adjustment effort and go far beyond the threshold above which he no longer has to share the fruits of his investment with the creditor.

Whether the drop in problem debtors' investment is attributable to their debt overhang or to changes in external resource transfers has important consequences for international debt strategy. If the debt overhang were responsible for the drop in investment, new money would not reduce debt-related disincentives. Debt reduction would then hold out most hope of an upturn in investment. If, however, the lack of external liquidity was mainly respon-sible, the debtor countries would then need new money in order to exploit profitable investment opportunities. Debt reduction alone would not achieve an investment upswing.

Empirical studies of the secondary market for LDC debt could not con-firm the debt relief Laffer curve.[14] Although these findings do not disprove the existence of a debt overhang, they imply that a debt reduction is not Pareto improving,[15] except for a very few countries with a large debt over-hang such as Bolivia, Peru, Nicaragua and the Sudan. It therefore follows that the Brady Initiative would not lead very far as a voluntary debt strategy; the empirical evidence shows that banks usually do not gain from waiving their claims and that there is therefore more to solve than the banks' free rider problem.

Econometric specifications of consumption and investment functions tend to confirm the importance of the liquidity constraint.[16] In a specification along the permanent income hypothesis, the debt overhang would have necessarily implied a greater marginal propensity to consume out of perma-nent income. This was not the case. Likewise, debt stocks proved to be insignificant in aggregate investment functions. On the other hand, the liquidity constraint was clearly significant, with positive values for the sav-ings and transfer variables in the investment functions and a significant re-jection of a negative correlation between the world interest rate and domestic investment.

Our results supplement the findings by Borensztein[17] who simulated the debt versus liquidity constraints for investment behaviour in a simple neo-classical growth model. The debt overhang effect was modelled as a tax on production, while the liquidity constraint was modelled to raise the domestic interest rate in order to balance domestic savings and investment. In Bor-ensztein's simulation model the liquidity constraint was found to exert a stronger negative effect on investment than the debt overhang tax unless the latter exceeded 20 per cent of a typical debtor country's GNP.

The literature dealing with debt-induced disincentives has failed to refer to the sovereign risk literature which had put the possibility of the debtor's default at the centre stage. The debt overhang hypothesis postulates that a reduction in the debt burden can induce the debtor to pay *and* to invest (reform the economy), as long as the creditor leaves the debtor with a part of the marginal yields from his efforts. It cannot explain what prevents the debtor from investing and from still *not* paying.

According to the sovereign risk approach debtor behaviour depends on the level, incidence and probability of the sanctions which the creditor can impose on the debtor in the event of default. The sanctions open to creditors are placed in two categories:[18] a) the threat to intervene in the debtor's international transactions (trade penalty; b) the threat to stop the debtor from obtaining further loans (reputation penalty). These *ex ante* threats, however, are not sufficiently credible to prevent default. The cost of *ex post* negotiated solutions for the creditor are usually lower than the costs of a clash with the debtor.[19]

Eight years of interrupted negative transfers have, from the debtors' perspective, also increasingly detracted from the credibility of the reputation penalty. Reputation-based models cannot explain why Latin America debtors have not completely stopped their payments. The limited explanatory power of the sovereign risk literature is probably due to the fact that the incentive effects of international debt relations on the debtor *governments,* which actually take the decisions, have been disregarded. When deciding whether to default, debtor governments must, for instance, also take into account the repercussions on the risk premiums which their nationals demand when purchasing domestic government bonds.

The Mexico Test Case

Can the Brady Initiative provide positive adjustment incentives for severely indebted developing countries? It has been discussed here that indebted governments compare the savings from default with the surpluses they can obtain from negotiations under the Brady agreement:

- in the case of public finances, the aim is to minimize total public debt service and hence to limit the tax burden, inflation and the rise in local interest rates as a result of growing domestic debt;

- with regard to foreign relations, the resource transfer to creditors must be kept to a minimum or even reversed by reducing debt service, gaining access to new loans and encouraging expectations of future capital inflows;

- the decision will also be based on the economic return from the debt reduction agreement by comparing it with the opportunity costs of the resources to be spent on debt relief operations. The parameters for such a cost-benefit analysis are interest rate levels and capital productivity.

On these criteria, the discussion of the Brady Initiative's incentive effects has been too narrow in scope. First, the financial press has focused on the contraction in the face value of foreign debt, although it is financial transfers

Table 4.1   Mexico: effects of the Brady Agreement

		Early 1990	March 1990
1.	External position, $ billions		
	Face value of gross foreign debt[1]	95.1	93.8
	Foreign exchange reserves	6.0	4.7
	US zero bonds and other assets	—	7.0
	Face value of net foreign debt	89.1	82.1
II.	Debt burden, $ billions		
	Market value of gross foreign debt[2]	34.2	38.0
	Present value of debt relief[3]	—	14.1
	Net resource transfer per year[4]		-3.7
	New debt		+0.3
	Repayment		-2.1
	Interest service		-1.3

and their net present value which matter for the economic implications of foreign debt. Second, the theoretical debate has overemphasized the importance (and efficiency) of the secondary markets. One side fears that the Brady Initiative will increase moral hazard, by encouraging debtors to implement policies that raise the discount on the secondary markets. The other side maintains that the marginal value of foreign debt is worth less (or nothing) than its average price on the secondary markets. The debtors would therefore be at a disadvantage and the banks would benefit since a) the banks would siphon off economic rents and b) the market value of the remaining debts would rise. Both viewpoints overlook the fact that the Brady Initiative works largely independently of the secondary market. Firstly, a creditor bears no further country risk on the discounted debt after the sale of his claims on the secondary market, while a creditor taking part in the Brady Initiative exchanges old for new paper at a lower discount depending on the remaining country risk. Secondly, the discount under the Brady agreement is

III. Announcement effects

	June 1989	August 1989
Real interest rates on CETES (Mexican paper with 28 day maturity) annualized	36	19

	February 1989	March 1990
Secondary market price (cents/$ 1)	36	40.5

[1] The decrease in face value is due to a debt waiver of $6.96 million (0.41 x 0.35 x 48.5), minus "enhancement" money from the IMF, World Bank and Japan ($1.64 + 2.06 +2.05 billion) for the acquisition of US zero bonds and other securities. The new money option ($1.45 billion between 1990 and 1992) is not included here.

[2] Prior to the announcement of the Brady Initiative (February 1989) and the conclusion of the agreement, the secondary market price was 36 cents per US dollar. Following the announcement, it "overshot" to 44 cents and after the agreement stood at 40.5 cents, the figure which was used to calculate the market value.

[3] The new money option does not involve any debt relief; the interest relief option produces debt relief worth 31.3 per cent on the basis of 9.1 per cent LIBOR (World Bank projection) (1-6.25/9.1); the debt reduction of 35 per cent is equivalent to debt relief worth 35 per cent with an unchanged spread over LIBOR.

[4] Over the period 1990-94 (period of validity), the reduced net transfer includes: $288 million a year in new inflows, yearly savings on the repayments which would have been due in this period, and interest savings of $650 million from interest reduction and $630 million from debt reduction.

Sources: Secretaria de Hacienda y Credito Publica: The renegotiation of Mexico's debt, Mexico City 1990; Banco de Mexico: Indicadores Economicos; own calculations.

the outcome of negotiations between creditors and debtors, independently of the secondary market.

While debt-reduction agreements under the Brady umbrella have also been concluded for Costa Rica, the Philippines and Venezuela, it is Mexico that has been seen as the important test case.[20] The table shows that the Brady agreement has indeed raised the market value of Mexico's gross foreign debt while leaving its face value unchanged,[21] but on the other hand has reduced the face value of net foreign debt by $7 billion and the dis-counted present value of future debt service by $14.1 billion. The net re-source transfer has been reduced by $3.7 billion a year, although this includes the repayments deferred until 2019 which would also have been postponed under the previous conventional restructuring process. The yearly reduction in interest for Mexico amounts to $1.3 billion, which is equivalent to an economic return from the official resources put up for this purpose

($7 billion by the World Bank, the IMF, Japan and Mexico) of 18.6 per cent. This is a reasonable yield even for an undercapitalized country such as Mexico, which is likely to have a high capital return on investment (the shadow price of the official resources provided for debt relief). The Mexican government estimates the net resource transfer implied by foreign debt at 2.43 per cent of GDP for the current sexennial (89-94), as compared with 5.57 per cent of GDP in the sexennial 1982-88.

After the announcement of the agreement at the end of July 1989, the annualized inflation-adjusted interest rates for Mexican government bonds (CETES) fell from about 36 per cent to 19 per cent; they have remained at this level since then. At this juncture the government's domestic debt amounted to $54 billion, on which interest payment was reduced by over $9 billion (about 4.5 per cent of GDP) as a result of the decrease in CETES rates. Assuming no change in the private savings of 26 per cent of GDP, the aggregate savings ratio (public and private) would therefore rise by the amount of interest saved (from 18.9 to 23.4 per cent of GDP). This would mean that Mexico's investment ratio could be 6.9 per cent of GDP higher than prior to the Brady agreement, since the postponement of amortization and new loans would result in an increase in foreign savings of 2.4 per cent of GDP. Capital formation in real terms would therefore be about 30 per cent higher than before the Brady agreement.

Without detailed empirical studies, however, the question of how far the fall in CETES interest rates can be attributed to the debt agreement must remain debatable. The shallowness of the Mexican financial market thwarts any attempt at quantifying foreseeable inflation by analysis of the term structure of interest rates. Reduced expectations of currency depreciation can only partly explain the decrease in interest rates since the debt agreement has only moderately lowered the net transfer abroad; in fact the Mexican peso has been further devalued in real terms since June 1989.

The return of flight capital after the Brady deal supports the assumption that the debt agreement has improved the government's credibility and that accordingly lower default risk premiums are being demanded by Mexican bondholders. The Mexican government's fiscal discipline, which transformed the earlier primary deficit into a primary surplus of 8 per cent of GDP, had not been enough in itself to overcome the government's credibility problem. Calvo (1989)[22] has recently shown the possibility of dual equilibria introduced by high public debt in determining interest and inflation rates. Since high interest rates increase government indebtedness, they not only reflect but also determine inflation expectations. With high public debt, only the government's credibility decides whether the economy ends up with high interest rates, high default risk and high inflation or with low equilibrium values. In this specific situation the Brady Initiative therefore could help to improve confidence and exerted considerable leverage in the form of an automatic improvement in Mexico's public finances that far exceeded its direct effects.

Fiscal Rigidities

It is not to be expected that the Brady Initiative will also immediately restore confidence in other debtor countries, in particular where the political situation creates lasting fiscal rigidities.[23] Fiscal rigidities originate when every social group is powerful enough to obstruct taxation or cuts in subsidies, but has not enough political clout to shift the costs of fiscal adjustment onto other groups. Accordingly, the Brady Initiative can be successful only in countries where competing demands for budget resources are not very pronounced, or where one political group is in firm control of economic policy decisions and is therefore able to shift the government debt burden onto groups not represented in the government.

Despite the fact that the Brady Initiative can only have decisive effects on fewer than the 19 middle-income countries concerned, it remains underfunded for the time being. Total public debt of these countries can be reduced only if 'enhancement' money for debt reduction is provided from abroad. Of the $30 billion in resources approved so far, $5.7 billion have already been granted to Mexico.

Taking the negotiation with Mexico as an example, the debt burden of the remaining countries works out as follows: the remaining enhancement resources of $24 billion are available for the negotiation of bank claims amounting to $166 billion (48.5 x 5.7/7 x 24) with a 35 per cent bargaining discount (assuming a residual country risk). Net debts can thus be reduced by $58 billion and interest reduced burden with LIBOR at 9.1 per cent, by $5.3 billion. The total foreign interest of this group of countries (excluding Mexico) amounted to $47.6 billion in 1989;[24] their interest payments would therefore be cut by a mere 11 per cent.

If the available official resources, however, were concentrated on quite a small number of countries, the Brady Initiative would encounter other limits. Market-based debt agreements of the Brady type will probably never restore the debtors' full creditworthiness, for two reasons. First, the commercial banks would find themselves in the prisoner's dilemma: with the expectation that the market value of their claims will again draw closer to their face value, no individual banks would still be prepared to waive their claims; they would then prefer to keep their book claims rather than to sell cheap. Second, every market-based debt reduction would then become too expensive for the debtor: the dwindling bargaining discount would depress the economic return from debt reduction under the opportunity costs. Debtors would prefer to use available official resources for investment instead of replacing their commitments to private banks by those to the IMF and the World Bank, without achieving any appreciable relief in the process.

NOTES

1. Cf. Jeffrey Sachs (1989): 'The Debt Overhang in Developing Countries', in J. Sachs, (ed.), *Developing Country Debt and Economic Performance*, vol. I, Chicago University Press; Paul Krugman (1988), 'Market-Based Debt Reduction Schemes', *NBER Working Paper* no. 2587, Cambridge, Mass.
2. The decision to invest rather than to consume stands for the wider concept of economic reform, i.e. foreign trade liberalization, privatization and tax reform. Both investment and economic reforms are expected to raise future output and accordingly the debt service capacity. A short description of the debt overhang hypothesis is given later in this article.
3. The Brady Initiative refers to debts owed to commercial banks. Debt and debt service reduction are to be achieved mainly by converting old bank debts into new loans or by buying back bank debts — in each case with a considerable discount — and by swapping old bank debts for new paper with the same value but lower interest rates. The specific country risk of this new paper is reduced by the provision of official funds (IMF, World Bank, Japan).
4. Helmut Reisen (1987), *Über das Transferproblem hochverschuldeter Entwicklungsländer*, Nomos-Verlag, Baden-Baden.
5. Helmut Reisen (1989), 'Public Debt, External Competitiveness, and Fiscal Discipline in Developing Countries', *Princeton Studies in International Finance* no. 66, Princeton, New Jersey.
6. W. Max Corden (1988), 'Debt Relief and Adjustment Incentives', *IMF Staff Papers*, 35 (4), pp. 628-643.
7. Vito Tanzi and Mario Blejer (1988), 'Public Debt and Fiscal Policy in Developing Countries' in K. Arrow and M. Boskin (eds), *Economics of Public Debt*, St. Martin's Press, New York.
8. Helmut Reisen (1989), 'Public Debt, North and South' in I. Hussain and I. Diwan (eds), *Dealing with the Debt Crisis*, The World Bank, Washington D.C.
9. Sebastian Edwards (1989), 'The International Monetary Fund and the Developing Countries: A Critical Evaluation', *NBER Working Paper* no. 2909, Cambridge, Mass.
10. J. Sachs, op. cit.
11. Krugman, op. cit.
12. The debt overhang can be illustrated by the so-called debt relief Laffer curve. The curve relates the market value of debts to their book value. It starts with zero; it first rises at pari to the book value, and then continues to rise, although at a slower rate; it finally reaches a maximum, after which the market value continually decreases towards zero, while the book value stretches to infinity. The debt overhang is 'weak' when it is to the left of the curve maximum and 'strong' when it is to the right.
13. W. M. Corden, op. cit.
14. See in particular Daniel Cohen, 'How to Cope with a Debt Overhang: Cut Flows Rather Than Stocks' in I. Hussain and I. Diwan (eds), op. cit.
15. Kenneth Froot (1988), 'Buybacks, Exit Bonds, and the Optimality of Debt and Liquidity Relief', *NBER Working Paper* no. 2675, Cambridge, Mass.
16. Bert Hofman and Helmut Reisen (1990), *Debt Overhang, Liquidity Constraints, and Adjustment Incentives*, OECD Development Centre Technical Paper no. 32, Paris.

17. Eduardo Borensztein (1989), 'The Effect of External Debt on Investment' in *Finance and Development*, September, pp. 17-19.
18. Jonathan Eaton, Mark Gersowitz and Joseph Stiglitz (1986), 'The Pure Theory of Country Risk', in *European Economic Review*, 30 (3), pp. 481-513.
19. Martin Hellwig (1986), 'Comments on the Eaton, Gersowitz and Stiglitz paper', in *European Economic Review*, 30 (3), pp. 521-527.
20. Helmut Hesse (1990), 'Aktuelle Probleme der Internationalen Verschuldungskrise' in Deutsche Bundesbank: Auszüge aus Presseartikeln, Frankfurt, 20.2.1990.
21. The renegotiation of Mexico's external debt covered $48.5 billion. The commercial banks faced three options. 41 per cent of the claims chose debt principal reduction, with an exchange of debt for bonds bearing a 35 per cent discount. 47 per cent selected interest reduction, with an exchange of debt instruments at par, but subject to a fixed rate of 6.25 per cent. The remaining 12 per cent chose the 'new money' options.
22. Guillermo Calvo (1989), 'Servicing the Public Debt: The Role of Expectations' in *American Economic Review*, vol. 78, no. 4, pp. 647-661.
23. Alberto Alesina (1989), 'The End of Large Public Debts' in F. Giavazzi and L. Spaventa (eds), *High Public Debt: The Italian Experience*, Cambridge University Press, Cambridge; Helmut Reisen (1989), 'Public Debt, North and South', op. cit.
24. World Bank (1989), World Debt Tables 1989-90, vol. 1, Analysis and Summary Tables, Washington D.C.

5. Public Finance in Developing Countries and the Attraction of Foreign Capital*

1. Introduction

This chapter summarizes some of the analytical and empirical evidence on supply and demand determinants of foreign direct investment (FDI) and discusses how public finance in developing countries may affect FDI flows.

There has been a tendency recently to view FDI as a way of resolving three problems common to many developing countries. First, FDI would be an important source of foreign finance so badly needed after the breakdown of commercial bank lending. Second, FDI would contribute to development by promoting a more efficient risk-sharing than foreign debt has done, and by transfer of technology. Third, FDI would respond to improved government policies, notably to an efficient mix of effective tax burdens on foreign capital and the provision of local public goods. While this chapter does not explore any of these propositions in great detail, it aims at providing empirical evidence for a balanced view on the role of FDI and the effect of tax policies. The chapter also points to urgent gaps in research. First, the variation of global FDI activity (rather than the existence of FDI per se) has been left quite unexplained by the literature. Second, a detailed exploration of tax avoidance strategies, both by resident and foreign investors, rather than an analysis based on statutory taxes seems needed to arrive at hard conclusions about the impact of taxation to FDI flows towards the South.

2. Supply Determinants of Foreign Direct Investments: A Theoretical and Empirical Survey

Unlike for foreign trade, economics has not managed to develop a general theory of the determinants of capital flows. It has been customary to treat different types of capital flows in isolation. This has resulted in a separate literature on short-term capital, long-term capital and foreign direct investment, the latter on which this paper will focus. Even a general theory of

---

*   Originally published in OECD (1990), *Taxation and International Capital Flows*, Paris.

FDI has not developed. But hypotheses on supply and demand factors abound, though public finance and tax issues do not feature prominently in the literature [for surveys, see Agarwal (1980) and Clegg (1987)].

The first group of hypotheses assumes *perfect markets*. Capital investment would be governed by (a) cross-country differences in the rates of return, and (b) by portfolio diversification to minimize foreign exchange and sovereign risk. The differential rates of return hypothesis (a) and the portfolio hypothesis (b) have found surprisingly weak empirical support, but both encounter a similar empirical test problem. Investment decisions are based on *expected risks and returns*, while the empirical verification can only be based on *ex post* and reported profit data. The conclusion thus is that (i) risks and returns matter less than economists presume (hard to believe) or, (ii) that reported profits are systematically distorted as a result of tax avoidance strategies, or (iii) that most FDI decisions have been based on return expectations that did not materialize.

The second group of hypotheses, pioneered by Hymer (1960), assumes *market imperfections* to explain cross-border capital investment. FDI is explained by the exploitation of comparative advantages that investing firms hold over local firms: cheaper sources of financing, brand name, patented technology, managerial skills, and other *firm-specific assets*. Firms save costs when they internalize certain markets for intermediate inputs because these markets often are highly imperfect or inefficient. Horizontal international investments are motivated by the firm's desire to internalize a market for intangible assets like brand names or technologies, while vertical investments are mainly governed by the firm's desire to internalize markets for intermediate products.

The *product cycle hypothesis* puts market imperfections into a dynamic setting. New products originate in rich countries where demand conditions allow firms to engage in research and development. Eventually, these products are imitated and become standardized (with the relative research content embodied in these products declining and the labour content rising). The change in relative factor intensities is mirrored by foreign direct investment, the product innovation is followed by locational innovation towards developing countries where labour is cheap. The product cycle hypothesis has found considerable empirical support for German and Japanese FDI.

A third group of supply factor hypotheses, relating to the firm's *propensity to invest*, has not found any empirical support. The *liquidity hypothesis* states that there is a positive correlation between the internal cash flows and the investment outlays of a firm. It seems, however, that only internal cash flows of the foreign subsidiaries have exercised a substantial influence on the new investment outlays of multinational enterprises active in developing

Debt, Deficits and Exchange Rates

countries (Reuber *et al.*, 1973). The *currency area hypothesis* presumes that portfolio investors tend to underestimate the risk premium involved in investing abroad and therefore foreign direct investors are able to borrow at low costs and capitalize their earnings on their FDI in 'softer' currency areas at higher rates than local firms.

Dunning's (1980) *eclectic theory* draws on various schools of thought within international economics, industrial organization, and location theories. A country is predicted to be a net supplier of FDI as a result of (i) net ownership advantages of home firms over foreign firms, (ii) the relative efficiency to the firm of internal versus external market exploitation of its ownership advantages, determining the choice between directly-owned production (exports plus direct foreign production) versus licensing; and (iii) the relative location of home versus host-country production, motivating the choice between exports and foreign direct investment. These factors determine cross-country differences to undertake FDI: today's ownership advantages are a reflection of yesterday's locational advantages. The eclectic theory may also explain the different pattern of US and Japanese FDI. Japanese investment is in labour-intensive production and export-oriented, while US investment is in high-technology and more oriented towards the domestic market.

Table 5.1   *Shares of selected DAC countries in net[1] FDI flows to developing countries (1970-1987)*

Country	1970	1980	1987
Total DAC ($bn) of which (%)	3.7	10.9	19.8
US	51.2	30.9	40.4
UK	9.2	17.6	9.5
Japan		15.4	36.5
FRG	8.6	14.5	3.4
Netherlands	5.0	1.2	1.3

[1] After allowance for repatriated earnings and disinvestment.

The supply of foreign direct investment to developing countries has, in dollar terms, very much concentrated on a few OECD countries. The US has always been the principal investor with a share of about one half in 1970 and now roughly 40 per cent of all FDI flows from the OECD area. Japan comes next with a share of 37 per cent in 1987. The UK, a traditional investor in the South, has directed FDI flows increasingly to other OECD countries, but it still provides about 10 per cent of all FDI flows from the OECD to developing countries. Other important investors have been Germany and the Netherlands. (See Table 5.1.)

Figure 5.1   Trends in foreign direct investment

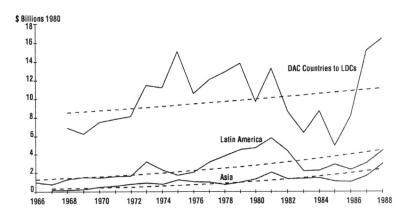

Figure 5.1 shows trends in foreign direct investment, defined as new investments plus reinvested earnings minus repatriation, (in constant US$) during 1966-1988 to a selection of important host-countries in *Latin America and East Asia*. Although most observers would agree that economic policy and performance have widely diverged between the two country groups, trends of FDI into these two regions have been *strikingly similar*. In fact, the correlation coefficient between FDI to Latin America and East Asia is

0.71, and only little lower with respect to world FDI activity. This finding suggests that supply factors matter more than demand factors, and that differences in policy performance may well have less impact on the attraction of capital flows than is often presumed, although at the margin government policies are significant.

Figure 5.1 shows also a considerable variability in FDI activity worldwide which is mostly left unexplained by the literature surveyed above. This literature is rather devoted to the explanation of why FDI exists per se, but it seems unable to explain its global fluctuations. An ad hoc theory, stressing the importance of swings among key OECD currencies, may be ventured here. It starts from the observation that the breakdown of the Bretton Woods exchange rate agreement (1972) marks an increase of FDI variability around a time trend which itself has not changed. Turning points are closely related to turning points in the exchange rates among the dollar, the yen, and European currencies. An appreciation of one of these currencies, say the yen, forces Japanese companies to outlocate production to survive world competition, to areas whose currencies are more closely related to the depreciating currency areas, possibly along the lines predicted by the product cycle hypothesis. The resultant FDI flows can be compared to a stock adjustment process (as in portfolio theory) in response to a change in the price of key currencies. Since a currency cannot appreciate forever in real terms, FDI flows should be interpreted as temporary stock adjustments (of course, sluggish and stretching over several years) from old to new equilibria in the locational pattern of industrial production.

Table 5.2   Trends in foreign direct investment (based on constant US dollars)

	From DAC to all LDCs	Latin America	Asia
1. Time trend, 1966-88, compound annual growth rate	1.40	5.90	9.90
2. Variability, coefficient of variation		0.41	0.37
3. Correlation coefficient, — DAC with region		0.52	0.59
— Latin America with Asia			0.71

3. Demand Determinants: Evidence

Developing country governments compete for internationally mobile capital by offering *club goods* besides other *immobile factors* which are used as input factors by firms. The immobile factors are not influenced (at least in the short term) by government policies and include (i) the geographic location, (ii) urban agglomerations, (iii) natural resources, (iv) domestic market size, (v) labour and other factor supply among others. Club goods are defined as public goods within, and as private goods outside the national jurisdiction. They include (i) the political and institutional setting for the enforcement of law and contracts, social stability, and the regulation as well as bureaucratic operation of foreign investment, and (ii) past, current and expected economic policy with respect to macroeconomic stability, foreign trade regime, foreign exchange regime, public debt management, taxation, regulation and competition as well as positive growth disparities.

The relative importance of all these factors has been found difficult to establish. There is no 'super-indicator' for locational attractiveness and competitiveness. This is hardly surprising, since profit functions of firms differ and their asset demand is not homogenous. Foreign direct investment in the primary commodity sector has been motivated by the investor's desire to secure access to important material inputs, especially in times of perceived raw commodity shortages. In the case of manufacturing, the *market size hypothesis* has found strong empirical support. Firms want to secure access to a big and growing market, perhaps also to circumvent trade restrictions. In a study for the OECD Development Centre, Reuber and associates (1973) found that the flow of FDI (on a per capita basis) into developing countries was strongly correlated with the size and growth of their respective GDP. In spite of its strong empirical content, however, the market size hypothesis can only apply to FDI for sales in the host country, not to export-oriented FDI. For the latter, cost considerations should prevail, in particular differences in *unit-labour costs*. The relevance of labour costs may have suffered recently due to increasing robotization of production processes.

Table 5.3 may suggest that the local market size and raw commodity supply has mattered more for the attraction of FDI than economic policies and cost considerations. Brazil has received more FDI than any other country. At the end of 1986, the stock of FDI in Brazil totalled \$22.4 billion. This is a large amount, even allowing for the size of Brazil compared with other developing countries. In the next largest FDI recipients, in oil-rich Mexico and Indonesia, the stock was only half that size. It is also interesting to note that Argentina, a relatively small economy which has experienced a secular economic decline due to misguided policies, ranks fourth in the list of FDI

Table 5.3 FDI from DAC countries: 1986[1]

RANK	Stock end 1986 ($ billion)	Percentage of net FDI in LDCs
1. Brazil	22.4	15.4
2. Mexico	13.2	9.1
3. Indonesia	10.3	7.1
4. Argentina	7.4	5.1
5. Singapore	6.7	4.6
6. Hong Kong	6.7	4.6
7. China	5.3	3.6
8. Malaysia	4.3	3.0
9. Venezuela	4.2	2.9
10. India	3.3	2.3
11. Taiwan	3.3	2.3
12. Peru	3.1	2.1
13. Nigeria	2.8	1.9
14. Colombia	2.6	1.8
15. Chile	2.5	1.7
16. Egypt	2.4	1.6
17. Philippines	2.4	1.6
18. Korea	2.3	1.6
19. Saudi Arabia	2.0	1.4
20. Thailand	1.9	1.3

[1] FDI into major offshore banking centres is excluded from the statistics: the stock of DAC countries' FDI in these countries (Panama, Bermuda, Netherlands Antilles, Bahamas and Liberia) amounted to $36.2 billion at end-1986.
Source: OECD.

recipients. Reviewing the environment for FDI, the World Bank Development Report 1985 thus concluded: 'Countries with large internal markets and import-substituting strategies are among those that have received the largest amount of foreign direct investment. They are also the countries where prices have been most distorted and where complaints about the development contribution of direct investment have been most common' (p. 129).

Since the debt crisis erupted in 1982, highly indebted countries have received relatively less FDI than before. Up to 1982, syndicated bank lending, often irrespective of country risk, has allowed many developing-country governments to neglect policies to improve the locational attractiveness. This has been reinforced by the fact that bank lending has often complemented other types of foreign capital such as FDI. Debt-swap schemes, even when they took major proportions as they did in Chile, did not seem to compensate for the perceived country risk in attracting much FDI since the debt crisis.

Latin America, however, has retained its prominence as an FDI recipient. In 1987, it absorbed almost 50 per cent of DAC countries' flows to LDCs, up from 40 per cent in 1970 and down from two thirds in 1980 (see Table 5.4 where we show a matrix of net FDI flows from DAC countries to LDCs). This table also shows that Asian countries have persistently increased their share in LDCs' FDI inflows up to 37.5 per cent in 1987 (only 12 per cent less than the Latin American share during that same year). This can be partly explained by the fact that China became an important FDI recipient. Its share in total FDI to Asian LDCs increased from 0.2 per cent in 1980 to more than 6 per cent in 1987. Africa has practically disappeared from the map. Whereas in 1970 it was a more important location than Asia, primarily because of investments in extractive industries, by 1987 its share in total FDI to LDCs was only 1.5 per cent.

Table 5.4 also reveals that the presence of the US in Latin America is now being rivalled by Japan. This country, as pointed out earlier, comes closely after the US as a net contributor of FDI to LDCs in 1987. This same year, both the US and Japan devoted more than 50 per cent of their investments in LDCs to Latin America. Combining the 1987 percentage numbers of Tables 1 and 4 reveals the following: 22.8 per cent of total DAC countries investments in LDCs was undertaken by the US in Latin America, and the corresponding figure for Japan was 20 per cent. Also Germany, the UK, and the Netherlands, have shown a strong preference for undertaking FDI activities in Latin America.

The persistency of Latin America as the main region of FDI destination could be explained, at least in part, by the significance of tax havens such as

Table 5.4   Matrix of net[1] FDI[2] flows from selected DAC countries to selected developing countries (1970, 1980, and 1987)[3]

	DAC			USA			JAPAN[4]		
	1970	1980	1987	1970	1980	1987	1970	1980	1987
Developing countries	100	100	100	100	100	100	100	100	100
Latin America	41.7	66.7	49.5	54.8	77.7	57.4	20.1	41.5	55.5
Argentina	2.4	8.5	0.7	3.6	9.0	-1.0	0.5	0.5	0.1
Brazil	8.8	8.1	4.5	12.5	4.4	8.3	5.5	6.7	0.1
Mexico	4.4	18.5	1.8	13.3	21.9	3.0	68.5	32.1	-0.4
Asia	18.6	20.0	37.5	13.3	2.0	33.1	68.5	48.4	43.2
R. of Korea	0.3	-1.9	4.1	—	-3.3	2.5	3.2	-0.2	8.2
Singapore	0.4	5.9	3.3	—	5.1	4.0	1.7	7.0	5.3
Taiwan	0.6	1.4	3.7	—	1.6	5.5	5.7	2.2	3.8
India	1.2	0.7	0.7	0.6	0.7	1.0	0.0	0.2	0.2
Thailand	0.3	2.0	2.0	—	2.4	2.4	3.4	2.2	1.8
Malaysia	1.0	2.2	1.2	—	0.5	0.1	3.4	7.0	0.5
China	—	0.2	6.4	—	—	—	—	1.3	16.6
Africa	21.9	13.1	1.5	23.0	9.1	8.5	3.2	5.3	0.9

[1] The net is after allowance for repatried earnings and disinvestment, this accounts for negative signs in certain cases.
[2] Includes financial investments, which explains why shares to leading LDCs appear so low.
[3] Aggregae FDI was $3.7 bn, $10.9 bn, and $19.8 bn in 1970, 1980, and 1987, respectively.
[4] The figures show a large negative in the category "LDCs unspecified". To make the percentages given in the table meaningful, this number has been ignored in the total.
[5] The total FRG investment includes a large number for "unspecified" LDCs. Therefore, the shares appearing in the table are relatively small, adding to well over 100.
[6] OECD statistics do not provide detailed breakdown by recipient country.
— Signifies data is unavailable.

Source: Department of Economics and Statistics, OECD.

Table 5.4   *Matrix of net[1] FDI[2] flows from selected DAC countries to selected developing countries (1970, 1980, and 1987)[3]*

	UK			FRG[5]			NETHERLANDS[6]		
	1970	1980	1987	1970	1980	1987	1970	1980	1987
Developing countries	100	100	100	100	100	100	100	100	100
Latin America	31.3	22.8	61.3	19.8	20.3	84.3	41.5	25.9	47.4
Argentina	0.0	2.8	3.4	2.5	3.9	22.5	—	53.3	2.7
Brazil	8.5	5.1	19.2	8.2	9.6	16.3	—	27.4	28.1
Mexico	27.8	0.8	2.1	7.5	1.2	19.3	—	—	0.7
Asia	27.8	15.3	26.1	7.5	7.5	28.4	—	57.7	32.8
R. of Korea	—	—	0.4	0.0	0.3	1.7	—	—	0.0
Singapore	2.3	4.1	4.0	0.0	4.7	3.5	—	4.4	4.2
Taiwan	—	—	1.3	0.3	0.0	2.9	—	5.1	0.3
India	7.3	1.2	1.5	2.2	0.0	1.4	—	—	0.0
Thailand	0.0	0.0	5.6	0.0	0.1	0.8	—	9.6	1.1
Malaysia	7.6	3.3	-6.6	0.3	0.0	-2.8	—	—	1.1
China	—	—	—	—	—	1.7	—	—	2.3
Africa	28.7	19.0	6.6	10.7	2.9	10.4	—	-22.2	6.1

[1] The net is after allowance for repatried earnings and disinvestment, this accounts for negative signs in certain cases.

[2] Includes financial investments, which explains why shares to leading LDCs appear so low.

[3] Aggregate FDI was $3.7 bn, $10.9 bn, and $19.8 bn in 1970, 1980, and 1987, respectively.

[4] The figures show a large negative in the category "LDCs unspecified". To make the percentages given in the table meaningful, this number has been ignored in the total.

[5] The total FRG investment includes a large number for "unspecified" LDCs. Therefore, the shares appearing in the table are relatively small, adding to well over 100.

[6] OECD statistics do not provide detailed breakdown by recipient country.

— Signifies data is unavailable.

Source: Department of Economics and Statistics, OECD.

Table 5.5   *US direct investment abroad (1988). US direct investment into Bermuda, Dutch Antilles, Bahamas and UK Caribbean, as percentage of US investment in Latin America and Caribbean[1]*

		Percentage of total investment into:	
	Position (in US$ billion)	Latin America and Caribbean	Developing countries
Developing countries	76,837	83.8	100.0
Latin America and Caribbean	64,438	100.0	83.8
Bermuda	19,880	30.8	25.8
Dutch Antilles	-11,796[2]	-18.3	-15.3
UK Caribbean	3,577	5.5	4.6
Bahamas	2,244	3.4	2.9

[1] From US Department of Commerce Data, this figure is the sum of figures for South America and Central America and other Western Hemisphere. Other Western Hemisphere including: Bahamas, Bermuda, Jamaica, Dutch Antilles, Trinidad-Tobago, Caribbean and "other".
[2] The negative in this figure is due to unique legislation in the Dutch Antilles that facilitates the setting up of companies for investment into the US.
Source: US Department of Commerce Data.

the Netherlands Antilles, Bermuda, and the Bahamas (see Table 5.5 for the case of US FDI into these countries).

4. The Impact of Public Finance

Public finance is relevant to the attraction of capital flows via three channels. The first is the (intertemporal) government budget identity. Governments finance the provision of local club goods by levying taxes, spending cuts, bonds or monetary finance. Indebted governments participate in the competitive process with a disadvantage compared to less indebted governments.

The second channel is public finance as a club good. Sound public finances can increase the attractiveness of a country by providing price stability through fiscal-monetary discipline, by avoiding crowding-out effects of private investment, by improving the profitability of private investment through the provision of complementary infrastructure and services, and by avoiding distortions and excessive burdens in the tax system, hence contributing to growth. The importance of fiscal parameters became only apparent after 1982 when many developing countries had to undertake a sharp turnaround in the current account. Where fiscal adjustment did not fully accommodate the turnaround in the balance of payments (as in much of Latin America) a vicious cycle was initiated which discouraged all forms of non-concessional finance and often encouraged capital flight. Cuts in public investment bore the brunt of adjustment, while the residual was financed by domestic bonds and the inflation tax. Resulting in excessively high domestic interest rates as well as high rising inflation, public finance contributed, at least for a while, to the collapse of domestic and foreign investment. With negative growth disparities compared to other countries, the vicious cycle became complete. By contrast, countries which recorded fiscal discipline, also attracted a growing share of world foreign direct (and portfolio) investment [for details, see Reisen (1989)].

It should be noted, however, that the special treatment of foreign-exchange gains in OECD countries provides an opportunity for tax arbitrage, derived from differential trend inflation between the OECD and, say, most of Latin America. The strategy consists of borrowing in currencies which depreciate (peso) and carry high interest rates, and lending in low-interest, hard-coupon currencies. The (negative) net interest costs are taxed at the corporate income tax rate, while the foreign-exchange gain is either not taxed, or taxed when realized. If the foreign-exchange gain is taxed at the same rate as interest income but only when it is realized, profits from deferrals are still available [for examples, see Giovannini (1989) and OECD (1988)].

The third channel is the tax system of a country in relation to the tax systems of other countries. Firms will base locational innovations not only on the comparison of statutory tax rates, but also on the interdependence of jurisdictional rules, foreign tax credits, nexus and attribution rules, factors which determine the location of the tax base.

However, the direct statistical tests of the effects of taxes on FDI flows have been quite limited [for a review, see Caves (1982)]. Surveys that have given the most attention to tax variables have ranked them below quantifiable costs and political stability in importance. That tax factors do not contribute more to explaining key foreign-investment decisions may indicate that effective tax burdens vary less across countries than factors that govern pre-tax rates of return. But these results may also be due to weak data bases underlying research on the interdependence of taxation and FDI in developing countries. Boskin and Gale (1986) find for the most important provider of FDI to developing countries, the United States, that tax policy *has* an important effect on the international location of investment. They show that FDI in the US is very sensitive to after-tax rates-of-return available there and that US investment abroad is also affected, although to a lesser extent.

To identify how public finances impact on the international location of investment, a distinction of investment financed by retained earnings and investment financed from abroad has to be made. Hartman (1981) has emphasized this distinction for analysing the effects of tax policy on FDI flows. If a subsidiary in an LDC is investing out of retained earnings, the home country tax on foreign sources income does not affect the marginal investment decision, because *the repatriation of earnings* and not the earnings themselves are the tax base. The home country tax on foreign source income is unavoidable, and its present value does not depend on the length at which investors can defer taxation. Thus, the marginal investment decision for investment out of retained earnings should depend on the net returns available in the home country or in the host country. For firms that finance foreign investment by transfers from home, the home country tax on foreign source income does matter because no foreign earnings have accrued and thus the tax on foreign source income is avoidable.

REFERENCES

Agarwal, J.P. (1980), 'Determinants of Foreign Direct Investment: A Survey', *Welwirtschaftliches Archiv.* Vol. 116, Heft 4, Kiel, W.G., pp. 739-773.

Boskin, J., and William Gale (1986), 'New Results on the Effects of Tax Policy on the International Location of Investment', *NBER Working Paper* no. 1862, Cambridge, MA., March.

Caves, R. (1982), *Multinational Enterprise and Economic Analysis*, Cambridge University Press.

Clegg, J. (1987), *Multinational Enterprise and World Competition*, Macmillan Press, England.

Dunning, J.H. (1980), 'Toward an Eclectic Theory of International Production: Some Empirical Tests', *Journal of International Business Studies*, Spring/Summer, pp. 9-31.

Giovannini, A. (1989), 'National Tax Systems Versus the European Capital Market', *Economic Policy*, no. 9, October, p. 346-386.

Hartman, D. (1981), 'Domestic Tax Policy and Foreign Investment: Some Evidence', *NBER Working Paper* no. 784, Cambridge, MA, October.

Hymer, S.H. (1976), 'The International Operations of National Firms: A Study of Direct Foreign Investment', *MIT Monographs in Economics*, 14, Cambridge, MA.

OECD, (1988) 'The Tax Treatment of Foreign Exchange, Gains and Losses', *Issues in International Taxation*, no. 3, Paris .

Reisen, H. (1989) 'Public Debt, External Competitiveness, and Fiscal Discipline in Developing Countries', *Princeton Studies in International Finance*, no. 66, Princeton, N.J.

Part 2

The Macroeconomics of Financial Opening

The Macroeconomics of Financial Opening

The second part of this book collects essays dealing with various aspects of financial *opening* (implications of financial *openness* will be dealt with in Part 3). Monetary authorities in many developing countries are currently reflecting and implementing *de jure* liberalization of external capital flows. At least three reasons can be identified for policymakers' renewed interest in financial opening. First, there has been increasing *de facto* opening of the capital account: the effectiveness of controls has declined due to growing trade integration, financial innovation and financial opening elsewhere; and ten years after the debt crisis, credit rationing by commercial banks is fading away while flight capital is being repatriated. Second, some countries have become subject to pressure in bilateral trade talks to open up their financial systems and to let their currency float. Third, for those advanced developing countries considering future membership of OECD, the OECD Codes of Liberalization may constitute another reason to engage into financial opening; the Codes commit OECD member countries to eliminate any restrictions between one another on current invisible and capital movement operations.

The next essay, first presented at the 1991 annual meeting of the *Verein für Socialpolitik*, explores the interaction between financial opening, stabilization, the exchange rate regime and the real exchange rate. The essay shows for the Southern Cone countries in Latin America that the active crawling peg combined with high nominal interest rates was to be blamed for inducing excessive capital inflows. The other extreme, a fully flexible float of the exchange rate, can lead to overshooting exchange rates without excessive inflows, as demonstrated by New Zealand's experience. The Southern Cone and New Zealand's experience are finally formalized in a simple general equilibrium model to discuss appropriate macroeconomic management during financial integration.

The following essay, written jointly with Hélène Yèches, tries to establish an important policy issue, first raised by the US Treasury: How open are the capital accounts in Korea and Taiwan? Has there been a trend towards more financial openness, as is often claimed by the governments both in Korea and Taiwan? The essay aims at answering both questions by estimating a model of interest determination first outlined by Edwards and Khan, in an extension suggested by Haque and Montiel. Use is made of a time-varying parameter estimation based on the Kalman filter technique, instead of the usual constant parameter estimation. The findings indicate a low degree of capital mobility for both Korea and Taiwan, and no trend towards more financial openness (except recently in Taiwan's interbank market). The dismantling of capital controls and of internal financial restrictions is thus likely to impose an important loss of monetary autonomy in both countries.

The essay 'Towards Capital Account Convertibility', co-authored by Bernhard Fischer, is addressed to governments which opt for *de jure* liberalization of capital movements. Conceived and published as a nontechnical Development Centre Policy Brief, the essay seeks to draw lessons from two thorough studies* of capital account opening in OECD countries, Latin America and Asia. Advocating a positive strategy for capital account liberalization, the essay identifies macro- and microeconomic impediments to liberalization in developing countries. It then designs institutional and policy measures which should precede the abolition of various capital controls. The appropriate sequencing of capital account liberalization is finally outlined.

The final essay in Part 2 focuses on the relationship between financial opening and capital flows. Latin American countries which in the early 1990s — just like in the late 1970s — were again facing heavy capital inflows, looked at the option to dismantle capital outflows to dampen excessive net inflows. The essay warns about the possibility that such a move would raise rather than stem net capital inflows. By contrast, I recommend tightening government budgets, managing exchange rates (an advice to be detailed in the last essay of this book), and enforcing bank competition and prudential regulation.

---

* Reisen, Helmut and Bernhard Fischer (eds) (1993), *Financial Opening: Policy Issues and Experiences in Developing Countries*, OECD Document on Sale, Paris, and Fischer, Bernhard and Helmut Reisen (1993), *Liberalising Capital Flows in Developing Countries: Pitfalls, Preresuisites and Perspectives*, OECD Development Centre Studies, Paris.

6. On Liberalizing the Capital Account: Experiences with Different Exchange Rate Regimes

1. Introduction

Advanced developing countries, such as Korea and Taiwan, are now under pressure to liberalize their financial markets and to convert to market-oriented foreign exchange systems. In particular the US government is pursuing vigorously its efforts to remove foreign trade and investment barriers for US financial firms (witness US Department of the Treasury, 1990). Asian officials have tried to resist the US pressure by pointing to the lessons drawn from the failed Latin American liberalization experiences (see, e.g., Taiwan's minister of finance, Kuo, 1989). The failure of financial reform in Latin America is also evoked by those economists who advise Eastern European countries 'to focus their efforts on the achievement of current account convertibility, and to treat unrestricted convertibility as a luxury to be delayed until reconstruction has been achieved' (Bergsten and Williamson, 1990).

This chapter will focus on the exchange rate consequences of capital account liberalization. Our concern will be with low-frequency (real exchange rate misalignment), not with high-frequency (nominal exchange rate volatility) deviations from exchange rate fundamentals. The authorities of developing countries which enjoy a good reputation in international financial markets are particularly worried that free capital flows would send the real exchange rate of their currencies through the roof and hence deprotect their export industries. Most economists clothe the authorities' concern with intellectual respectability. The literature on the sequencing of economic reform typically advances three arguments against the early opening of the capital account during the process of economic reform: the *'immiserizing'* flows argument, the *resource shifting* argument, and the *'Dutch disease'* argument. That debate will be presented in Section 2 in order to examine its relevance for advanced developing countries. Particular emphasis is given to the role of different exchange rate regimes in determining likely outcomes.

Section 3 will revisit the experience of the Southern Cone countries, Uruguay, Argentina and Chile. All three countries experienced during 1978-82 a strong real appreciation of the currency, followed by balance of payments crises and collapsing exchange rates. The liberalization episode of the Southern Cone ended with capital flight, generalized loan defaults, banking crises, falling output and massive unemployment. I will focus on the real appreciation experience here which has been interpreted in two alternative ways. The first interpretation has highlighted the liberalization-induced pressure of capital inflows on the real exchange rate; it is firmly rejected for all three countries. The second interpretation, by contrast, is thoroughly confirmed: reduced depreciation achieved by an *active* crawling peg combined with high nominal interest rates attracted excessive capital inflows and sustained real appreciation.

Section 4 looks at a unique policy experiment which has been much neglected in the 'sequencing' debate. Since the mid-1980s, New Zealand has undertaken sweeping reforms, but very much in contrast to the order preferred by most economists. Financial reform came overnight and at the beginning, while progress in other areas has been gradual. In contrast to the Southern Cone countries, financial reform has been based on purely floating exchange rates. The pure float and fiscal discipline helped to choke off unsustainable capital inflows, but the real exchange rate displayed a tendency to 'overshoot' to changes in monetary policy as analysed in Dornbusch (1976). While New Zealand outperforms the Southern Cone with respect to external balances, the growth and employment performance has been disappointing, suggesting costs for resource allocation and export performance.

In Section 5 the Southern Cone and New Zealand's experience are formalized in a simple general equilibrium model laid out by Bruno (1983) to discuss macroeconomic management during financial integration. Blending Bruno's model with Rodriquez' preannouncement model and with Dornbusch's overshooting model, the paper concludes in favour of managed floating for liberalizing countries without obvious partners to peg on.

2. Opening the Capital Account: Exchange Rates and Optimal Sequencing

The fear that capital account liberalization would entail a real appreciation of the exchange rate may have been nourished by the way several economists have *modelled* capital account liberalization. Usually, capital controls have been assumed to act like a tax on capital *inflows* (not outflows) whence their dismantling would lead to net capital inflows [for an overview of the literature, see Edwards (1990)]. This modelling practice can be justified as long as (a) controls on capital inflows are more effective than controls on capital outflows; (b) only those countries open their capital account which need not tax their domestic financial system to generate government revenues by fixing interest rates at arbitrarily low or negative levels; and c) the announcement of liberalization measures and their credibility has not been fully anticipated in the exchange rate.[1] But it needs more than these (often implicit) assumptions to hold that liberalizing the capital account will appreciate the real exchange rate. Only to the extent that the liberalization induced capital inflows (a) will increase the net financial transfer to the economy from abroad, and (b) that this net transfer is partly spent on non-tradables, will the domestic currency appreciate in real terms (Harberger, 1985). If, by contrast, the increased resource transfer is completely spent on additional imports (or on foreign debt service), or if the transfer is used to build up foreign assets abroad (or to amortize foreign debt), the real exchange rate is likely to be quite immune against the new capital inflows. The authorities may also enjoy some short-term monetary independence after the liberalization of capital flows so that they can shield the domestic currency from capital inflows by way of open-market operations or intervention on the foreign exchange market.

Many economists [such as McKinnon (1982), Edwards (1984), Mathieson (1986)] have been concerned with the overshooting of the exchange rate that may occur during the liberalization of the capital account. To avoid capital outflows, the authorities may accompany the liberalization measures with a firm monetary policy, driving real interest rates up. In addition, financial portfolio structures must be brought into line during liberalization; there may be a once-and-for-all attempt by foreign lenders to increase their claims on the newly liberalized economy, and by domestic residents to bring back funds invested abroad. Real appreciation may be reinforced by a spending boom caused by the wealth effect due to the (sometimes euphoric) revaluation of domestic assets perceived by investors. These sudden shifts in portfolio preferences are expected to cause a temporary appreciation in the real exchange rate above its long-run equilibrium level. The argument assumes that financial market arbitrage (uncovered interest parity) occurs much faster than goods market arbitrage (towards purchasing power parity).

The problems of real exchange rate overshooting for developing countries are similar to the 'Dutch disease' effects of an important discovery of natural resources (Edwards and van Wijnbergen, 1989). Domestic welfare rises due to increased capital inflows, but at the expense of (relatively) falling output in the manufacturing sector (deindustrialization). The relocation of production from tradables to nontradables can imply employment losses when high import protection has made many consumer goods virtually nontraded. The temporary nature of capital inflows would be no problem with perfect capital markets: export firms would borrow and invest when the domestic currency is overpriced to be prepared for the time when the return of the real exchange rate to long-run equilibrium has increased their external competitiveness. But capital markets in developing countries are far from perfect. Thus temporary appreciation will cause suboptimal investments in the traded sector which are more costly to reverse than financial investments. Hence the conclusion for the sequencing of liberalization measures: the capital account should be opened only once trade liberalization is well in train (Frenkel, 1983).[2] That point is reinforced by Edwards and van Wijnbergen in the spirit of the recent literature on endogenous growth: productivity growth has been faster in trade-oriented than in inward-oriented economies: the learning-by-doing formulation first outlined by Kenneth Arrow implies that such productivity growth is a function of accumulated experiences; hence active trade promotion (implying a competitive exchange rate) is called for to capture these dynamic gains from trade. A final objection to real exchange rate overshooting involves capital flight. Once it is perceived that the current exchange rate is unlikely to persist, overvalued currencies breed capital flight, leaving less resources available for domestic investment and growth.

Both positive and normative analysis on the optimal order of liberalization have often failed to specify the exchange rate regime[3] when discussing the effects of and the policy prescriptions for the opening of the capital account. 'International monetarists' [such as Harberger (1985), and McKinnon (1991)] favour the nominal anchor approach, implying an active crawling peg or fixed nominal rates. They opt for using the exchange rate as an instrument of anti-inflation policy, as a way of constraining domestic policies and influencing private sector expectations. The second argument often advanced against flexible nominal rates is the difficulty of monetary targeting during financial (and overall) liberalization: inducing rapid shifts in money demand and implying new transmission mechanisms (expected wealth and relative prices rather than domestic credit guide expenditure decisions), financial reform forestalls autonomous monetary policy such as is needed with a floating rate. Third, it is often argued that floating rates would tend to generate sooner and higher misalignments of the real exchange rate than do pegged or fixed exchange rates.

Whoever, by contrast, opts for purely floating exchange rates is bound to opt for early liberalization of the capital account. A clean float requires free and open capital markets. The 'domestic monetarist' (minority) view has been advanced by Lal (1987). Liberalization generates uncertainty in the dynamics associated with the process of adjustment. To minimize the information required to set specific nominal values at optimal levels and hence to avoid nominal disequilibrium exchange rates, Lal concludes the need for an exchange regime with an *automatic* balance of payments mechanism: a firm fix or a clean float.[4] A clean float is preferred because it serves to choke-off excessive capital flows. Floating rates do not constitute the one-way bet for speculators that pegged rates at times do. Lal concedes, however, the possibility of overshooting exchange rates also under pure floating, but then overshooting will apply to capital account liberalization *at any time*.

There is little disagreement in the 'sequencing' debate that stabilization (both fiscal and monetary) as well as domestic financial liberalization should precede external liberalization. But 'domestic monetarists' disagree with the mainstream advice (see, e.g., Edwards, 1990) that trade liberalization should be well under way before the capital account is opened up. They (have to) opt for the early elimination of capital controls, accompanied by a free float of the exchange rate. To contain 'immiserizing' capital inflows, opening up the capital account must include the (credible) announcement of trade liberalization, to be realized later. In 1984, New Zealand chose quite precisely the 'domestic monetarist' approach to the sequencing of reform, accompanied by pure floating. New Zealand thus adds an important country experience that the 'sequencing' debate cannot afford to ignore.

3. The Southern Cone Revisited

After having followed development strategies that were heavily biased towards protectionism and a high degree of government intervention, Uruguay, Chile and Argentina moved in the 1970s towards the liberalization of their economies, including their capital account.[5] Michael Bruno (1985) has summarized the exchange rate experience of the three reform countries: 'A central accompanying feature was a substantial real appreciation of the exchange rate following massive capital inflows in response to sustained interest differentials, with a severe crisis in the export sector. This is a more general phenomenon that has become known as the "Southern Cone Syndrome", but it is also known from the experience of several other countries during the past decade' (p. 867). We will now revisit the historical evidence of each of these three countries in order to identify to what extent capital account liberalization *per se* may have contributed to their ill-fated reform experiments.

Uruguay[6]
Uruguay eliminated restrictions on private capital flows very early, in late 1974. Domestic residents were allowed to hold foreign exchange. Compared with Argentina, and especially with Chile, the sequencing of the Uru-

Figure 6.1   Uruguay: Balance of payments (millions of US$)

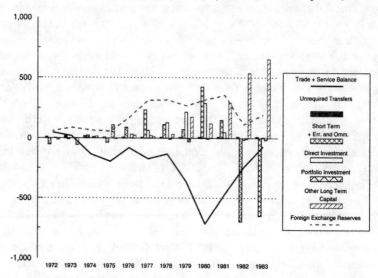

Source: IMF.

Figure 6.2   Uruguay: Real effective exchange rates IV:1972-IV:1983
AVG IV:72-III:74 = 100

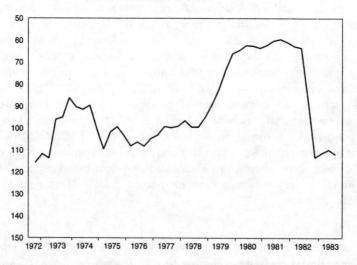

guayan reform program was unusual because the reforms of the financial markets were implemented more fully and often *preceded* those in commodity markets (Hanson and de Melo, 1985). External financial liberalization went along with domestic financial reform. Also in 1974, the ceiling on interest rates for peso loans and deposits was substantially raised (final elimination in September 1976). Sectoral credit allocation was abolished in 1975. In 1977, the barriers to entry into banking were lifted as competition for deposits with established commercial banks became allowed. Financial liberalization was accompanied by an orthodox stabilization program; the budget deficit as a fraction of GDP fell continuously, from 4.5 per cent in 1974 to 1.2 per cent in 1977, being almost nil thereafter until 1982. The fiscal deficit was largely financed by selling dollar-denominated government bonds to the public.

Figures 6.1 and 6.2 present the consequences of the reform package for Uruguay's balance of payments and the real effective exchange rate (inverted scale: rise of the curve denotes appreciation). The capital account of the balance of payments started to improve in 1975, but inflows were not excessive. Errors and omissions turned from negative to positive values, suggesting that capital flight was over. Argentinean investment into foreign-currency denominated deposits explain most of that turnaround. Note also that foreign direct investment inflows were important during 1977-1980. The turnaround in the capital account was reflected by a switch of the current account into deficit which remained modest up to 1979. The deficit was no cause for concern because exports were buoyant. Export incentives, a passive crawling peg ensuring stable real exchange rates and the capital inflows induced by liberalization and stabilization avoided the usual liquidity squeeze that accompanies orthodox stabilization packages. Thus, up to 1979, liberalizing the financial sector offered substantial benefits. In fact, Uruguay was the only oil-importing country to increase its average growth rate substantially after the 1973 oil price shock.

The link between increased capital inflows and the real effective exchange rate was weak between 1974 and end 1978. This evidence defies much of the analytical reasoning about the exchange rate implications of capital account liberalization, but it can be explained by several factors. First, Uruguay was especially hit by worsening terms of trade during that period, a result of the oil price shock and falling wool and beef prices since the cut off from the EEC market. Second, the financial system was largely dollarized; increased portfolio inflows were allocated into dollar assets after the removal of the prohibition to hold dollar assets, while peso-denominated financial assets rose only slowly. Third, official foreign exchange reserves rose during 1977 when short-term capital inflows became more important:

the increase in reserves amounted to a nonsterilized intervention on the foreign exchange market to dampen the appreciation of the peso. As a result of these factors, the real exchange rate was kept remarkably stable, at least by Uruguay's standard, after the capital account was opened (IV. 1974) up to IV. 1978.

But inflation remained stubborn. Thus, the authorities decided in October 1978 to use the exchange rate to bring down inflation. The government adopted the policy of announcing in advance future values of the exchange rate (the *tablita*) as a tool to reduce inflationary expectations. At the same time, financial liberalization was completed with the removal of legal reserve requirements and the banking tax. Only then did the real exchange rate start to shoot through the roof. From IV. 1978 to I. 1980, the peso appreciated in real effective terms by 50 per cent. The overvaluation was then maintained for another six quarters, up to III. 1982 (when Mexico defaulted on its foreign debt).

When the *tablita* was instituted in October 1978, the preannounced rate of crawl (a schedule of monthly devaluation of the peso against the dollar six to nine months in advance) was much below the domestic-foreign inflation differential. The *tablita* opened the opportunity of large profits from uncovered arbitrage, an opportunity which was actively exploited in particular in 1980, also by the Argentinean neighbours. The result was that during 1980 (when Uruguay experienced excessive capital inflows) peso deposit rates of 52.2 per cent a year combined with a devaluation rate to the dollar of 13.6 per cent a year (period averages). It then became possible for foreign capital to earn almost 40 per cent a year in dollars. Hanson and de Melo (1985) have estimated a simple model of uncovered interest parity to show that the *ex ante* spread between peso and dollar interest rates remained constant, implying a widening *ex post* spread (adjusted for exchange rate devaluation). The widening spread has been explained by a rising risk premium on Uruguayan assets, the increase in consumer borrowing, and the wealth effect caused by a land and real estate boom.

It is difficult to disentangle the final causes of the widened interest spread: the spread reflects both the lack of credibility of the *tablita* as well as the impact of rising capital inflows on asset prices and euphoric market perceptions. In any case, it was *not* the liberalization of the capital account *per se* which caused or deepened the subsequent difficulties. But as from 1979 on, portfolio inflows (in particular in 1980), foreign direct investment and foreign borrowing all combined to finance costly policy errors. First, the *tablita* continued with a slowing rate of crawl, although Argentina embarked on massive devaluations, and thus deepened recession in the tradables sector. The recession turned the government budget into deficit, because social security outlays rose while government revenues declined. With growing doubts about the exchange rate, private capital flew and official reserves declined. The government incurred foreign debt at an unsustainable rate to defend the exchange rate. That the Uruguayan authorities delayed devaluation for so long (up to November 1982) may also be explained by their perception that the country needed a fixed exchange rate were it to become an international financial centre. However, the liberalization episode ended with capital flight, generalized loan defaults, a banking crisis, falling output and massive unemployment. The real effective exchange rate collapsed during III. 1982 and I. 1983, down by 78 per cent.

Argentina[7]

Argentina eliminated most controls on capital movements between 1977 and 1979, later than Uruguay and earlier than Chile both for the timing as well as for the sequencing with respect to other reforms. The relaxation of capital controls was gradual. In March 1977, service payments and transfers were liberalized. During 1978, the ceiling on unrestricted purchase of US dollars was progressively raised from US$ 1,000 to US$ 20,000. At end 1978, the minimum maturity requirement for foreign loans was reduced from two years to one year. In July 1980, this maturity requirement was eliminated. By then, capital controls were completely relaxed. External financial reform went hand in hand with domestic financial reform. In mid-1977, deposit rates of interest were deregulated, banks' reserve requirements reduced and commercial banks were paid interest on their reserves with the central bank. All minimum deposit requirements on private financial borrowing were abolished in December 1978. From November 1976 (when a dual exchange market system designed to discourage capital outflows was abolished) to May 1978, Argentina had a passive crawling peg system. From May to December 1978, the exchange rate was floated freely. From December 1978 to June 1981, a *tablita* scheme similar to Uruguay's was introduced, announcing in advance a schedule of daily exchange rates. However, the *tablita* did *not* free speculation from foreign exchange risk because the government never prefixed the exchange rate for more than six months while foreign capital could not be repatriated until it had been in Argentina for a year (Calvo, 1983). When in 1981 the tablita got increasingly incredible due to pronounced overvaluation of the real exchange rate, the government provided direct exchange rate guarantees to stimulate foreign borrowing.

There is no obvious link between the level of *net* capital inflows (Figure 6.3) and the astounding real appreciation of the peso (Figure 6.4) which was sustained for almost four years, from II. 1977 to I. 1981. During 1976 and 1978 (when gross and net capital flows were small), there was a sizeable

Figure 6.3   Argentina: Balance of payments (millions of US$)

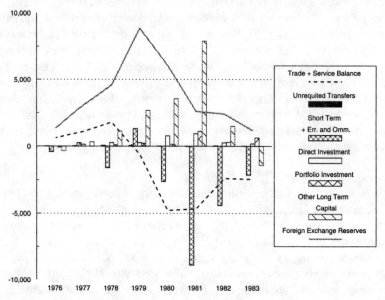

Source: IMF.

Figure 6.4   Argentina: Real effective exchange rate III:1976-IV:1983
AVG III:1976-II:1978 = 100

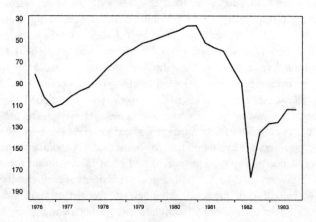

increase of international reserves held by the central bank. The increase of reserves is partly explained by current account surpluses, and partly by portfolio shifts by domestic residents. Calvo (1983) assigns the portfolio shift to the credible government commitment that private property would be fully respected as well as to the decontrol of domestic interest rates and to the widening set of attractive domestic assets. Thus, much of the increase of reserves came from private portfolios held by Argentineans, in many cases a straight shift from dollars held in private safety boxes into official reserves. A sizeable inflow of net capital occurred only in 1979 when the *tablita* policy of declining rates of devaluation had been announced and when fiscal and monetary policies both were tied. The 1979 stabilization policy was reversed in 1980 when several bank failures resulted in a sharp increase in central bank lending to the financial system, and when the (mostly central bank financed) public sector deficit rose from 5 to 11 per cent of GDP. The *tablita* schedule lost credibility. Rising interest rates on peso deposits could not make up for the growing foreign exchange risk, resulting in large official reserve losses and private capital flight. In 1981, measures were taken to retain or attract private capital. The government offered exchange rate guarantees (involving a significant implicit subsidy) to persuade domestic firms or banks to either borrow abroad or maintain their external debt rather than pay off their foreign loans. The exchange rate guarantees explain well the asymmetric capital flows in 1981 and early 1982: it was nothing but a round trip of capital flows — borrowed free of private exchange rate risk — into capital flight to avoid losses from the expected collapse of the exchange rate. The expected exchange rate collapse materialized from early 1981 on when the rate was repeatedly devalued.

In explaining the pronounced rise and fall of the exchange rate curve (Figure 6.4) one can choose among a bewildering variety of models that have been offered (after the event). Before the *tablita* policy was introduced — for the period 1976-78 — Calvo's (1983) portfolio shift model seems appropriate to explain the appreciation of the peso. Improved expectations about the honouring of property rights and an improved set of domestic assets trigger a portfolio shift from foreign exchange holdings towards domestic assets (say, land). The shift raises the price of land, and, consequently, wealth goes up. The wealth effect increases the demand for nontradables, hence their prices and, subsequently, the demand for domestic money. The central bank accumulates reserves, and the real exchange rate appreciates, even though the public was interested in land, not in domestic money. But real appreciation is only temporary in Calvo's model and one has to wonder why the rise of the peso was sustained for four years. That the peso appreciated further during 1979-80 seems best explained by Rodriguez'(1979) preannouncement model which reflects the *tablita* policy at that period. The short-term response to a credible announcement of lower devaluation rates is a fall of nominal and real interest rates under perfect capital mobility. Lower devaluation rates stabilize tradables prices earlier than prices of nontradables, hence producing a real appreciation. But the *tablita* cannot by itself affect relative prices in the long run. Thus, a real depreciation is to be expected later which requires positive real interest rates at a later date. From late 1979 on, positive real interest rates materialized, but not real depreciation. On the contrary, during 1980 the real exchange rate continued the appreciation trend started in 1976.

The 1980 appreciation of the Argentinean peso helps to clarify an important point of debate about the degree of endogenity of the real exchange rate. Real appreciation during 1980 did *not* occur with rising official reserves and rising inflation. The peso appreciated in real terms simply because the reform of the *tablita* schedule was delayed. Since the announced rate of crawl had become inconsistent with the hyper-expansionary fiscal and monetary policies pursued by the authorities, it had to be supported by declining central bank reserves and with a rising premium for exchange risk (increasing the spread between domestic interest rates and the world interest rate plus the announced rate of devaluation). According to Fernandez (1985), the stabilization plan could have been rescued with a rise in the devaluation schedule immediately after the banking crisis erupted in March 1980. Instead, the slowing rate of crawl was maintained for another three quarters, and thus heavy real appreciation of the exchange rate continued.

Chile[8]

Chile followed the widely recommended sequence of liberalizing the current account first and the capital account later. The staggering fiscal deficits of the Allende government had been steadily reduced and by 1978 the public sector was in surplus. Tight fiscal policy was accompanied by a monetary squeeze. Among the Southern Cone countries, Chile did most to abolish domestic price controls and it was the only one to liberalize foreign trade substantially. Chile followed the recommended sequencing with respect to financial reform, too. Domestic reform began by allowing nonbank intermediaries to operate without interest controls: the decontrol of interest rates was then gradually extended to commercial banks. State-owned banks were returned to the private sector. External financial reform was gradual, but lacked initially a clear direction. Global limits on medium-term external bank borrowing were eliminated in June 1979 only, and restrictions on monthly inflows in April 1980. But restrictions on short-term capital inflows were not dismantled until December 1981, when commercial banks were for the first time allowed to lend short term with external credit for purposes other than financing commercial operations. Note in particular that such restrictions were to ensure some control over domestic monetary policy. The government realized early that given high domestic interest rates, complete liberalization would induce excessive and destabilizing capital inflows (Ffrench-Davis, 1983).

Figure 6.5   Chile: Balance of payments (millions of US$)

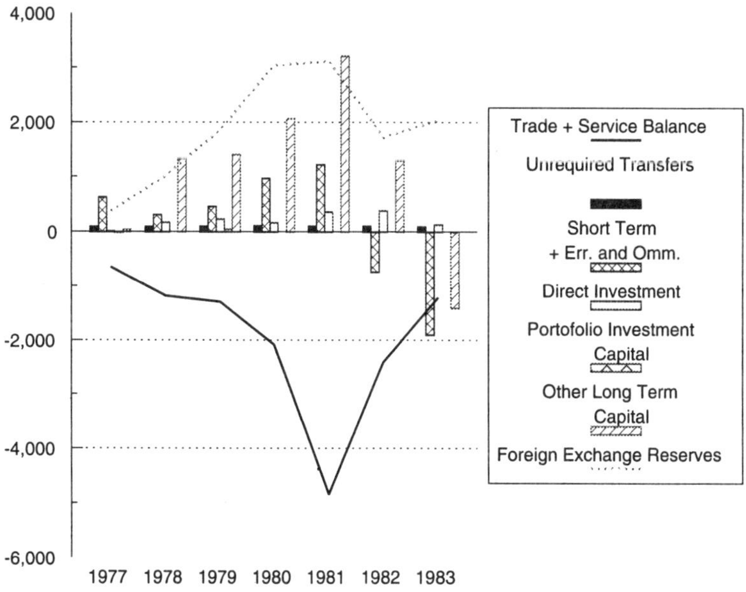

Source: IMF.

Despite the restrictions on capital inflows, the inflows proved massive, as seen from Figure 6.5. Most was medium-term borrowing passing through the banking system while foreign direct investment was unimportant. Subsequently, foreign exchange reserves rose tenfold during 1977 and 1981, up to a level worth round 7 per cent of GDP. In February 1978 Chile adopted the *tablita* policy of preannouncement of the exchange rate (the active crawling peg) to reduce inflation. The authorities devalued, at a decreasing pace, until June 1979 when the value of the peso was *fixed* to the US dollar. Inflation at that time was still around 20 per cent higher than inflation in the US Also in June 1979, the government introduced *backward wage indexation* stating that wages subject to collective bargaining (most outside agriculture and services) would have as a minimum the previous twelve months' rate of inflation.

Figure 6.6   Chile: Real effective exchange rate III:1977-IV:1983
AVG III:1977-II:1979 = 100

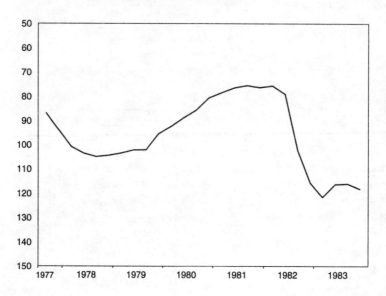

Figure 6.6 reveals that the real effective exchange rate was quite stable in 1978 and up to IV. 1979. Only then real appreciation set in, a trend maintained through I. 1982, accumulating in a fall of the real effective rate of 35 per cent. Disinflation (whence real appreciation with a nominal fix of the exchange rate) was slower than expected by the authorities, essentially for two macroeconomic reasons. The active crawling peg policy was, in particular in 1980 and 1981, partly thwarted by the inflationary pressures created by the capital inflows since their full sterilization could not be achieved by the monetary authorities. Part of the increased demand fell on nontraded goods, increasing their prices (while the prices of tradables were more stable because of the fixed exchange rate). The real exchange rate (remind definition 2 given above) appreciated. The second macroeconomic reason was the

full indexation of wages to consumer price inflation in the previous year which was, in the context of disinflation, bound to result in inertia inflation and real appreciation (remind definition 3).

What then did the lifting of capital controls contribute to the appreciation of the Chilean peso? Corbo (1987) has tried to settle that question by estimating a three asset portfolio model similar to Kouri and Porter (1974). The results show that capital inflows are largely explained by portfolio considerations, even in periods when controls on capital inflows were present. Again, the combination of reduced, and later, zero depreciation with high nominal interest rates (partly reflecting continuing inflation) attracted capital inflows, triggered by a portfolio shift toward dollar-denominated loans. Corbo reports also that on the supply side the lifting of capital controls (represented by an intercept dummy in the model) gave capital inflows a further push. But here, Corbo's estimate is misspecified. First, the intercept dummy although 'highly significant' is close to zero. Second, it makes little sense to represent capital controls by way of intercept dummies; rather the responsiveness to the world interest rate would be assumed to change in the portfolio model. Finally, Corbo has not addressed an important problem of multicollinearity: both the fixing of the peso to the dollar and the elimination of global limits on borrowing abroad happened at the same time, in June 1979 from when on the peso started to appreciate. There is thus no support for Harberger's (1985) proposition that 'it was probably the relaxation of restrictions . . . that permitted what in retrospect was . . . a significantly excessive inflow of capital in 1981' (p. 247).

In 1982, capital inflows and more so, the net transfer of resources were sharply reversed. Adjustment came through a sharp fall in income partly because of the combined depressive impact of the highly appreciated peso and of high interest rates on tradables production. In spite of declining reserves, the *tablita* was maintained until June 1982, adding to the high employment and output costs of the exchange regime experiment.

4. Financial Liberalization Down Under: New Zealand[9]

In mid-1984, New Zealand looked very much like a pre-reform Southern Cone country. The economy was weakened by extensive protectionism, government intervention and suppressed inflation. Macroeconomic imbalances were severe. Large government budget deficits since the mid-70s had been financed to an important extent by foreign borrowing, with gross debt as a fraction of GDP rising over that period from virtually nil to 73 per cent. Including loans to public enterprises, the public sector deficit approached 9 per cent of GDP in 1984. With a deficit in the current account of the balance of payments of also 9 per cent of GDP, and with official reserves of foreign exchange exhausted due to private capital outflows, New Zealand was in the middle of a classical foreign exchange crisis.

The newly elected (Labour party) government immediately started an ambitious program of macroeconomic stabilization and structural reform. The comprehensiveness and speed of that reform process is rivalled only by Chile's 1970s reform process, while the order of reform is more comparable to Uruguay's. Like in Uruguay, domestic and external financial reform preceded reform in other areas such as foreign trade or the labour market. Within eight months, virtually all controls on financial markets were removed. In July 1984, to combat the foreign exchange crisis, controls on interest rates were abolished, and the currency was devalued by 20 per cent. A month later, administrative controls on credit allocation were ended. The capital account was opened in December 1984 when virtually all controls on foreign exchange transactions were lifted. Finally, all reserve requirement and ratio controls on banks' portfolio went in February 1985. Within months, New Zealand's financial market had moved from being one of the most regulated in the OECD area to one of the most liberal. Somewhat later, from April 1987 on, the government also permitted foreign entry into the banking sector (but foreign presence had already been large before).

Like in Uruguay, financial reform came overnight while progress in other areas such as public sector reform, removal of trade protection and the freeing up of the labour market was gradual. Within 1984-87, the primary deficit was reduced by 6.2 per cent of GDP, and the financial deficit by 4.4 per cent. On a cash basis (i.e. including asset transactions), the improvement during 1984-87 was from a deficit of 8.3 per cent of GDP to a surplus of 1.1 per cent, reflecting raised efficiency in public enterprises and higher cost recovery for public services. Most of the fiscal consolidation happened in 1985, the government's first full year in office. Swift reductions in subsidies and a large increase in direct tax receipts (fiscal drag) had a major impact. The cut in subsidies partly reflected trade liberalization, with a withdrawal of agricultural subsidies which accompanied tariff cuts and the dismantling of import licenses for the manufacturing sector. But trade liberalization has worsened incentives for export production vis-à-vis import substitution with the speedy abolition of export subsidies and slower progress in lowering import protection. Other distortions remained, especially in the labour market. Labour market competition and flexibility has been impeded by legislation stipulating compulsory union membership, a minimum membership of 1,000 employees, and asymmetric negotiation rights for unions versus employers. Different tax treatments for different types of investment income encourages investors to invest for capital gains in financial speculation and property.

Financial reform was accompanied by tight money (except late 1985 to late 1986, see below) and, from March 1985 on, by a pure float of the exchange rate. In contrast to the Southern Cone countries, New Zealand's authorities quickly realized that, with open capital markets and confidence in the prevailing exchange rate peg, private capital flows could easily undermine monetary targets by fueling the reserve component of base money. New Zealand's authorities opted for the move from pegged to floating rates for several reasons (Spencer and Carey, 1988). First, to support disinflation by targeting zero trend growth from year to year in the supply of *primary liquidity* which consists of settlement cash and securities discountable with the Reserve Bank. Second, the authorities thought to facilitate future real exchange rate adjustments with less adverse output and employment consequences than under the crawling peg. Third, there was a desire to avoid future taxpayer funded foreign exchange losses (as happened in 1984 when the preceding government tried to defend an overvalued exchange rate). To peg the New Zealand dollar to a trade-weighted basket has proved to be very difficult because export markets are so diverse (Australia and the United States for manufactured goods and the EEC and Japan for primary commodities) and because of sharp shifts in the cross-rates between the currencies of New Zealand's major export partners.

Capital flows are not seriously reported by the New Zealand balance of payments statistics. The data do not provide sufficient information for a comprehensive classification of capital account flows into portfolio and other transactions and into short-term and long-term transactions. Moreover, available data on capital account flows are inconsistent (do not add up) with the residual items of New Zealand's balance of payments. To identify the link between liberalization, capital flows and the real exchange rate, we have substituted the figure on the balance of payments reported for the other sample countries by a table similar to Harberger (1985) to measure the capital market pressure on the real exchange rate (Table 6.1).

Table 6.1 assumes that an increase in net capital inflows will cause the real exchange rate to appreciate (to the extent to which the inflows are spent on nontradables), and that two main forces operate to offset the capital market pressure on the real exchange rate. First, net factor payments abroad represent a flow of funds in the opposite direction. Second, if the capital inflow is acquired by the central bank and accumulated as foreign currency holdings, there is again no pressure on the real exchange rate (at least, in the shorter term). These two offsetting forces have been taken into account in Table 6.1 by subtracting the relevant flows for each year from the corre-

Table 6.1   Capital market pressure on New Zealand's real exchange rate,
                1983-1988

Items	1983	1984	1985	1986	1987	1988
(a) Inflow of capital NZ$, bn.	2.19	5.93	3.52	6.38	1.10	1.35
(b) Net factor payments abroad NZ$, bn.	1.28	1.91	2.69	2.21	2.75	2.73
(c) Accumulation of reserves NZ$, bn.	0.27	2.22	-0.82	3.81	-1.69	-0.41
(d) Net pressure on the real exchange rate [(a) - (b) - (c)]	0.64	1.80	1.65	0.36	0.04	-0.97
(d) Relative index of exchange rate pressure [(d): GDP], percentages	1.86	4.64	3.69	0.67	0.07	-1.52

(a) Equals the current account deficit, SNA definition, plus change in foreign exhange reserves.
Sources: OECD; own calculations.

sponding inflow of capital. The resulting net figure is given in row (d), and
is expressed as a percentage of GDP in (e). Obviously, New Zealand did not
experience excessive capital inflows after having opened up the capital account. To the contrary, cross-border flows combined to exert the strongest
pressure on the real exchange rate just *before* the capital market was opened,
in 1984 when the government borrowed foreign funds worth 2 per cent of
GDP to defend the exchange rate. After financial reform, we observe the
index of exchange rate pressure to continuously tail off. During 1985-88 the
index goes down from +4.6 to -1.5, a swing of almost 6 per cent of GDP.
Other observations support our findings. The current account deficit fell
steadily from 8.5 per cent of GDP in 1984 to less than 2 per cent in 1988.
Net foreign debt remained stable over that period, and slightly declined in
terms of national income and exports.

   In Chile, by contrast, the index of exchange rate pressure had jumped up
to 10 per cent of GDP in 1981 (Harberger, 1985). One explanation that net
capital inflows never became excessive in New Zealand may be found in the
nature of the interest rate adjustment process following financial liberalization. As has been shown above for Chile, for example, the lack of conver-

gence of domestic interest rates to world rates has been an important determinant of excessive capital inflows. Although real rates of interest were never excessively high after liberalization in New Zealand, nominal effective devaluation fell considerably short of nominal short rates, providing important *ex-post* returns to portfolio inflows (Table 6.2). High returns *ex post* were in particular available during 1985 and 1987, when short-term rates were well above long-term rates, giving a steep inversion of the yield curve.

Table 6.2　　*Elements of uncovered interest parity, New Zealand, 1984-1989*

Fiscal year (March-March)	Short-term interest rate (90 day bank bills)	Long-term interest rate (5 year gov. bonds)	Inflation (CPI)	Percentage change in nominal effective exchange rate
1984/85	17.9	14.3	8.7	-15.8
1985/86	24.5	18.1	15.3	-3.1
1986/87	20.6	15.9	14.6	-10.2
1987/88	18.9	14.9	13.4	6.2
1988/89	14.8	13.0	5.2	-0.4
1989/90	13.6	12.3	7.3	-2.7

Source: OECD, 1991.

Thus, pure uncovered interest parity did not hold for at least three years, providing good opportunities for portfolio investment also in New Zealand. In an empirical study on the determination of New Zealand's short and long-term interest rates, McNelis, Grimes and Wong (1989) attribute the observed deviation from interest parity to the slow learning process in the capital markets. In particular, the impact of government debt and of the real value of securities discounted with the Reserve Bank (a proxy for the monetary stance) lost impact on interest determination only from 1987 on. Since then, there is a move towards greater *effective* international openness (towards uncovered interest parity).

The fact that the observed important *ex-post* returns to portfolio inflows were only little exploited thus seems partly explained by the perceived risk derived from the high level of government debt already in existence when financial reform was started. By contrast, debt levels were comparatively low in the Southern Cone countries when they started the financial opening. Another distinguishing feature is, of course, the exchange rate regime under which financial reform was carried out. The pure float has acted to absorb speculative flows by way of exchange rate adjustment and thus reduced incentives for, and the size of, net capital inflows. The observed deviation from interest parity has been partly driven by the exchange rate risk premium. Firstly, New Zealand's authorities had made it clear that they were strongly committed to monetary targeting, not to exchange rate targeting. Secondly, the New Zealand dollar has been shown (largely for seasonal reasons) to display greater short-term volatility than the major currencies and the close substitute, the Australian dollar (Spencer and Carey, 1988). Thus, the pure float did not provide the possibility of a one-way bet for portfolio speculation that was provided, as shown above, by the active crawling peg in the Southern Cone.

The 20 per cent devaluation of the New Zealand dollar in III.1984 was quickly eroded during 1985 when the currency appreciated back to pre-devaluation levels. The New Zealand dollar softened again in 1986 only to appreciate in turn from late 1986 to mid-1988. By that time, the New Zealand dollar had appreciated in real effective terms by 41 per cent since the capital account had been opened and the exchange rate been floated. But late 1988, the currency weakened again and since then has stabilized in real effective terms. All in all, the New Zealand dollar provided, five years after financial reform, the same level of external competitiveness as it did before the 1984 devaluation.

A recent study on the determination of New Zealand's exchange rate (Blundell-Wignall and Gregory, 1990) rejects a tendency to purchasing power parity. It is shown that the real effective value of the New Zealand dollar has traditionally been closely determined by movements in the commodity terms of trade, both before and after the capital account was opened. Both under pegged and floating exchange rates, the real exchange rate has adjusted to accommodate changes in New Zealand's terms of trade. But with the pure float of the New Zealand dollar, the real exchange rate moved more closely in line with the terms of trade: the immediate change in the nominal rate, rather than the inflation differential with trading partners, brought about the adjustment. Capital account liberalization is likely to have speeded up the exchange rate adjustment since liberalization translates 'news' about commodity prices quickly into portfolio readjustment.

The study by Blundell-Wignall and Gregory has not investigated the relative importance of money. Figure 6.7 suggests that the sharp shifts in the real effective exchange rate reflected above all monetary policy. In particular, there was a close correlation between the real exchange rate strength and the spread of short-term interest rates over long-term rates. The 1985 appreciation reflects the tightening of monetary policy from end 1984 on. The appreciation may also be interpreted as a move of the real exchange rate back to longer-run equilibrium because the 1984 devaluation of 20 per cent involved some arbitrariness and may have been too sharp. The 1986 softening of the New Zealand dollar reflected the abrupt (and premature) easing of the monetary stance, as the subsequent strengthening of the currency reflected the monetary re-tightening after September 1986. When evidence of rapid disinflation became apparent in early 1988, monetary conditions eased again with declining short-term interest rates, a flattening of the yield curve and a sharp slide of the New Zealand dollar. Since late 1988, both money and the exchange rate have been successfully kept on a flat trend. This has coincided with the shift of emphasis towards the exchange rate as a guide to monetary policy (Spencer, 1990). Since August 1988, the trade-weighted New Zealand dollar has become the Reserve Bank's principal monetary indicator. The shift in emphasis between the indicators acknowledges the experience that the money supply is a poor indicator of the effective monetary stance during financial liberalization. With more weight given to the exchange rate, monetary policy is likely to exert a more consistent degree of disinflationary pressure while creating a more stable trading and investment environment.

Labour market legislation has resulted in wage levels exceeding those which would have been set in a more competitive setting of the labour market (Spencer and Carey, 1988). Apart from slowing the process of disinflation, higher wages have supported the sustained real appreciation of the New Zealand dollar up to 1988. Finally, by fostering the stickiness of wage-price adjustment, labour market legislation has contributed to a Dornbusch (1976)-style overshooting of the exchange rate. With sticky wages and prices, an unexpected reduction in monetary growth is likely to produce an initial over-appreciation of the exchange rate and a contraction in the tradables sector. While money has no impact on the equilibrium exchange rate in the Dornbusch model, the New Zealand experience suggests that in practice monetary shocks can affect the real exchange rate over one to two years.

Distortions in New Zealand's tax system and labour market have supported the sustained appreciation of the currency during disinflation. As long as inflation was comparatively high, it has introduced an important bias into the taxation of investor income. While there is no capital-gain tax, interest income has been highly taxed because the inflation component of interest rates was not exempted from taxation. Tax distortion has encouraged investment for capital gains in construction and financial assets. The distortion has thus created excess demand for nontradables, raising the relative price of nontradables and supporting real appreciation.

The 'most comprehensive economic reform programme undertaken by any OECD country in recent decades (p. 38)' has 'so far failed to deliver the long-term increases in output and employment which were its ultimate objectives (p. 9)', writes the OECD (1991) in its recent country survey on New Zealand. Table 6.3 scrutinizes the disappointing performance in output and employment. Arguably the best single summary performance indicator is GDP per head, expressed in purchasing power parity (PPP) equivalents. During 1975 and 1985, with terms of trade broadly flat, per capita GDP declined from 97 to 82 per cent relative to the OECD average. After reform, with terms of trade up, the comparative decline continued, with GDP per head down to 75 per cent of the OECD average in 1988. The unemployment rate which has been traditionally low in New Zealand rose from 3.6 to 6.8 per cent during the reform period, at a time when the OECD area managed to bring unemployment rates down; for the first time ever, unemployment rates (in spite of considerable emigration) are now higher than on OECD average.

Unlike before reform, New Zealand's decline in comparative income level has not been due to poor productivity. Table 6.3 suggests considerable improvements of capital productivity to which the business sector has quickly reacted by raising investment rates. Investment (and the growing labour force) raised potential output which was not translated into higher actual output due to declining capacity utilization, explaining roughly 75 per cent of the deterioration in comparative per capita income during 1985-88. Since the OECD has also estimated that the complete elimination of agricultural support in OECD countries (which has not been built up during 1985-89 alone) would lead to a one-time gain of 2.7 per cent in real income, more than half of the output gap since 1985 must be explained by other factors. The OECD report is silent on exchange rate misalignment and sequencing of reform. Can they explain anything about New Zealand's disappointing performance so far?

Table 6.4 provides some preliminary evidence which seems to confirm concerns about longer-run costs of exchange rate overshooting, though not concerns about costs of early capital account liberalization. The 'immiserizing capital flows' objection to early capital account liberalization (unrelated to exchange rates) is clearly rejected by the facts. The Spearman rank estimate, produced for nine industries (for which estimates on effective rates of assistance are available), yields a significantly negative correlation coefficient for both 1984/85 and, even more so, 1989/90. This finding indicates

Table 6.3   New Zealand: indicators of comparative performance

	Pre-reform		Post-reform
	1975	1985	1988
1. GDP per head, current PPPs OECD = 100	97	82	75
		1985	1989
2. Unemployment rate — New Zealand — OECD		3.6 8.0	6.8 6.4
		1975-84	1985-89
3. Rates of return on business capital — New Zealand — OECD		10.3 13.9	15.3 15.6
		1975-84	1985-89
4. Investment rates in the business sector — New Zealand — OECD		15.5 16.1	18.8 17.2

Source: OECD, 1991.

that investment has not been guided by prevailing distortions but was channelled into those sectors which received the lowest level of protection.

There is, however, evidence available from Table 6.4 that resources were shifted away from tradables. It is a common approximation to treat services as nontradables and the rest as tradables. Within the tradables sector, agriculture and mining are subject to special factors such as weather or terms of trade, so it will make more sense to concentrate on manufacturing. Table 6.4

gives a clear indication that when the NZ dollar was strong capital has been reallocated away from the manufacturing sector. Both measures, the share of manufacturing investment in GDP and its share in total fixed investment, display a clear downward trend for the post-reform period. The relocation of

Table 6.4　　*New Zealand: indicators of factor reallocation and trade performance*

	Pre-reform	Post-reform
	1984/85	**1989/90**
1. Investment rates and effective rates of assistance, Spearman Rank Corr. Coeff.	-0.70	-0.82
	1976-85	**1986-89**
2. Fixed investment in manufacturing as a share of GDP;	0.048	0.031
and of total investment	0.202	0.148
	1982-85	**1986-89**
3. Employment in manufacturing as a share of total employment	0.324	0.269
	1983-85	**1986-88**
4. Manufactured exports as percentage of manufactured exports of all OECD countries	1.47	1.31

Sources: OECD Secretariat; own calculations.

investment from tradables towards nontradables implied considerable employment losses. During 1986-89, employment levels have shrunk by 83,000 (equivalent to more than 2 per cent of total employment), and the manufacturing sector contributed 73,000 to the loss. At the same period, employment in manufacturing contributed on average a fourth to total employment, while it still had contributed a third during the three-year period before the NZ dollar strengthened in real terms. Chapter 10 will report a test similar to Krugman and Baldwin (1987) to explore whether the strong NZ dollar has produced sustained effects on trade. Table 4 demonstrates that during the reform period, New Zealand has not only lost income compared to the OECD area, but also market shares in manufactured exports. Incidentally, both losses, comparative income and comparative exports of manufactures, amounted to around 10 per cent from original levels in the mid-80s.

Polak (1990), summarizing a conference on experiences with different exchange rate regimes, has recently brought New Zealand's experience to the point: 'Since floating is the prevailing regime . . . the cost of it seems to be underplayed — namely, that the resulting ups and downs of the real rate play havoc with resource allocation and hamper export diversification. The coun-

Figure 6.7   The Bruno model

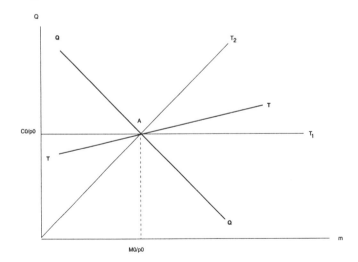

tries are told to overcome this problem by developing "competitiveness less dependent on relative prices" — a neat trick if you can do it (p. 386)'.

5. Modelling the Evidence

Chronicling some liberalization experiences may not be sufficient to draw 'hard' conclusions, but it helps to discriminate between irrelevant models and relevant ones. The experience of the four countries surveyed above can serve to qualify a common objection to capital account liberalization: that opening the capital account induces 'excessive' capital inflows which appreciate the domestic currency so as to hamper the development of tradable activities. It is rather the exchange rate regime which shapes events after the financial opening of an economy. The interaction between financial opening, stabilization, the exchange rate regime, and the real exchange rate seems appropriately formalized by the framework laid out by Bruno (1983). Using a slightly simplified and modified version of Bruno's model, I will discuss the most important insights derived from the chronicling performed above.

The general equilibrium A of the economy is represented in Figure 6.8 in which the real exchange rate ($q = e/p$) and real money balances ($m = M/p$) are given on the two axes. The goods market equilibrium is given by:

$$(1) \qquad Q^d - Q^s = f_1(q, m, U_1)$$
$$\qquad\qquad\qquad\quad + + +$$

where U_1 stands for a vector of various exogenous shift factors such as real income, expected inflation, real wages and government spending. The equilibrium schedule QQ gives the combinations of the real exchange rate and real money balances that keep the good market in equilibrium with excess demand (raising inflation) above and right to the schedule and with unemployment below and left to it. An increase of any of the shift factors will move the schedule inward.

Next we define the basic balance (T_1) as the current account plus exogenously given long-run capital flows, such as foreign investment. As long as capital controls are effective enough to allow autonomous monetary policy, the real exchange rate stays undetermined by real money balances. Hence the basic balance is represented by the horizontal line T_1 in Figure 6.7, at a given real exchange rate $q_0 = e_0/p_0$. Equilibrium in the basic balance is given by:

$$(2) \qquad T_1 = T_1(q_1, U_2)$$

where U_2 is another shift factor. T_1 shifts up with a long-run fall in import protection, foreign investment or deteriorating terms of trade, for example. Below the T_1 line, the basic balance is in deficit, above it is in surplus.

The private sector holds three financial assets: domestic money M_1 domestic bonds B carrying a nominal interest rate i, and a foreign currency asset Z carrying an interest rate i^*. The money market is in equilibrium with given money supply (M) when

$$(3) \qquad M^d/p = \lambda(i)Q = M/p$$
$$\text{--}$$

where money demand (M^d) is proportional to domestic output (Q) and a negative function of the domestic interest rate (i). The relative demand for foreign assets (Z^d) is assumed to be driven by the expected rate of depreciation, ε:

$$(4) \qquad eZ^d/M^d = qZ^d/m^d = k(\varepsilon)$$
$$+$$

where k is a coefficient for the degree of substitutability between domestic and foreign assets. Once total asset demand is given, the demand for domestic government bonds can be derived as a residual. The asset market equilibrium is represented by the line T_2 in Figure 6.7. The relationship between the real exchange rate and real money balances is given by rearranging equation (4) so that $q/m = k(\varepsilon)/Z$ is the slope of the short-run (or quickly reversible) capital account balance, the line T_2.

Capital controls — when effective — prevent the private sector to hold foreign assets (or foreigners to hold domestic assets) to the extent *desired*. The *actual* change in the privately held foreign assets ($\Delta(Z)$) is proportional to the desired change $Z^d - Z_0$ from the initial level, Z_0

$$(5) \qquad \Delta Z = \beta[k(\varepsilon)m/q - Z_0]$$

according to the effectiveness of capital controls, β. A low level of β means that capital controls are rather binding.

The overall balance of payments is the sum of the basic balance T_1 and the short-run capital account T_2 (which equals $-\Delta Z$)

$$(6) \qquad T = T_1(q, U_2) + \beta[Z_0 - k(\varepsilon)m/q]$$

The curve TT in Figure 6.7 represents the overall balance of payments (T = 0). With binding capital controls, the TT curve is relatively flat and close to T_1. With increasing financial openness, the TT curve rotates counter-clockwise towards T_2. Above TT, there is net accumulation of foreign exchange reserves by the central bank, while below TT foreign exchange reserves are being depleted. Foreign exchange reserves may or may not be determined by the central bank, depending on the exchange rate regime.

Liberalizing the capital account implies that the asset market assumes a growing role in the short-run determination of the exchange rate. The crucial channels through which monetary policy acts on the exchange rate are then:

− the effectiveness of remaining capital controls (β)

− exchange rate expectations (ε)

Figure 6.8   The active crawling peg

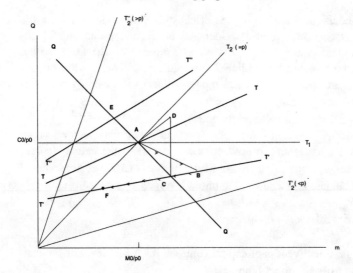

–   the sustitutability between foreign and domestic assets (k),

–   and the stickiness of prices (wages).

The Southern Cone experience is illustrated in Figure 6.8. The government switches from a passive crawling peg ($\varepsilon = p$) to an active crawl ($\varepsilon < p$). Assume that the preannounced exchange rate is credible and that the degree of asset substitutability is not yet affected (k stays constant). We then have a clockwise rotation of T_2 to T_2', and with imperfect capital mobility, a downward shift of the overall balance of payments from TT to T'T'. The active crawling peg induces excessive capital inflows which exceed the sterilization capacity (or willingness) of the central bank. The system moves from the old equilibrium A to a temporary equilibrium B, reflecting increased real money balances by a horizontal rightward move, and reflecting nominal depreciation lagging behind the inflation differential by a downward move (real appreciation). The resulting excess demand on the goods market can be eliminated, and the macroeconomic consistency of the active crawl can be restored by fiscal or income restraint which would shift the QQ schedule rightward. (The opposite is likely to happen because excessive inflows tend to undermine support for restrictive policies). Without restraint, inflation will rise. The move back toward QQ is achieved with higher prices eroding real money balances and further appreciating the real exchange rate. During the process and at point C, the country has been running up external short-term debt. Foreign lenders (and domestic residents) will eventually perceive greater exchange risk and will demand higher returns. The asset equilibrium curve rotates back upward to, say, T_2 and the overall balance will shift back to T. These moves may reflect the public's expectation that the government has to return to a passive crawling peg.

If the government reacts immediately by nominal devaluation, keeping money constant, from C to D, rising inflation (because the devaluation has created excess demand in the goods market) can bring the economy back to equilibrium at point A. Expectations will stabilize at ($\varepsilon = p^*$) if devaluation is sufficient and rapid enough. But the governments in the Southern Cone stuck to the active peg. The situation at this point was typically characterized by falling foreign exchange reserves, and by a deepening slump in the tradables sector caused by sustained overvaluation of exchange rates. Growing expectations of real devaluation ($\varepsilon > p^*$) rotate the asset market equilibrium schedule towards T_2" and shift the overall balance of payments schedule towards T" T". Contracting real money balances raise interest rates, but limited downward price flexibility prevents sufficient deflation to restore the system at a sustainable equilibrium such as at point E. The sys

Figure 6.9   Exchange rate overshooting

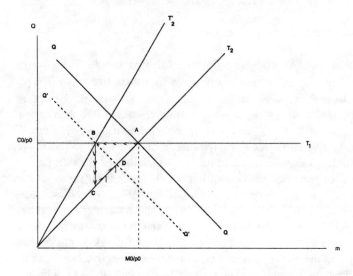

tem moves to F instead, with unemployment (excess supply) in the goods market, and with further foreign capital flows financing the basic deficit until credit rationing may set in. It is obvious that the movements of the real exchange rate are driven by the exchange rate regime. Further financial opening would merely magnify the ups and downs.

Let us finally use the Bruno framework to consider the essential features of New Zealand's experience (Figure 6.9). After full financial liberalization, the exchange rate is fully determined on asset markets (T_2). There is also full exchange rate flexibility, with no intervention on the foreign exchange market (as in New Zealand at least up to 1988). At point A, (repressed) inflation indicates excess demand in the goods market. The authorities tighten monetary policy, implying a shift from A to β (where they assume the new goods market equilibrium to hold, at Q'Q'). Two things may now happen: overshooting and, less sure, misalignment of the exchange rate.

With full capital mobility and a pure float of the exchange rate, the monetary contraction (if unexpected) leads to a real appreciation (point C). As in Dornbusch (1976), reduced money balances send the interest rate up before disinflation will gradually set in, expanding real money balances towards D and lowering interest rates on the way. The New Zealand dollar overshoots to point C at which expected depreciation will just offset the rise in interest rates. The overshooting occurs because if disinflation succeeds, investors will require lower interest rates than those produced by the current monetary stance. To restore equilibrium, the currency must appreciate to more than its long-term value — to a point from which it is expected to depreciate. However, disinflation has proven slow to come in New Zealand (after decades of high inflation). Inflationary expectations and implicit indexation in New Zealand's economy have for many years produced high stabilization costs. The economy was slow to move from C to D because prices were not downward flexible, resulting in excessive unemployment.

Even at point D, the real exchange rate (as determined by the asset market) may be misaligned. Unless the stabilization-induced drop in imports or improved terms of trade shift the basic balance T_1 downward (so as to inter sect with D), the real exchange rate is overvalued with respect to the fundamental equilibrium rate.[10] Here we may have the explanation why New Zealand's authorities have abandoned the pure float in 1988 and have moved to a managed float instead. Intervention in the foreign exchange market (like tax on capital imports) can succeed in rotating the asset market equilibrium. In Figure 6.9, for example, a purchase of foreign exchange by the central bank, by raising foreign exchange reserves and by reducing Z, succeeds in rotating T_2 counter-clockwise to T_2'. In spite of monetary tightening, the managed float helps to restore the long-run equilibrium at point β where the real exchange rate is competitive enough to reduce unemployment and external imbalances.

6. Some Tentative Conclusions

The experience of the four countries surveyed above can serve to qualify a common objection to capital account liberalization: that opening the capital account induces 'excessive' capital inflows which appreciate the domestic currency so as to hamper the development of tradable activities. It is rather the exchange rate regime which shapes events after the financial opening of an economy. The active crawling peg can be dismissed for liberalizing developing countries as an inappropriate exchange regime. Rather than the opening of the capital account, it was the *tablita* policy in all three Southern Cone countries which made the liberalization programmes inconsistent. By providing vast opportunities for portfolio investment, the *tablita* induced excessive capital inflows and fed a sustained real appreciation of the exchange rate. The active crawl was unable to exert the inflation discipline hoped for by its proponents. The induced capital inflows exceeded the sterilization capacity of central banks; the inflows created wealth effects which fed the inflation process; and they undermined the necessary support for a peg of a consistent government budget, monetary stance, and wage policy.

Capital controls did not prevent excessive capital inflows when the *tablita* was operated. By contrast, capital account liberalization did not induce 'excessive' capital inflows with a passive crawling peg and a pure float of the exchange rate. Both regimes did not offer speculators a one-way option that invites speculative attacks, because neither the passive crawl nor the float invite the government to hold on to specific nominal rates for too long.

The link between capital flows and the real exchange rate is also found weaker (or even reversed) than is often assumed these days. For major currencies, the 1980s have displayed a widely-observed tendency for real exchange rate misalignments to be much greater under nominally floating exchange regimes than under fixed regimes, due to exchange market speculation (Krugman, 1989). This observation must not hold for the less-observed currencies of the developing world. First, due to heavy raw commodity orientation or oil dependence as well as thin foreign exchange trading, real shocks tend to dominate exchange rates and probably also the expectations formation about them. Second, with lower tax enforcement and more prone to accept higher inflation rates, currency substitution and unsterilized intervention on the foreign exchange market tend to loosen the link between capital flows and the real exchange rate more than in OECD economies. Finally, any credible liberalization policy is apt to lead to real exchange rate appreciation even if cross-border capital flows are not involved. Improved property rights, higher domestic rentability or a better supply of domestic portfolio opportunities all lead to a revaluation of assets, generating a wealth effect at least partly spent on nontradables. Real appreciation will follow as long as euphoric investor sentiment is inevitably involved.

In stabilizing and liberalizing countries, the convergence of domestic interest rates towards international levels has been hard to achieve, quite independent of the exchange rate regime and even of the degree of independence of the central bank. Long-lasting deviations from uncovered interest parity suggest that the dismantled capital controls have been partly replaced by imperfect asset substitutability. This suggests some, but decreasing along the learning curve, room for sterilized foreign exchange market intervention to reconcile monetary and real exchange rate targets. The case for managed floating is also supported by New Zealand's experience which suggests more emphasis for the exchange rate as a monetary indicator when financial liberalization makes monetary aggregates a less reliable indicator of the monetary stance.

Governments which are committed to thorough economic reform are likely to start the reform process where it meets least political resistance. In New Zealand, with heavy foreign bank presence already in place, financial reform was a natural candidate to start the reform process. More gradual financial reform might have undermined the government's credibility with respect to the sustainability of the overall reform process. Thus, gradual financial reform could have implied no or little reform for the other sectors. With my revisionist reading of the Southern Cone experience and with the fresh insights from New Zealand, the following conclusion may be ventured: the benefits of getting away with pre-reform distortions by whatever order of reform will outweigh the welfare costs of a 'wrong' sequencing. But, as Chile and New Zealand suggest, the benefits will be slow to come.

NOTES

1. When discussing policies to influence the real exchange rate, one must realize that the real exchange rate is an endogenous variable. Both a flexible exchange system and a fixed rate system bring about *longer-run* adjustment through their influence on the real exchange rate. While with a flexible rate policy the adjustment occurs through movements of the nominal exchange rate, a fixed rate policy works through the differential of domestic and foreign inflation. In any case, the real exchange rate does move in the longer run, in response to real disturbances, to bring about a new real equilibrium under both fixed and flexible rate policies.

    The real exchange rate has many guises. Among them are (1) the nominal exchange rate (say, peso/dollar) multiplied by a foreign price index and divided by a domestic price index; (2) the internal (that is, within the country) price level of tradable goods deflated by the internal price level of nontradables (such as many services); and (3) the ratio of the nominal exchange rate to an index of wages. If the foreign price index corresponds with the internal price level of tradables, and if the domestic price level goes with the price level of nontradables, the real exchange rate as defined by (1) moves the same way as the one defined by (2). Likewise, (3) can be seen to approximate (2) given that the nominal exchange rate is the predominant local variable in determining the internal price of goods traded on the world market, and that the wage level is the principal component of the price of nontradables.

2. Another objection to early capital account liberalization is unrelated to exchange rates. As long as distortions in domestic commodity markets prevail, capital inflows into the distorted economy may be 'immiserizing' (Brecher and Diaz-Alejandro, 1977). Thus the reduction of distortions should precede capital account liberalization to avoid foreign capital to flow into industries with high private profitability but low social profitability.

3. See, however, the framework laid out by Bruno (1983) and Kenen (1993) to analyse exchange rate effects of financial opening.

4. The choice of the exchange regime may depend critically on the degree of labour mobility as was reckoned early by Bob Mundell and witnessed recently by the East German slogan: 'Kommt die DM, bleiben wir. Kommt sie nicht, gehn wir zu ihr!' (Claassen, 1991).

5. The arguably best single source for a description of the reform process is to be found in the Special Issue of *World Development*, August 1985: 'Liberalization with Stabilization in the Southern Cone of Latin America'.

6. The section on Uruguay draws on Hanson and de Melo (1985), and de Melo (1987).

7. The section on Argentina draws on Calvo (1983), Fernandez (1985), and Phylaktıs (1988).

8.   The section on Chile draws on papers by Ffrench-Davis (1983), Harberger (1985), Corbo (1987), and Velasco (1988).
9.   The section on New Zealand draws on OECD (1989, 1991), Spencer and Carey (1988) and most useful discussions with economists at the Economics and Statistics-Affairs Department of OECD, in particular with Paul Atkinson and Peter Sturm.
10. Note that this is due to the shift in the goods market equilibrium. If the shift of the QQ schedule had not occurred and if prices were downward flexible, the system would move back to long-term equilibrium at point A.

REFERENCES

Bergsten, C. Fred, and John Williamson (1990), 'Currency Convertibility in Eastern Europe', in The Federal Reserve Bank of Kansas City (ed.), *Central Banking Issues in Emerging Market-Oriented Economies*, pp. 35-49.

Blundell-Wignall, Adrian, and Robert G. Gregory (1990), 'Exchange Rate Policy in Advanced Commodity-Exporting Countries: Australia and New Zealand', in V. Argy and P. de Grauwe (eds), *Choosing on Exchange Rate Regime: The Challenge for Smaller Industrial Countries'*, IMF, Washington, D.C., pp. 224-271.

Brecher, Richard, and Carlos Diaz-Alejandro (1977), 'Tariffs, Foreign Capital, and Immiserising Growth', *Journal of International Economics*, vol. 7, no. 4, pp. 317-322.

Bruno, Michael (1983), 'Real Versus Financial Openness Under Alternative Exchange Rate Regimes', in P. Aspe, R. Dornbusch, and M. Obstfeld (eds), *Financial Policies and the World Capital Market: The Problem of Latin American Countries*, Chicago, University of Chicago Press, pp. 131-149.

Bruno, Michael (1985), 'The Reforms and Macroeconomic Adjustments: Introduction', *World Development*, vol. 13, no. 8, pp. 867-869.

Calvo, Guillermo (1983), 'Trying to Stabilize: Some Theoretical Reflections Based on the Case of Argentina', in P. Aspe, R. Dornbusch, and M. Obstfeld (eds), op. cit. pp. 199-216.

Claassen, Emil Maria (1991), 'Sequencing and Timing of Stabilization Policies in the East', mimeograph.

Corbo, Vittorio (1987), 'The Use of the Exchange Rate for Stabilization Purposes: The Case of Chile', in M. Connolly and C. González-Vega (eds), *Economic Reform and Stabilization in Latin America*, New York, Praeger, pp. 111-138.

De Melo, Jaime (1987), 'Financial Reforms, Stabilization, and Growth under High Capital Mobility: Uruguay 1974-83', in M. Connolly and C. Gonzáles-Vega (eds), op. cit., pp. 229-252

Dornbusch, Rudiger (1976), 'Expectations and Exchange Rate Dynamics', *Journal of Political Economy*, vol. 84.6, pp. 1161-1176.

Edwards, Sebastian (1984), 'The Order of Liberalization of the External Sector in Developing Countries', *Princeton Essays in International Finance*, no. 156.

Edwards, Sebastian (1990), 'The Sequencing of Economic Reform: Analytical Issues and Lessons from Latin American Experiences', *The World Economy*, vol. 13, no. 1, pp. 1-14.

Fernandez, Roque B. (1985), 'The Expectations Management Approach to Stabilization in Argentina during 1975-82', *World Development*, vol. 13, no. 8, pp. 871-892.

Frenkel, Jacob (1983), 'Remarks on the Southern Cone', *IMF Staff Papers*, vol. 30, no. 1, pp. 164-173.

Ffrench-Davis, Ricardo (1983), 'El Problema de la Deuda Externa y la Apertura Financiera en Chile', *Colección Estudios CIEPLAN*, no. 11.

Hanson, James and Jaime De Melo (1985), 'External Shocks, Financial Reforms, and Stabilization Attempts in Uruguay during 1974-83', *World Development*, vol. 13, no. 8, pp. 917-938.

Harberger, Arnold C. (1985), 'Lessons for Debtor-Country Managers and Policymakers', in G.W. Smith and J.T. Cuddington (eds), *International Debt and the Developing Countries*, World Bank, Washington, D.C., pp. 236-257.

Kenen, Peter (1993), 'Financial Opening and the Exchange Rate Regime', in H. Reisen and B. Fischer (eds), *Financial Opening: Policy Issues and Experiences in Developing Countries*, OECD, Paris, pp. 237-262.

Krugman, Paul (1989), *Exchange Rate Instability*, MIT Press, Cambridge (Mass.).

Kuo, Shirley (1989), 'Liberalization of the Financial Market in Taiwan in the 1980s', *Economic Review* (Taipei, Taiwan), no. 250, pp. 1-20.

Lal, Deepak (1987), 'The Political Economy of Economic Liberalization', *The World Bank Economic Review*, vol. 1, no. 2, pp. 273-299.

Mathieson, Donald J. (1986), 'International Capital Flows, Capital Controls, and Financial Reform', in H. Chang (ed.), pp. 237-260.

McKinnon, Ronald (1982), 'The Order of Economic Liberalization: Lessons from Chile and Argentina', in K. Brunner and A. Meltzer (eds), *Economic Policy in a World of Change*, Amsterdam, North-Holland.

McKinnon, Ronald (1991), *The Order of Economic Liberalization: Financial Control in the Transition to a Market Economy*, Baltimore, the Johns Hopkins University Press, forthcoming.

OECD (1989), *Economic Surveys: New Zealand*, Paris.

OECD (1990), *Progress in Structural Reform*, Paris.

OECD (1991), *Economic Surveys: New Zealand*, Paris.

Phylaktis, Kate (1988), 'Capital Controls: The Case of Argentina', *Journal of International Money and Finance*, vol. 7, no. 3, pp. 303-320.

Polak, Jacques J. (1990), 'Summary', in V. Argy and P. de Grauwe (eds), op. cit, IMF, Washington, D.C., pp. 378-388.

Rodriguez, Carlos (1979), 'El plan Argentino de estabilizacion del 20 de diciembre', *Documento de Trabajo, CEMA*, no. 5.

Spencer, Grant, and David Carey (1988), 'Financial Policy Reforms — The New Zealand Experience, 1984-1987', Reserve Bank of New Zealand.

Spencer, David (1990), 'Comment', in V. Argy and P. de Grauwe (eds), op. cit, IMF, Washington, D.C., pp. 277-284.

US Department of the Treasury (1990), National Treatment Study, Washington, D.C.

Velasco, Andrés (1988), 'Liberalization, Crisis, Intervention: The Chilean Financial System, 1975-1985', *IMF Working Paper*, WP/88/66.

7. Time-Varying Estimates on the Openness of the Capital Account in Korea and Taiwan*

1. Introduction

The loss of monetary autonomy implied by financial opening worries Korea's and Taiwan's authorities; it is this worry which motivates this chapter. In the past, capital controls have helped Korea's and Taiwan's authorities to successfully target monetary aggregates and, at the same time, the real exchange rate. The degree to which concerns about loss of monetary autonomy are warranted depends very much on how interest rate determination in Korea and Taiwan have evolved during the recent past. If existing capital controls have been sufficiently effective, interest rates should have been largely determined by domestic monetary conditions, not by world interest rates. In this case, the removal of existing controls and restrictions would indeed reduce the effectiveness of monetary policy unless exchange rates were purely floating. However, the effectiveness of capital controls is widely questioned. If capital controls have not prevented international interest arbitrage in Korea and Taiwan, the official dismantling of these controls would not imply important modifications for macroeconomic policy.

This chapter will assess how the openness of the capital account and curb market interest determination have evolved during the 1980s in Korea and Taiwan. It will use a model first outlined by Edwards and Khan (1985) and an extension recently suggested by Haque and Montiel (1990) to estimate the degree of openness of the capital account (Section 2). It then presents a time-varying parameter estimation based on the Kalman filter technique, instead of the usual constant parameter estimation, to obtain information about how openness has evolved during the period 1980-1990 (Section 3). The findings indicate a low degree of capital mobility for both countries. The index of financial openness has been somewhat higher in Korea than in Taiwan, but has displayed more instability and even a tendency to decline dur-

* Originally published in *Journal of Development Economics*, vol. 40, no. 3, August 1993.

ing the second half of the 1980s. The dismantling of capital controls and internal restrictions is thus likely to imply an important loss of monetary autonomy in both countries.

2. Interest Rates in Semi-Open Economies

Financial semi-openness can be defined as lying between two extremes. The one extreme is the completely open economy with no impediments to capital flows. In such an economy, there should be full arbitrage between domestic and foreign interest rates, both being market-determined. Arbitrage under full openness should lead to convergence of risk-adjusted nominal rates of return on financial assets denominated in different currencies or issued in different countries. For a small open economy it would imply that domestic interest rates are solely determined by foreign interest rates, after taking into account exchange rate expectations (or the forward premium). The other extreme is the economy which is completely closed to the world. If market-determined, a change of interest rates in the closed economy are thought to result from domestic money market disequilibrium with excess money demand raising domestic interest rates.

Most developing countries are neither wholly closed in financial terms, nor wholly open. Edwards and Khan (1985) have proposed a model of interest determination for semi-open economies in which both domestic and world influences play a role. Haque and Montiel (1990) have recently extended that model. The approach assumes the domestic (nominal) market-clearing interest rate (i) to be the weighted average of the uncovered interest parity rate ($i*$) and the domestic market-clearing interest rate that would be observed if the private capital account were completely closed (i')

(1) $\qquad i = \psi i* + (1 - \psi)i' \; ; \qquad 0 \le \psi \le 1$

The parameter ψ serves as an index of financial openness. Running from zero to one, the parameter rises when a country strengthens its integration with world financial markets. With $\psi = 0$, external factors play no role in the determination of the domestic interest rate — this is only possible with the private capital account effectively closed. If $\psi = 1$, the domestic market-clearing interest rate is equal to its uncovered parity value, and capital mobility is assumed to be perfect.[1]

The hypothetical closed economy interest rate i' is derived in two steps, starting with the demand for money

(2) $\ln(M^D/P) = \alpha_0 + \alpha_1 i + \alpha_2 \ln(y) + \alpha_3 \ln(M/P)_{-1}$

             $\alpha_1 < 0; \ \alpha_2, \alpha_3 > 0$

where y is real output, P is the domestic price level and M^D is the demand for money. Assuming equilibrium in the money market $[ln\ (M^D/P) = ln\ (M^s/P) = ln\ (M/P)]$, an expression for the observed domestic interest rate is obtained

(3) $i = -(\alpha_0/\alpha_1) - (\alpha_2/\alpha_1)\ln(y) - (\alpha_3/\alpha_1)\ln(M/P)_{-1} + (1/\alpha_1)\ln(M/P)$

The money supply which would correspond to the hypothetical situation with a closed private capital account is:

(4) $M' = M - KA_p$

the actual money supply less the portion of reserve flows accounted for by private capital movements (KA_P). The hypothetical interest rate i' is the value of i which satisfies the money-market equilibrium condition

(5) $ln\ (M'/P) = ln\ (M^D/P)$

or, using equation (2):

(6) $i' = -(\alpha_0/\alpha_1) - (\alpha_2/\alpha_1)\ ln(y) - (\alpha_3/\alpha_1)\ ln(M/P)_{-1} + (1/\alpha_1)\ ln(M'/P)$

Replacing this hypothetical closed economy interest rate in equation (1) we obtain:

(7) $i - i' = \psi\ (i* - i')$

Equation (7) can be estimated directly to determine the key parameter ψ as an index of financial openness. Direct estimation of equation (7), however, requires the observation of domestic market-clearing interest rates. In most developing countries, like still in Korea and Taiwan, organized securities markets are shallow or absent, and interest paid on bank assets are subject to legal controls (such as ceilings, 'window guidance', etc.). Therefore, the only domestic market-clearing interest rate is commonly found on the unorganized curb market. Estimates along the Edwards/Khan approach based on curb market rates may pose two problems. First, published curb market rate data are rarely available. To circumvent this problem, Haque and Montiel (1990) have recently extended the Edwards/Khan approach, assuming that the unobserved true domestic interest rate is an argument of the money demand function given in equation (2). The second problem arises when data on curb market rates are available — as is the case in Korea and Taiwan — so that estimates of the index of financial openness can be based on direct tests of interest arbitrage. Curb market risks and other institutional characteristics drive a substantial wedge between domestic market-clearing interest rates and uncovered interest parity. This markup of curb market over foreign interest rates reflects differences in the quality of underlying assets and not lack of financial openness.

Figure 7.1   *Interest differentials and exchange rate changes*

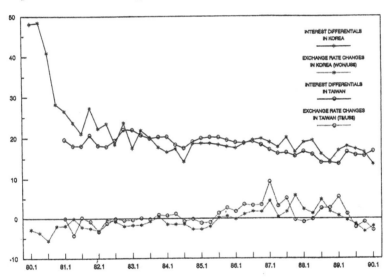

Figure 7.1 shows two series for each country: the solid curve denotes the difference between nominal curb market rates in Korea, resp. Taiwan, and the three-month LIBOR interest rate on the US dollar; the broken curve is the quarterly percentage change of the won/dollar rate, respectively the Taiwan dollar/US dollar rate. The spreads between curb market rates and the US dollar LIBOR rate have remained significant and persistent during the

1980s. Note in particular that the spread persisted during the second half of the 1980s when both the Korean won and the Taiwan dollar appreciated against the US dollar. To account for different asset quality, we introduce a constant markup α to the uncovered interest rate parity term in equation (1):

(1') $i = \psi(i* + \alpha) + (1 - \psi)i'$

Re-expressing equation (1') changes the estimation equation (7) into:

(8) $i - i' = \psi\alpha + \psi(i* - i')$

Since α is hardly observable, we make the assumption and impose the restriction that α_0 equals $\alpha\psi$. The deviation of the observed curb market rate from the hypothetical closed economy interest rate is proportional to a constant markup which captures different asset qualities plus the divergence of uncovered interest rate parity from the closed economy interest rate.

3. Time-Varying Estimates: Methodology and Results

Usually, estimates of the index of financial openness ψ have been presented as a constant for a given period. Since the aim of this chapter is to reveal how effective financial integration in Korea and Taiwan has changed during the 1980s, it is recognized here that ψ is a variable coefficient with its value varying due to various measures of financial liberalization (or repression). The time-varying parameter estimation is done using the Kalman filter. Explanations to this statistical technique are available in, and its application in this paper are based on, McNelis and Neftçi (1982), Gourieroux and Monfort (1983), and Browne and McNelis (1990).

The domestic interest rate element of our estimates of financial openness have been based on curb market rates in both countries. Two fundamental reasons have guided our choice to base these estimates on the curb market: (1) the degree of market determination of reported interest rates, and (2) the persistent importance of the curb market for domestic fund intermediation. In Korea, interest rates other than those yielded on the curb market cannot be qualified as 'market-clearing': government bonds are sold at yields below market rates to captive buyers; deposit money banks are still subject to quantitative ceilings on lending and loan rates; and Korean authorities still tend to intervene when they judge market-determined interest rates going too high. In Taiwan, the largely government-owned banking system has not yet become an important source of investment financing, and the corporate bond market is virtually nonexistent. According to flow-of-funds accounts for private business enterprises, the ratio of curb market to total bank borrowing was 48 per cent in 1986 (Fry, 1990).

The low degree of international tradability in informal curb market assets, however, gives rise to an important problem of data interpretation. Time-varying estimates on linkages with foreign interest rates may thus reflect time-varying factors specific to the curb market (such as varying degrees of financial dualism) rather than changes in financial openness. To handle this interpretation problem, we will supplement our estimates based on curb markets with estimates based on the official money market in Korea and on the market for interbank call loans in Taiwan. The assets traded on these respective money markets are generally qualified by the highest degree of international tradability; it is not easy to judge *a priori*, however, to what extent interest rates on these markets are free of government intervention in the case of Korea and Taiwan.

To obtain preliminary information with constant parameters, we first performed an Ordinary Least Squares (OLS) estimation of the money demand function given in equation (2). Using quarterly data for the period for which curb market rates were available — 1980:1 to 1990:1 in the case of Korea, and 1981:1 to 1990:1 in the case of Taiwan — the estimates produced the following results:[2]

Korea:

$$\ln(M^D/P)_t = 0.715 - 0.005\, i_t + 0.447\, ln(y)_t + 0.436\, \ln(M/P)_{t-1}$$
$$(0.766)\ (-1.916)\ (3.231)\qquad (3.300)$$
$$R^2 = 0.896,\qquad h = 1.298$$

Taiwan:

$$\ln(M^D/P)_t = -1.183 - 0.019\, i_t + 0.486\, ln(y)_t + 0.654\, \ln(M/P)_{t-1}$$
$$(-0.591)\ (-4.016)\ (2.027)\qquad (6.423)$$
$$R^2 = 0.991,\qquad h = -0.023$$

In both equations, i_t stands for the domestic curb market interest rate (in per cent). Curb market rates which were quoted on a per month basis have first been annualized and subsequently been based on quarterly averages. $(Y)_t$ is the local currency GDP (Korea), resp. GNP (Taiwan) at constant 1985 prices. $(M)_{t-1}$ is the lagged money stock defined as M_1 denominated in national currency. In both countries, the interest, income and lagged money parameters are correctly signed and significant (t-values in brackets). The corrected regression coefficient $\bar{R}^2$ shows a good fit, and Durbin's h statistic to test for first order autocorrelation in the presence of a lagged dependent variable shows absence of autocorrelation.

The parameters in the money demand functions seem to have remained constant during the observation period in both countries, in spite of officially announced measures of financial opening and liberalization. In Korea's money demand function, a break could have occurred from 1985 on when financial intermediaries were allowed, within a given range though, to determine their own lending rates and when current account surpluses led to a gradual relaxation of capital outflow controls. In Taiwan, the most important liberalization measure was the removal of foreign exchange controls in July 1987. However, in neither country's money demand function can Chow tests reject the hypothesis of parameter stability over the 1980s:

Korea   (1980:2 – 1985:4) $\chi_2(4) = 3.84$ (< 9.49),

Taiwan   (1981:2 – 1987:3) $\chi_2(4) = 8.74$ (< 9.49).

The forecast Chow tests reject at the 95 per cent confidence level the hypothesis that the above mentioned liberalization measures caused a structural break in Korea's and Taiwan's money demand function.

The estimates of the money demand function described above allowed us to estimate the hypothetical closed economy interest rate i'. Equation (3) was first estimated employing the nonlinear least squares method. Then, we inserted the coefficients estimated in equation (3) into equation (6) and calculated the closed economy interest rate i' by replacing the observed money supply by the hypothetical closed economy money supply for each current period t. The money supply which would correspond to the hypothetical situation with a closed private capital account was defined as M_1 less foreign direct investment, portfolio investment, other short-term capital and errors and omissions. These various steps prepared the ground for the estimation of equation (8).

In the estimation of equation (8), the definition of i^*, the uncovered interest parity rate, posed the usual conceptual problem. In view of the continuing strong impact of the US dollar for both countries, the three-months LIBOR interest rate of the dollar was used to reflect world interest rates. Expected devaluation was proxied by the actual rate of devaluation of the respective currency vis. the US dollar at the end of the corresponding period. This simplifying assumption, consistent with the perfect foresight variant of the rational expectations view, can be justified by the nature of the exchange regime prevailing in both Korea and Taiwan during the 1980s (basket peg first, later managed float).

Since our aim is to analyse the stability of ψ during the process of financial opening, it is important that equation (8) satisfies tests for autocorrelation, heteroscedasticity and normality of residuals based on the assumption of constant parameters before we can apply the Kalman filter. To this end, equation (8) was first estimated using OLS techniques, incorporating the error term Σ_t $(0, \delta^2)$. The test revealed homoscedasticity and normally distributed residuals, but autocorrelation in the error term in the case of Korea. For Korea then, serial correlation was eliminated by using the Cochrane-Orcutt procedure. The results obtained by the autoregressive process of order one (AR1) for Korea, and by OLS for Taiwan,[3] were:

Korea: $(i - i')_t = 10.498 + 0.594 \, (i* - i')_t$

                    (6.452) (7.945)

         $RHO1 = 0.554 \quad R^2 = 0.807, \quad h = -0.258$

            (7.888)

Taiwan: $(i - i')_t = 6.687 + 0.353 \, (i* - i')_t$

                  (9.970) (10.202)

      $\overline{R}^2 = 0.747, \quad DW = 1.523$

The regression results will be interpreted and put into perspective in Section 4. It will suffice here to note that the parameter ψ satisfies the theoretical *a priori* bounds (0,1) and that they are highly significant. The constant term and the estimate of ψ imply a constant markup α of 18 per cent in Korean curb market rates and 19 per cent in Taiwan. Durbin's h statistics are consistent with the absence of serial correlation in the residuals. The corrected regression coefficient $\overline{R}^2$ indicates that the model fits the data fairly well. Note also the high and significant value of the constant which proxies the markup to capture different asset qualities.

The main interest of this chapter is to identify how the parameter ψ has changed over the 1980s in response to major financial policy developments. The Kalman filter requires some *a priori* specification of the movement of ψ_t over time. We assumed the following motion process

(9) $\psi_t = A\psi_{t-1} + v_t \, ;$

with the null hypothesis of parameter constancy, i.e. assuming an identity matrix A = 1.

Without repeating the Kalman technique employed here to arrive at time-varying estimates of ψ in any great detail, some points peculiar to the procedure used in this paper need to be stressed [for further explanation, see McNelis and Neftçi (1982)].

–   For the AR1 estimation of Korea, all observed variables were trans-
     formed with the filter $F(L) = 1 - \rho L$. Under the null hypothesis of time-
     invariant parameters which is done at the starting point of the
     application of the Kalman procedure, the use of a fixed ρ is defensible
     even if it could be objected that ρ should vary along with the other
     parameters of the equation (9). Under the assumption of an invariant ρ,
     the Cochrane-Orcutt procedure yields a consistent estimate of ρ which
     in turn is used to produce a consistent estimate of parameter ψ in equa-
     tion (9). Therefore, the results obtained by the AR1 estimations are the
     starting point for the Kalman filter iterative process.

–   The Kalman filter technique is quite sensitive to the specifications of
     equation (9). For the specification of the variance-covariance matrix of
     the transition equation (9) estimate, we have to assume different values
     beforehand in order to represent various degrees of uncertainty in equa-
     tion (9). We multiplied the variance-covariance matrix by $\sigma = 0.1$,
     $\sigma = 0.01$, $\sigma = 0.001$ and $\sigma = 0.0001$; all values result in estimates for ψ
     which do not violate the theoretical *a priori* assumptions for ψ. We
     choose $\sigma = 0.001$ as our preferred value of σ as indication of our con-
     fidence in the underlying Edwards/Khan model (McNelis and Neftçi,
     1982).

After these checks, we applied the Kalman iterative procedure. The test of Student was used to determine if the variation of the estimated values of ψ obtained by the Kalman filter was significant. In order to assess the variability of ψ, we plotted the Kalman filter estimates (Figures 2 and 3) with OLS (Taiwan) and AR1 (Korea) constant estimates and the 95 per cent confidence intervals obtained. Under the null hypothesis of a constant parameter, the Kalman filter estimates show significant differences from the constant coefficient, and thus significant variability over the observation period if the estimate falls outside the 95 per cent confidence interval.

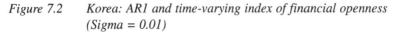

Figure 7.2   Korea: AR1 and time-varying index of financial openness (Sigma = 0.01)

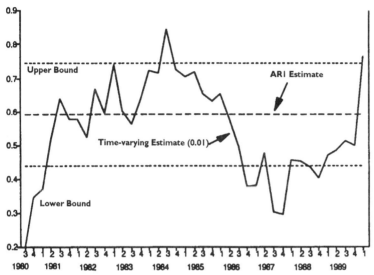

Figures 7.2 and 7.3 chart the time-varying parameter for the index of financial openness in Korea, resp. Taiwan. In both countries, and throughout the complete observation period, the parameter estimates satisfy the theoretical interval between zero and one. For Korea, the Kalman filter estimates show 'significant' differences from the constant AR1 estimate under the four σ specifications. The estimates display a wide variability in the index of financial openness. By contrast, the hypothesis of parameter constancy cannot be rejected for Taiwan for any of the four σ which specify different degrees of uncertainty for the estimation of ψ in equation (9). Note also that the constant AR1 estimate tends to overestimate the degree of financial openness in Korea for most of the observation period (except during 1984-85).

Figure 7.3   *Taiwan: OLS and time-varying index of financial openness*
            (Sigma = 0.01)

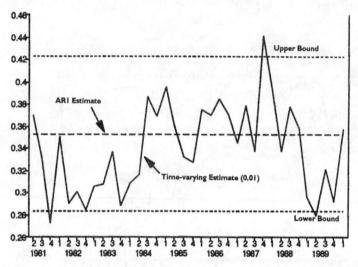

To facilitate the interpretation of the curb market based results, we finally report estimates based on money markets. For Korea, estimates have been based on money market rates for which data have been published from 1984:1 on. For Taiwan, we used interbank call loan rates for which data have been available throughout the observation period 1980:1 to 1990:1. Again, the degree of market determination and the importance of these money markets for domestic fund intermediation guided our selection among markets.

OLS estimation of money demand functions produced the following results:

Korea:

$$\ln(M^D/P)_t = 0.041 + 0.013\, i_t + 0.608\, \ln(y)_t + 0.307\, \ln(M/P)_{t-1}$$
$$(-0.035)\quad (1.087)\quad (3.435)\quad (1.707)$$
$$R^2 = 0.742, \quad h = 0.206$$

Taiwan:

$$\ln(M^D/P)_t = -2.819 + 0.011 \; i_t + 0.464 \ln(y)_t + 0.763 \ln(M/P)_{t-1}$$
$$(-1.494) \; (-3.883) \quad (1.905) \qquad (7.462)$$
$$\overline{R}^2 = 0.991, \quad h = 0.480$$

In Korea's money demand function, the interest rate coefficient is wrongly signed but insignificant. An alternative specification of the money demand function including expected inflation did not change the sign of the interest coefficient (which stayed insignificant). This suggests that the official money market rate is irrelevant as an opportunity cost to hold M_1, in contrast to the informal curb market rate. This result prevents us from pursuing any meaningful estimation of the index of financial openness based on the Korean money market.

Table 7.1   *Constant estimates of financial openness in dynamic Asian economies*

Country	ψ	t-value	Period
Indonesia	0.865	8.537	1969-87
Korea	0.594	7.945	1980-90
Malaysia	0.638	2.930	1969-87
Taiwan	0.353	10.202	1980-90
Thailand	0.590	6.300	1978-90

Sources: Haque and Montiel (1990) for Indonesia and Malaysia; Robinson *et al.* (1991) for Thailand; see text for Korea and Taiwan.

The results for Taiwan's money demand function satisfy the theoretical *a priori* expectations. The interest, income, and lagged money parmeters are correctly signed and significant; the corrected regression coefficient $\overline{R}^2$ shows a good fit and Durbin's h statistic shows the absence of autocorrelation. These results enabled us to move on to estimate the index of financial openness in equation (8) based on the interbank call loan rates. The whole estimation procedure was exactly as described above for estimates based on curb market rates. Since OLS estimation of equation (8) revealed autocorrelation in the error terms, serial correlation was eliminated by using the Cochrane-Orcutt procedure. The result obtained for the AR1 estimation was:

Taiwan $\quad (i_i - i'_t) = -0.789 + 0.464 \ (i_t* - i'_t)$
$$(-1.46) \quad (6.030)$$
$$RHO = 0.534, \quad \overline{R}^2 = 0.741, \quad h = -0.258$$

In comparison with the curb market based estimates performed above, two observations on the money market based estimates are noteworthy. First, the constant in the money market based estimate is insignificant and close to zero while it was substantial and significant in the curb market based estimate of equation (8). This confirms the importance to account for different asset quality when estimates on financial openness are based on curb market rates; by contrast, assets traded on Taiwan's interbank call loan market do not seem to display a lower asset quality than foreign (US) inter-bank traded assets. Secondly, we note that the constant estimate of Taiwan's financial openness is only slightly higher when estimates are based on the official interbank market (0.464) rather than on the informal curb market (0.353). Both values are significantly different from zero, but also significantly different from one, excluding for Taiwan both polar cases of full capital mobility and immobility.

*Figure 7.4   Taiwan (interbank call loans): AR1 and time-varying index
of financial openness (sigma = 0.01)*

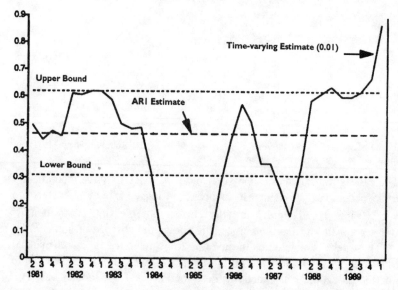

The time-varying parameter for the index of financial openness based on Taiwan's interbank market (see Figure 7.4) reveals a further divergence with estimates based on the curb market (Figure 7.3). While the hypothesis of parameter constancy could not be rejected for Taiwan's curb market based estimates, there is a clear trend movement towards increasing financial openness from early 1987 on when estimates are based on Taiwan's interbank market. By end 1989, the index of financial openness rises beyond the upper confidence bound for all uncertainty specifications except for $\sigma = 0.0001$.

4. Interpretation

The interpretation of our results must be subject to two important caveats. First, the estimates along the Edwards/Khan and Haque/Montiel approach are based on curb market rates. We have allowed for a presumably low quality of assets underlying the curb market by correcting interest arbitrage relationships with a constant markup of curb market over foreign interest rates. The constant markup cannot capture, however, factors specific to curb markets which tend to prevent speedy arbitrage with foreign interest rates. Such factors include, e.g., the dualism between the formal and the informal sector which could explain the existence of the curb market even under full capital mobility, or informational imperfections which give rise to such problems as moral hazard and adverse selection. Wherever possible, empirical tests of interest arbitrage should be based on assets and liabilities whose degree of international tradability is higher than those subject to the curb market.

The second reason for caution is the widespread failure of uncovered interest parity to hold even for highly liberalized OECD economies (see Blundell-Wignall and Browne, 1991). A low estimate of the index of financial openness may thus reflect a high currency risk premium, irrational expectations in the foreign exchange market, or the peso problem, rather than low capital mobility. Since our results are based on curb market rates, however, it seems plausible to assume that exchange rate considerations are largely neglected due to the low tradability of curb market assets. The absence of free forward exchange markets and of market-clearing interest rates other than on the informal curb market currently precludes any more reliable estimates as the one performed here on the degree of financial openness in Korea and Taiwan.

Table 7.1 puts our constant estimates of parameter ψ into comparable Asian perspective. All results cited in Table 7.1 have been obtained with the Haque/Montiel specification of the Khan/Edwards approach. Perfect capital mobility cannot be ruled out for Indonesia and Malaysia, with the index of financial openness significantly different from 0, but only insignificantly different from 1. For Korea, Taiwan and Thailand, by contrast, both polar cases of perfect capital mobility and immobility can be ruled out. At least in these three countries, the government seems to have retained partial control over domestic interest rates and the money supply during the 1980s.

Our time-varying estimates based on curb market rates in Korea and Taiwan (shown in Figures 7.2 and 7.3) display no upward trend of financial opening during the 1980s. For Taiwan, there is no trend movement in the ψ parameter through the period. Korea, by contrast, shows a strong upward movement from 1981:1 to 1985:1, and then a return to the lower confidence bound (at 0.44) which stops in 1987:4 from whereon the trend is flat. These findings are, obviously, not consistent with a move to greater financial openness. As Figure 7.1 had visualized, the lack of curb market rates to react to US dollar movements against the Korean won and the Taiwan dollar may provide a key to the interpretation of our results.

To examine this issue further, we estimated a correlation matrix (not reported here) for the quarterly values of parameter ψ, the domestic curb market rate, the three-months LIBOR interest rate on the US dollar, and the nominal exchange rate (US dollar in domestic currency units). The correlation coefficient between parameter ψ and the won/dollar rate was positive and important (0.63 for $\sigma = 0.001$ specification), while the correlation between ψ and the Taiwan dollar/US dollar rate was small and negative (-0.13 for $\sigma = 0.001$). Since the won and the Taiwan dollar had moved quite in tandem against the US dollar, reflecting the rise of the US dollar up to 1985 and its subsequent decline, the different outcome for Korea and Taiwan is likely to be found in characteristics of their domestic financial systems rather than in developments on the foreign exchange market.

A recent description of Korea's financial sector is found in Park (1991). The up and down of the index of financial openness estimated in our paper (Figure 7.2) is well reflected by Park's overview of Korea's financial sector: 'despite numerous and often confusing reform measures, deregulation of the financial sector has been slow, uneven, and most of all limited in scope and degree' (p. 30). Specifically, the rise in Korea's index of financial openness from early 1981 to early 1985 corresponds well with the financial deregulation package on which the monetary authorities embarked in 1981 as part of the overall liberalization of the economy. The deregulation led to privatization of the existing nationwide commercial banks and to the creation of new banks and nonbank financial institutions. In the same year a commercial paper market free of government control was established. The creation of the commercial paper market and the encouragement of nonbank financial institutions seems to have introduced a higher degree of foreign determination on curb market rates during the first half of the 1980s.

The subsequent downturn in Korea's index of financial openness (during the years 1985 to 1987) corresponds to the period when the Korean won appreciated in every quarter against the US dollar without inducing any narrowing in the respective interest differentials. While this result is probably due to the low international tradability of curb market assets, it is noteworthy that some official interest rates stayed fixed during the same period in Korea. Interest rates on bank deposits have been unchanged since end 1984, except on maturities of more than two years which have been liberalized in 1988. The same observation holds for interest rates offered by nonbank financial intermediaries. According to many observers, this interest rate behaviour (in spite of reform) is largely explained by intrabank collusion and pressure exerted by the government which gives up its attitude of benign neglect as soon as interest rates start to move onto unwanted levels.

In Taiwan, officially proclaimed interest rate deregualtion during the 1980s has not had a significant impact on the nature of interest determination. Figure 7.3 shows that the index of financial openness remained low (OLS estimate = 0.353), and the hypothesis of parameter constancy could not be rejected for estimates based on curb market rates. Estimates based on interbank call loan rates (Figure 7.4) display a slightly different impression. Since 1988 or 1989 (according to the specification of σ) there is a clear trend towards higher financial openness, a move which seems to be linked to the liberalization and internationalization of Taiwan's securities market. In July 1989, the authorities revised the basic banking law which allows private acquisition of government-owned banks, the creation of privately-held new banks, and setting deposit and lending rates in line with market conditions (OECD, 1990). Until then, nearly all domestic banks had been owned by the government; moreover, half of these banks had been established as specialized banks to service particular sectors with little competition from other financial institutions. This explains why the curb market has stayed an important source of finance for small-scale businesses which have enjoyed little access to institutional credit.

Official liberalization measures undertaken in Korea and Taiwan during the 1980s have thus largely failed to strengthen interest links with the rest of the world. The capital account of both countries seems still quite closed, with the possible exception of Taiwan's interbank market in very recent years. Therefore, the authorities in both Korea and Taiwan have continued to enjoy considerable scope for an independent short-term monetary policy. This conclusion, however, must not hold even for the near future, given recent reform measures in Taiwan and announced reform in Korea. The authorities' concern about a possible loss of monetary autonomy is confirmed by our results.

APPENDIX

Data Definitions and Sources

Korean data were first converted into billions of won. For the estimation of the money demand function, income was proxied by the annual GDP at constant prices (IFS line 99bp) and when quarterly data were unavailable GDP has been weighted by a production index (IFS line 66c). Money stock at the end of the period was proxied by M1 (IFS line 34). The hypothetical closed economy money demand M' was defined as M1 less direct investment (IFS line 77bad), portfolio investment (IFS line 77bbd), other capital nie (IFS line 77gd) and net errors and omissions (IFS line 77ed) not accounted for by the resident official sector. Real money stocks M1 and M' were calculated by dividing nominal stocks by the consumer price index at end of period (IFS line 64). For the uncovered interest parity rate, the LIBOR on three month US dollar deposits was used, corrected for the subsequent change in the exchange rate (local currency units per US$) at the end of period (IFS line ae). Curb market rates have been received from the Korea Development Institute (courtesy Sang-Woo Nam), in percentage per month and have then be annualized. Money market rates are from IFS, line 60b.

For Taiwan all data are converted into millions of NT dollars. For the estimation of the money demand function, income was proxied by the annual GDP at constant prices from Directorate-General of Budget, Accounting and Statistics, The Republic of China, *Monthly Statistics of The Republic of China*. The same source was taken for data on M1 and the consumer price index. The hypothetical closed economy money demand M' was calculated as for Korea, from the source publication of the Central Bank of China, *Balance of Payments - Taiwan District The Republic of China*. For the uncovered interest parity rate, the LIBOR was obtained from IFS (line 111601dd) and the exchange rate from *Monthly Statistics of the Republic of China*. Curb market rates and interbank call loan rates were obtained from the Bank of China, *Financial Statistics Monthly, Taiwan District, The Republic of China*.

NOTES

1. Note that most empirical studies reject uncovered interest parity to hold even in indus-trialized countries (Frankel, 1989). While covered interest parity has been largely found valid, the rejection of uncovered interest parity allows two different interpretations: either foreign exchange speculators are bad forecasters, and the rational expectations hypothesis does not hold; or, alternatively, the finding is evidence in favour of the existence of an exchange risk premium which explains the difference between the forward discount and expected depreciation. Thus, a low index of financial openness may reflect nothing but an important exchange risk premium. Notwithstanding this conceptual deficiency of the Ed-wards/Khan approach, the lack of forward exchange markets in most developing countries precludes its estimation based on covered interest parity.
2. The inclusion of an inflation variable (as another opportunity cost item to hold money) did not add much information about money demand functions in Korea and Taiwan. Expected inflation proved more relevant than current inflation. Being an unobserved variable, we assumed expected inflation to equal the actual next-period inflation. For Korea, expected inflation proved to be a significant determinant of money demand. However, the inclusion of the inflation variable introduced autocorrelation into Korea's money demand function. Moreover, estimates of the index of financial openness based on parameters of the ex-tended money demand function were similar to those reported below. In the case of Tai-wan, the coefficient for expected inflation was not significantly different from zero.
3. For the sake of comparability of results, we also performed an AR1 estimate for Taiwan which did not significantly change the index of financial openness (4). The result was

$$(i - i')_t = 5.933 + 0.313 \ (i - i')_t$$
$$(6.581) \quad (6.842)$$
$$RHO1 = 0.326 \quad \overline{R}^2 = 0.747, \quad h = -0.452$$
$$(1.870)$$

REFERENCES

Blundell-Wignall, Adrian, and Frank Browne (1991), 'Increasing Financial Market Integration, Real Exchange Rates and Macroeconomic Adjustment', OECD, *ESD Working Papers*, no. 96.

Browne, Francis and Paul McNelis (1990), 'Exchange Controls and Interest Rate Determination with Traded and Non-Traded Assets: the Irish-United Kingdom Ex-perience', *Journal of International Money and Finance*, 9, pp. 41-59.

Corbo, Vittorio, and Andres Solimano (1989), *Chile's Experience with Stabilization Revisited*, The World Bank, Country Economic Department.

Edwards, Sebastian (1988), 'Financial Deregulation and Segmented Capital Markets: The Case of Korea', *World Development*, 16.1, pp. 185-194.

Edwards, Sebastian and Moshin Khan (1985), 'Interest Rate Determination in De-veloping Countries: A Conceptual Framework', *IMF Staff Papers*, 32.3, pp. 377-403.

Frankel, Jeffrey (1989), 'Quantifying International Capital Mobility in the 1980s', *NBER Working Paper*, no. 2856.

Fry, Maxwell (1990), 'Nine Financial Sector Issues in Eleven Asian Developing Countries', *University of Birmingham, International Finance Group Working Papers*, 90/09.

Glick, Reuven, and Michael Hutchinson (1990), 'Financial Liberalization in the Pacific Basin: Implications for Real Interest Rate Linkages', *Journal of the Japanese and International Economies*, 4, pp. 30-48.

Gourieroux, Christian, and Alain Monfort (1983), *Cours de séries temporelles* (Economica, Paris).

Haque, Nadeem, and Peter Montiel (1990), 'Capital Mobility in Developing Countries — Some Empirical Tests', *IMF Working Paper*, WP/90/117.

McNelis, Paul and Balih Neftçi (1982), 'Policy-Dependent Parameters in the Presence of Optimal Learning: An Application of Kalman Filtering to the Fair and Sargent Supply-Side Equations', *The Review of Economics and Statistics*, 64, pp. 296-306.

OECD (1990), *Financial Market Trends*, Paris, no. 47.

Park, Yung Chul (1991), 'Growth, Liberalization, and Internationalization of Korea's Financial Sector, 1970-89', mimeo.

Robinson, David et al. (1991), 'Thailand: Adjusting to Success — Current Policy Issues', *IMF Occasional Papers*, no. 85, August.

8. Towards Capital Account Convertibility*

1. Introduction

The 1980s will be remembered as a decade of rapid integration of financial markets in the industrialized world. However, while most OECD countries have removed capital controls, these controls still persist even in the most advanced developing countries. Some of the advanced developing countries find themselves increasingly involved, albeit sometimes reluctantly, in a debate which urges them to remove existing capital restrictions without further delay. Since liberalization failed in, for example, some of the Southern Cone economies of Latin America, views on capital account opening — a complex topic which does not lend itself to simple statements — have become increasingly diversified.

For those advanced developing countries considering future membership of OECD, the OECD Codes of Liberalization may constitute another reason for ambivalence on financial opening. One of its first acts after the OECD was established in October 1961 was the adoption of the Code of Liberalization of Current Invisible Operations and the Code of Liberalization of Capital Movements. The Codes commit OECD Member countries to eliminate any restrictions between one another on the current invisible and capital movement operations listed in the Codes. Since 1989, the Codes cover all capital movements, including money-market and other short-term financial activities, as well as banking and financial services. The Codes now also contain provisions for national treatment of nonresident financial institutions. Although the OECD Codes of liberalization have the legal status of OECD decisions which are binding on all the members . . . (they allow) . . . reasonable scope for countries in different circumstances to move towards the ultimate objective in different ways and at varying speeds, taking account of the specific economic circumstances they face (OECD, 1990, p. 13).

*   Originally published as OECD Development Centre Policy Brief no. 4, Paris, 1992.

While the ultimate objective of financial reform is to increase efficiency and growth, the reform process must be carefully designed to achieve these results. This chapter will explain:

- *why* it can be beneficial to liberalize capital movements;

- *when* different capital controls should be dismantled; and

- *how* the process of capital account liberalization should be implemented.

The rationale for the liberalization of capital movements (Section 2.1) will be considered in the context of the mixed reform experiences in both OECD and non-OECD countries (2.2).

While there is general agreement on the desired results, the potential dangers during the opening process necessitate careful examination of the timing of reform (2.3). This chapter identifies the most pertinent macro-economic and financial sector constraints that must be removed to ensure the success of financial opening (3.1 and 3.2). The impediments to capital account opening should not lead to delay in reform; rather, they should encourage the implementation of policies promoting financial openness.

The policy guidelines (4.1-3) for financial openness will stress the need and suggest solutions for the:

- establishment of solid fiscal consolidation and prior stabilization;

- problem of finding the right monetary-fiscal policy mix to dampen the loss of monetary autonomy, with emphasis on exchange rate management;

- building of primary and secondary securities markets for monetary policy implementation and financial stability;

- enforcing of domestic competition to foster allocative and operational efficiency within the financial sector;

- strengthening of prudential regulation and supervision, legal and accounting systems to cope with systemic risks of financial systems;

- restructuring of the domestic banking system to remove excessive bad loans, so enabling unfettered competition on level playing fields.

Most policy recommendations tend to assume that governments must liberalize all capital controls simultaneously. Instead, this policy brief recommends — based partly on OECD country experience — a sequential process of capital account liberalization. At the outset, important distinctions of capital controls such as whether they impact on capital inflows or outflows, short-term or long-term (sustainable) flows, bank or nonbank relationships, have to be recognized. This policy brief identifies the best timing for each capital account liberalization measure in view of progress made in the macroeconomic and domestic financial sector performance previously outlined. The aim is to avoid disruption and to ensure that financial opening achieves its ultimate objectives: to raise efficiency and growth without compromising stability.

2. Why Liberalize, and When

2.1. The Rationale for Opening the Capital Account

Dismantling capital controls is generally presumed to generate economic benefits through increased opportunities for intertemporal trade and cross-border portfolio diversification in both assets and liabilities, by imposing macroeconomic discipline on national governments, and from the rising costs and ineffectiveness of controls as economic development proceeds.

Economists argue that gains from intertemporal trade occur because time and liquidity preferences differ across countries. What does that mean? It means, for example, that ageing economies tend to post excess savings and hence a surplus in the balance of payments on current account which they will run down later (when old) in the form of net inflows. Or, a country which receives a temporary shock (such as bad harvests) will prefer to run a current account deficit to smooth consumption over time, instead of keeping consumption at all times equal to current income. Opening capital markets relieves such liquidity constraints.

Allowing portfolios in assets and liabilities to be diversified across borders enables a country's borrowers to find lower funding costs and its savers prospects for higher yields. Benefits from increased competition may be even more important than static gains from financial integration. If opening breaks oligopolistic market structures, competition among financial intermediaries will be intensified. Intermediation margins are squeezed, costs of funds to borrowers decrease and returns to lenders rise. In addition, transaction costs for nonfinancial market participants decrease due to the dissemination of financial innovation initially developed in other countries. The quality of financial assets increases as a result of the greater liquidity due to the development of deeper markets with well capitalized market participants.

Homogenous pricing as well as better tailoring in terms of liquidity and special-purpose instruments takes place through separation, hedging and risk spreading. For example, a Korean investor, whose portfolio is confined to Korean assets runs more risk than one who can diversify into international assets. The counterpart is the foreign investor who places some of his portfolio in Korean assets. Since international trade in financial assets is largely a wholesale market, improved asset quality and risk diversification mainly benefit institutional investors, such as pension funds.

Capital controls have often been used to preserve monetary autonomy. With fully floating exchange rates, the nominal money supply can be controlled at any desired level by the central bank, and balance of payments adjustment is achieved, in the main, through exchange rate movements. Hence, national monetarists claim that the government can enjoy simultaneously both monetary independence and external balance, provided they accept a pure float of their currency. In such a world, exchange controls are obsolete. When the exchange rate is fixed in nominal terms and capital is freely mobile, monetary policy independence is lost. Those in favour of abolishing exchange controls argue that such policy independence is actually undesirable: inflationary policies become untenable with free capital flows because capital flows abroad and official foreign exchange reserves run dry. As a result, greater discipline is imposed on both monetary and fiscal policy. Fundamental imbalances are never inevitable and capital flight provides a clear signal that policies must be changed. Conversely, when controls over capital inflows are used to maintain an undervalued exchange rate, large current account surpluses and the buildup of foreign exchange reserves are likely to pose policy problems. Opening the capital account helps dampen inflationary pressures arising from any inability to sterilize excess liquidity. The abolition of capital outflow controls provides new opportunities to invest, thus raising the return to (lower) investment at home and (higher) investment abroad.

There is a close link between capital controls and industrial policy which is often implemented through government credit allocation. However, as countries move from an early to an advanced stage of development, the industrial-policy rationale for capital controls gradually fades away. As countries move up the product cycle towards more complex and sophisticated goods, governments are less likely to pick winners better than the market and more likely to saddle the domestic banking system with nonperforming loans.

On a more pragmatic note, disillusion over the effectiveness of existing capital controls may be another reason for dismantling them. Growing trade integration and the increased presence of multinational businesses produce closer financial links, opening up many ways of circumventing existing controls. Consequently, capital controls may well not produce the desired effects; yet their very existence might generate uncertainty about the possibility of further tightening and thus stem capital inflows and induce outflows beyond the level envisaged by the authorities.

2.2 Goodbye Financial Repression, Hello Financial Crash?

In the late 1970s and early 1980s, several countries in Latin America (Argentina, Chile and Uruguay) and Asia (Indonesia and Malaysia) embarked on financial deregulation as part of a broader liberalization strategy. The results differed so much in each case that predictions about the effects of financial liberalization in countries where financial repression prevails are hardly possible. Experience with financial opening of small open OECD economies (Australia and New Zealand) also indicate mixed results.

Having followed development strategies that were heavily biased towards protectionism and a high degree of government intervention, Uruguay, Chile and Argentina moved towards liberalizing their economies, including their capital accounts, in the 1970s. The liberalization episode of the Southern Cone ended with capital flight, generalized loan defaults, banking crises, falling output and massive unemployment. Capital controls were reintroduced. The Southern Cone experience is highlighted by sustained interest differentials inducing excessive capital inflows, appreciating real exchange rates which exerted a major profit squeeze on the traded goods sector, as well as financial institution failure and anything but increased growth.

Real interest rates in the Southern Cone stayed extremely high after financial opening, reaching 40 per cent in Chile. Theory predicted that domestic liberalized interest rates would converge to world levels. Several micro- and macro-explanations have been advanced to explain sustained interest differentials. First, there was a substantial increase in demand for credit, triggered by an increase in perceived wealth due to overall liberalization and improved private property rights. Second, domestic credit market segmentation prevented interest arbitrage between specialized lending institutions and across sectoral uses of funds: the spread between lending and borrowing rates was not reduced and reflected oligopolistic price behaviour. Third, lack of supervision and interlocking ownership between banks and firms led to the accumulation of bad loans; as a consequence, banks increased interest charges on viable borrowers to compensate for losses. Fourth, nonperforming loans caused further distress borrowing and added to credit demand. Fifth, because of increasingly overvalued currencies, foreign lenders and domestic residents eventually perceived greater exchange risk and demanded higher returns.

A central accompanying feature was a substantial real appreciation of the exchange rate following massive capital inflows in response to sustained interest differentials. Real exchange rates in the Southern Cone became overvalued once attempts were made to stabilize inflationary expectations by pre-announcing future devaluation rates below current inflation rates (active crawling peg). Anchoring inflationary expectations to the exchange rate did not work: excessive capital inflows exceeded the sterilization capacity of the central bank and loosened fiscal and wage discipline, hence eroding the very foundations on which the nominal anchor approach is built.

The highly publicized experiments by the Southern Cone countries with financial opening ended in financial crash. Other country experiences indicate, however, that financial opening can be beneficial, although it always involves substantial risks. Proponents of early capital account liberalization point to the experiences of Malaysia and Indonesia.

Singapore's financial centre has traditionally been to Indonesia and Malaysia what the informal curb market is to so many developing countries. Hence, capital controls could not have been effective in these two countries. The Indonesian and Malaysian authorities simply had to cope with open capital accounts. Both countries have been successful in fostering growth, diversifying exports and keeping inflation at low levels. While open capital accounts have certainly imposed restraints on fiscal and monetary policies in both Indonesia and Malaysia, they imposed a healthy discipline, notably on government budgets, which maintained macroeconomic stability.

The sequencing of reform in Indonesia defies all orthodoxy established in the development literature. The capital account was opened first (1971), trade was gradually liberalized in the early 1980s, interest rates were freed in 1983 and institutional aspects of the fnancial system were deregulated in 1988. Only since then does one observe a pattern of events familiar from other reform episodes (in both OECD and non-OECD countries) which can be stylized as follows.

True financial reform relieves the existing liquidity constraints for consumer and construction borrowing. Rising prices produce a positive wealth effect, further raising demand for credit. Eventually, the Central Bank worries about rising money supply and tries to stabilize. Interest rates rise and companies borrow offshore to avoid high interest rates at home. The countrys current account deficit rises, but a rising country risk premium is not sufficient to curb offshore (distress) borrowing. If the Central Bank sustains its stabilization programme, real activity slows down, unveiling the first business failures. Banks now find out that some of their assets are doubtful and that they are overexposed in some areas, typically in half-empty real estate. Only now does the government start to worry about bank supervision and prudential regulation.

It is worth noting some institutional explanations for Malaysia's and Indonesia's success in keeping inflation low and exchange rates competitive in spite of open capital markets. In the past, both governments controlled a large share of foreign exchange earnings from oil and gas exports. These could be used to counteract movements in the private capital account of the country. On the other hand, until recently the Indonesian private sector in particular lacked creditworthiness in offshore markets. Growing exports have allowed Indonesian companies to gain international credit standing while the government share in foreign exchange has been shrinking. These developments increased the need to manipulate the liquidity of the domestic banking system.

In such a situation, it helps if the LDC central bank commands a large share of domestic financial assets, either through state banks or through public enterprises if the latter run financial surpluses. Recently, the Indonesian authorities withdrew large amounts from the bank deposits of state-owned companies and used the funds to buy Bank Indonesia certificates. These quantity-oriented directives (as opposed to price incentives) to reduce domestic credit have been effective (though not efficient) in defending the Indonesian rupiah. In Malaysia, institutions such as the Employee Provident Fund (which holds 20 per cent of domestic financial assets) have also played a crucial role in the management of domestic liquidity. This did not prevent a sharp recession in the early 1980s from turning into a generalized financial crisis. These events galvanized the government, so that Malaysia now serves as a model for bank supervision and prudential regulation.

The evidence of financial fragility in the reforming countries does not necessarily imply that financial crises are the inevitable price of financial liberalization. The causes of financial crises have been manifold, including severe external macroeconomic shocks, extremely high real interest rates, imprudent or fraudulent behaviour of bank management, inadequate regulation and supervision of financial institutions, deposit insurance, new entrants with no bank experience and concentration through conglomerate takeovers.

The fear of financial institution failure has slowed the process of financial opening in economies such as Korea and Taiwan. Their authorities take a cautious approach towards capital account opening, in line with the experience of many OECD countries. Indeed, the OECD countries move towards financial market integration has been neither straightforward nor uniform. During the Bretton Woods period (up to 1973) with fixed but adjustable exchange rates, only a few countries such as the United States, Canada, Germany and Switzerland operated without significant capital controls. During

the 1960s and 1970s, even liberal OECD countries continually resored to
capital controls. A well known example is the interest equalization tax
which the United States introduced in 1964 to deter capital outflows. Widespread measures to defend exchange rates and autonomous monetary policy
during the Bretton Woods days included dual exchange rates, closed-circuit
payments channels and restrictions on the overall foreign position of financial institutions. Long after the breakdown of the Bretton Woods system, a
number of countries still introduced temporary measures to dampen capital
inflows: for example, Japan, Germany and Switzerland in 1977 when speculative pressures developed against the US dollar and Spain in 1990 to damp-
en the rise of the peseta. It was only during the 1980s that the majority of
OECD countries achieved comprehensive financial opening.

Financial opening of most OECD countries has been *gradual*. A speedy
transition from rather restrictive to open financial regimes occurred only in
the United Kingdom (1979), Australia (1983) and New Zealand (1984).
These countries first tried to maintain monetary autonomy through a pure
float of the exchange rate. They finally understood, however, that a regime
of purely floating rates does not reduce economic interdependence with open
capital markets; it only alters the form of interdependence. The stylized experience of financial opening, accompanied by a pure float of the exchange
rate, is overshooting exchange rates following stabilization which burdens
export performance, often with persistent effects. Japan, by contrast, represents the gradual approach to financial opening. Maintaining extensive restrictions when it joined the OECD in 1964, Japan gradually removed its
capital controls during a period which lasted until 1980. First to go were
restrictions on foreign direct investment, securities transactions and personal
capital movements; then real estate operations, Japanese direct investments
abroad and commercial lending were liberalized; finally, all remaining restrictions were removed in December 1980. The process of gradual financial
opening was achieved in most European OECD countries in the second half
of the 1980s, reflecting the efforts by the European Community to establish
complete freedom of capital movements across EC member states.

The country experiences summarized here — in particular those in OECD
and Asian countries — show that capital account opening does not inevitably
lead to real exchange rate appreciation or to financial crash. Much depends
on the timing of capital account opening relative to prerequisite institutional
and policy measures.

2.3 Timing of reform

What are the indicators available to the policymaker with which to judge the
appropriate moment for opening up the capital account? A major rationale

for liberalizing capital flows in the OECD areas was the move to generalized exchange rate floating in 1973. At that time, the (now discredited) majority view was that flexible exchange rates would buy economic independence. Indeed, a number of OECD countries dismantled most of the temporary restrictions (mostly on inflows) they had imposed during the final years of the Bretton Woods system. Those countries which maintained controls were increasingly disillusioned over their effectiveness.

In particular, the dismal performance of the Southern Cone countries has provided the policymakers in developing countries with more lessons on the appropriate timing of reform. There is little disagreement in the so-called sequencing literature (on how best to sequence different reform steps) that stabilization, both fiscal and monetary, as well as domestic financial liberalization should precede external liberalization. High inflation reduces the information content of prices, so worsening the allocation of resources. Excess demand, resulting in unsustainable current account deficits or exchange rate fluctuations, reduces the credibility of liberalization measures. The problem of weak government finances (often implying a weak tax effort in developing countries) has to be addressed first to obviate the need for domestic financial repression.

Many economists have been concerned about real exchange rate overshooting that may occur during the liberalization of the capital account, and the risk of falling output in the manufacturing sector (deindustrialization). Since capital markets in developing countries are far from perfect, temporary appreciation causes excessive investment (which is costly to reverse) in the nontraded sector.

Another objection to early capital account liberalization is unrelated to exchange rates. As long as distortions in domestic commodity markets prevail, capital inflows into the distorted economy may be immiserizing. Thus the reduction of distortions should precede capital account liberalization to prevent foreign capital from flowing into industries with high private but low social profitability. All these considerations lead to the mainstream advice that stabilization, domestic price deregulation, financial sector reform and foreign trade liberalization should all be well under way before the capital account is opened up.

One deficiency of the sequencing literature is that it is apt to discourage liberalization and to ignore policies needed to prepare the ground for successful opening. The nature of the capital controls is rarely specified and no distinction is made between inflows and outflows of capital; it assumes that countries have to liberalize controls on both outflows and inflows simultaneously. A second reservation about the sequencing literature is that it stems from the experience of countries that liberalized at a time when funds were in abundant supply on the international capital markets. The sequencing literature also ignores the political economy of reform. Any move from a restricted to a liberalized financial regime implies a redistribution of income, rents and decision-making powers. Therefore it is likely to meet opposition from the affected groups, such as favoured borrowers under domestic credit rationing, companies entitled to subsidized foreign exchange and banks enjoying a comfortable life as a national monopolist.

This policy brief advocates a positive strategy for capital account liberalization. The first step is to identify impediments to liberalization which must first be removed. The next section distinguishes salient characteristics differentiating such impediments in advanced developing countries and OECD countries. This leads to the identification of institutional and policy measures which must precede reform in each group of countries. The final section outlines the appropriate sequencing of capital account liberalization in the two country groups, giving special emphasis to the interaction between the prerequisite institutional and policy measures, on the one hand, and the sequential opening process on the other.

3. Impediments

3.1 Loss of Macroeconomic Autonomy
There are three characteristics typical of developing countries which may pose a particularly important impediment to the dismantling of capital controls on macroeconomic grounds. First, regular tax effort is often weak and replaced by the repression of the domestic financial system. Second, since poor domestic markets necessitate strong reliance on world demand, developing countries rely on capital controls to prevent undesired appreciation in the real exchange rate. Third, the shallowness of domestic securities markets for indirect monetary control and a fragile international credit standing complicate the smooth absorption of shocks. This section discusses each of the three impediments in turn.

First, tax ratios of developing countries tend to be much lower than those of industrial countries — less than half on average. Failure to broaden the tax base is the main cause of weak tax effort in most developing countries. Administrative and technical defects in tax assessment and collection prevent tax revenues from rising, and powerful interest groups often prevent tax legislation reforms aimed at abolishing tax holidays and exemptions. This also explains the widespread objection to multi- or bilateral tax treaties which would prevent the tax-free ownership of foreign assets.

Money creation and domestic financial repression result directly from weak government finances. Base money is an interest-free liability of the public sector which can finance real spending to the extent that the private sector holds domestic currency and the domestic banking system holds reserves with the central bank against its deposit liabilities. Removal of capital account controls reduces the seigniorage base. Interest-free minimum reserve requirements on demand and savings deposits are important in providing the government with direct access to bank credit. As long as the government relies on this source of finance, free entry of banks is resisted. If financial repression does not give the government enough resources at a stable price level, inflation develops and interacts with the reserve requirements to impose an 'inflation tax' that gives the government more revenue. High inflation tends to shorten maturities of financial assets, to reduce the information content of relative prices and to stimulate capital flight. Capital controls may serve (for a while) to ameliorate these ills. An additional public finance aim of capital account controls is to accommodate the stock of government debt. Controls serve this purpose by maintaining captive buyers — like pension funds which cannot easily escape controls — at home, forced to buy government debt at below-market interest rates.

Second, capital controls can help the monetary authorities target monetary aggregates and, at the same time, the exchange rate. With increasing openness of the capital account, the effectiveness of monetary policy depends critically on the degree to which a flexible exchange rate is maintained. However, a country such as Korea, whose companies are structured to exploit scale economies on the world market on low profit margins, cannot afford to ignore the exchange rate. Real appreciation induced by capital inflows tends to bite quickly into low margins while the benefits of industrial upgrading are slow to emerge. Sterilized intervention by a central bank to counteract private capital flows and to manage the exchange rate can only be effective when the substitutability between foreign and domestic assets is sufficiently imperfect to replace the dismantled capital controls. In other words, only the existence of an exchange risk premium which causes deviations from uncovered interest parity can be exploited by managed floating to reconcile monetary and exchange rate targets when the capital account is open. Moreover, during the process of financial *opening*, the world's pent-up demand for a country's assets may easily exceed the sterilization capacity of its central bank.

A further complication for echange rate management arises when stabilization does not precede financial opening. Inflation tends to be built into expectations, via implicit (or even explicit) indexation in goods and labour markets. This makes goods prices and labour costs sticky, while financial markets tend to be forward-looking. This asymmetry of response between the labour market and financial markets raises stabilization costs by producing real exchange rate overshooting. Stabilizing the economy while some capital controls (notably on borrowing abroad and portfolio flows) are still in place is the way to avoid burdening exchange-rate sensitive industries because stabilization then only affects domestic demand. With a clean float of the exchange rate and no capital controls, the effectiveness of monetary policy is enhanced through both domestic demand (tight credit) and foreign demand (strong currency). But the effectiveness of monetary policy comes at an immediate and often persistent cost in terms of external competitiveness. Implying over-investment in nontraded and under-investment in traded goods sectors, as well as missed opportunities for diversifying away from unproductive product ranges, real exchange rate overvaluation exerts a strong negative impact on long-term growth performance.

Third, while OECD countries can spread the costs of external shocks and financial crises through time (witness the recent crisis of US savings and loan institutions), most developing countries do not have this option. They risk losing international creditworthiness, inhibiting consumption smoothing based on foreign borrowing (even Korea was on the brink of losing access to voluntary lending in 1985). And domestic securities markets are too small to absorb shocks through variations in domestic liquidity; liquidity shocks often end up in the central bank as hidden losses. Therefore, full financial opening requires the establishment and deepening of money and securities markets. Otherwise, while using indirect monetary tools for daily operations when everything goes well, the monetary authorities of the typical advanced developing country will tend to resort to direct credit rationing to combat capital flight and recession, implying the need for capital controls.

The failure to establish and deepen domestic money and securities markets is often the simple result of ongoing domestic financial repression. Interest rate deregulation, for example, threatens the soundness and safety of banks which have been saddled with nonperforming loans through government credit allocation. Interest regulation also inhibits the development of domestic money markets, bond markets, and secondary securities markets — all important ingredients for open market operations. Equally, when much central bank lending consists of the automatic rediscounting of subsidized loans made by the banking system, the discount window can only play a limited role in indirect monetary control. The undercapitalization of domestic banks often inhibits changes in the required minimum reserve ratio as a monetary policy investment for influencing domestic liquidity.

3.2 Domestic Financial Sector Constraints

Domestic financial markets in developing countries can be stylized as follows: credit markets are segmented, competition among banks is weak, joint ownership between the corporate sector and financial institutions predominates, asset quality in banks' balance sheets is low, and institutional arrangements for prudential supervision and regulation are inadequate. While some of these features may at times be shared by OECD financial markets, their joint existence in developing countries is likely to increase financial instability, particularly in the presence of macroeconomic disequilibria. Financial opening, unless carefully designed, would be unlikely to generate interest rate convergence towards world levels, to enforce competition within the banking sector and to improve allocational and operational efficiency. Financial stability can be threatened in such a situation through the increased possibility of financial institution failure, inasmuch as the entry of new foreign banks undermines the viability of domestic banks saddled with bad loans and foreign exchange exposure of domestic banks rises.

Even in countries which have deregulated domestic interest rates, credit market segmentation has persisted, discriminating against small and rural financial institutions. Since international capital markets are largely wholesale markets, access to foreign capital is restricted in practice to firms linked to principal banks and to the export sector. With these financial market imperfections, financial opening may result in a distorted relief of liquidity constraints and in misallocated resources. Moreover, the lack of information and difficulties in monitoring small and rural sectors as well as specialized institutions servicing specific sectors impede the interest rate convergence predicted in economic textbooks.

Restrictions on domestic and foreign bank entry, restrictions on foreign ownership of domestic financial institutions and government ownership of domestic banks typically produce an oligopolistic structure of the banking industry in developing countries. If capital account opening excludes the entry of foreign banks, high operating costs and large spreads between lending and borrowing rates are likely to persist until the impact of foreign competition begins to work. This will be felt particularly in high-inflation countries where banks exhibit very high spreads and cost ratios due mainly to the increased paper work caused by inflation and to the expanded branch network used to capture low-cost deposits. Moreover, privileged banks can borrow long-term funds cheaply abroad and relend short-term funds to domestic borrowers excluded from the wholesale world capital market at high interest rates. Again, the presence of cartelized or concentrated banks impedes the reduction in domestic lending costs in spite of financial opening.

The prevalence of joint ownership of financial, industrial and commercial firms in developing countries risks jeopardizing the desired results of financial opening. Typically such holding companies or groups are not capable of adjusting quickly to a market-determined cost of credit which financial opening entails. Without prudential regulation and supervision, banks may extend credit to insolvent but related firms in order to protect their own capital. Increased interest rates, which often accompany financial opening, do not reduce demand for credit as expected, but stimulate 'distress borrowing', particularly when interlocking ownership relations are prevalent. Interlocking ownership strengthens domestic lobbies against free entry of foreign banks enabling doubtful lending practices to continue.

Interlocking ownership, and the resulting credit risk of excessive loan portfolio concentration leading to excessive nonperforming loans in the banking system, can only be prevented by independent and tightly enforced prudential regulation and supervision. However, in contrast to the industrial countries, even the advanced developing countries rarely possess the necessary components, such as private credit rating services and uniform accounting standards and practices. The failure of appropriate supervision and regulation will become more serious, since financial opening implies stronger competition and brings financial institutions into areas of new risk, such as interest risk, foreign exchange risk and position risk in securities trading.

A critical impediment to financial opening, in particular to foreign bank entry, is the overhang of nonperforming loans in the domestic banking system. The size of the bad loan problem is easily underestimated. Data on bad debts generally do not include large but doubtful debtors (particularly those with interlocking ownership) for whom the banks are capitalizing the arrears into new loans. Questionable accounting and supervisory practices also help to obscure the hidden losses. Inclusion of such nonperforming loans would often increase total bad debts significantly. While domestic interest liberalization often makes the existence of doubtful loans apparent, it can also contribute to underestimating the extent of the problem. As deposits grow (thanks to higher interest rates), the debt-asset ratio seems stable or even to decline over time. Yet, the banking system may be based on bad debt, with the central bank providing the necessary reserves. Once the monetary authorities maintain a restrictive monetary stance, bankruptcies in the nonbank sector and subsequent financial institution failure will force the government to consolidate the whole banking system. The costs involved in the rescue operation of ailing banks impose a heavy burden on central banks and/or the government budget. The actual cost of the rescue depends — apart from the size of bad loan portfolios to be handled — on the type of rescue scheme and on the timing of intervention. Experience in the Southern Cone of Latin America in the early 1980s suggests that the costs of rescue operations are far from negligible. In Chile, for example, these costs incurred over the period 1982-85 have been estimated at 44 per cent of Chile's 1985 GDP.

4. Policies Towards Capital Account Convertibility

4.1 Macroeconomic Management and Market Deepening
In the macroeconomic sphere, careful distinction has to be drawn between *opening* of the capital account and *openness*. Opening requires solid fiscal consolidation as a *sine qua non* for durable macroeconomic stability and the establishment of financial markets to provide instruments for cushioning the loss of monetary autonomy implied by opening. Neither area is amenable to a quick fix; both require institution building which takes time and commitment. Openness requires policy instruments to avoid both inflation and overvaluation, notably careful public debt and exchange rate management and new ways of monetary policy implementation, in part to foster interest rate convergence to world levels.

In the short term, government budget control is achieved by cuts in public outlays for consumption and investment, by eliminating subsidies and by privatizating or closing public enterprises running deficits. Long-term government budget control, however, usually needs supply-side tax reform, preferably by broadening the tax base, simplifying tax structures and setting tax rates at competitively low levels. Tax reform also has to compensate for the loss of explicit and implicit taxes on financial intermediation which is inevitable if dismantling outflow controls is not to produce capital flight.

The preparation, drafting and implementation of a tax reform takes time, if it is to be an economic and fiscal success. Tax reforms in developing countries have often failed because the period allowed for preparation and implementation was too short. Indonesia's tax reform, which took effect in 1983, has been a rare exception to widespread tax reform failure, in that a broadened tax base (away from oil) lowered tax rates. The simplified tax system succeeded in raising the tax ratio by several percentage points of GDP. The Indonesian tax reform plan allowed a two-year period for the necessary administrative and technical changes (modernization of the accounting system, training of tax officials, and changes in administrative structure) before implementation. Since powerful interest groups often prevent legislative reforms aimed at abolishing tax holidays and exemptions, credible commitment to reform on the part of the authorities is absolutely essential. Jail sentences for tax fraud have to become part of the culture, as happened recently in Mexico.

Tax reform and government budget control do not immediately remove the heritage of past budget deficits, i.e., large stocks of public debt. Dismantling capital controls undermines the government's ability to keep interest rates on its domestic debt low if capital flight is to be avoided. Domestic banks are often very important captive lenders to their government and continued implicit taxation in this discriminatory form weakens their position in the face of new competition from foreign bank entry. Taxing domestic bond returns would help only if the tax did not raise bond yields required from the savers commensurately. With open capital markets, domestic savers would compare after-tax yields at home and abroad, and would simply demand higher gross yields on any domestic government debt they held. Much depends in practice on the extent to which financial opening precludes the option of forcing captive buyers to hold domestic government debt. To the extent that captive buyers are lost, more fiscal discipline will be needed to preserve (or restore) a government's creditworthiness and credibility on open financial markets. Just how much discipline will be required is difficult to say because of changing market perceptions and unstable lending conventions. A more modest approach is to determine the government budget balance needed to stabilize debt ratios and simultaneously to meet other macroeconomic targets. More fiscal discipline is needed to avoid inflation and rising debt ratios when the demand for base money is low, when GDP growth is low relative to real interest rates (when public debt is high relative to GDP) and when real depreciation raises the real value of net foreign debt. Only when real GDP growth exceeds real interest rates and accumulated debt is low relative to seigniorage can the government run a noninterest deficit without raising the debt ratio.

Sound government finances are also a precondition for a more activist fiscal policy for managing domestic demand. As experience in Singapore and Indonesia shows, manipulating the flow of domestic liquidity into the banking system (using government excess savings) partly frees the interest rate from demand management purposes so that it can be used for exchange rate management. This avoids the overcommitment of policy instruments — maintaining exchange rates at competitive levels and using interest rates to manage domestic demand — which cannot be reconciled in the absence of capital controls.

To absorb speculative shocks to domestic liquidity (varying levels of foreign exchange reserves in the monetary base), small open economies typically resort to credit rationing measures, implying the need for controls on short-term capital flows. To obviate the need for these capital controls, domestic money markets have to be established and deepened to equip the monetary authorities with market-based policy instruments. For example, to avoid inflation (through a boost in the reserve component of base money) and unwarranted exchange rate appreciation when a country becomes a popular destination for portfolio inflows, the most important instrument of exchange rate management will be sterilized intervention by the central bank on domestic money markets. A sterilized purchase of foreign currency leaves the money supply unchanged, because the central bank sells domestic assets of equal value to the private sector. As long as domestic securities markets are shallow (as indeed they still are even in advanced developing countries), a direct (contractionary) supply effect is felt much quicker than in OECD countries. The sectoral distribution of the domestic credit squeeze is sharper, working capital costs for unpreferred lenders in the residual curb markets rise faster, the liquidity position of financial markets is quickly affected (especially if instruments used, such as government bonds, carry below-market rates), and the resulting crowding out rapidly depresses the shallow corporate bond market.

The origin of domestic money markets is usually trading in short-term government bonds. Other money market instruments — interbank deposits, bankers' acceptances, certificates of deposits, and corporate bond issues — then develop. The reluctance of finance ministries to pay market rates on their debt is usually the biggest obstacle to the development of a domestic money market. Obviously, heavy reliance of government revenues on concessional borrowing and aid tends to create a shortage of government paper on the domestic market. Lax enforcement of corporate income taxes is another public finance impediment to establishing markets for both private bonds and equities. Evading corporate taxes by showing very low profits is incompatible with creating the investor confidence needed for successful equity and bond issues. Setting up independent credit rating agencies may overcome these obstacles to sound market judgments on private debt issues. Subsidized bank lending is another important obstacle to be removed in order to develop domestic money markets. The time needed to establish and deepen money markets depends crucially on how quickly domestic financial repression is overcome.

4.2 Bank Competition and Supervision
Credit market segmentation, lack of competition in the domestic banking sector and insufficient prudential regulation and supervision have complicated financial opening and frustrated intended outcomes. This policy brief identifies three policy areas to help achieve successful liberalization.

Credit market segmentation can be overcome by abolishing restrictions imposed on banks and specialized financial institutions. Institutions should be allowed to extend their business over a wider range of financial activities; for example, industrial sector banks should be allowed to lend to other sectors. Bank management autonomy from government policy guidance can be fostered by making risk-averse management and cultures more profit oriented. Governments should stop restricting the creation of new financial instruments that provide a wider range of financial substitutes better tailored to the needs of clients.

Measures to stimulate competition among existing financial institutions include the abolition of interest ceilings, the abolition of subsidized loans to and credit floors for priority sectors, and the privatization of government-owned financial institutions. An effective way to intensify competition is to encourage the establishment of direct securities markets. The success of privatization is tied to the ability of privatized banks to of exercise independent credit judgments. Hence, banks must be able to protect their own capital position against loan losses forced upon them by past and ongoing government credit allocation. This cannot happen before the existing balance sheets are cleaned up by writing off bad loans and by injecting new capital (see next section for details).

New domestic as well as foreign bank entry should be allowed and encouraged, subject to adequate prudential requirements. New entrants should not be allowed to exacerbate the problem of interlocking ownership between financial, industrial and commercial sectors. In developing countries, powerful business interests are often in a position to finance new entrants into the domestic banking system. When domestic competition is a remote option, foreign competition on a level playing field becomes all the more important. A prerequisite for undistorted competition between domestic and foreign banks is to end domestic financial repression. For example, excessive minimum reserve requirements give a competitive edge to foreign banks which can more easily raise funds abroad that are not subject to these reserve requirements. Another obvious disadvantage for domestic banks arises from their obligation to buy government bonds and to make high-risk policy loans at below-market interest rates. Equal treatment also requires that the existing stock of nonperforming loans is largely consolidated before the refreshing winds of foreign competition start to blow. After the banks' balance sheets have been cleaned up, the authorities might consider the merger of some banks with the foreign entrants. This would help domestic banks to obtain an international reputation as well as open opportunities for diversifying into a broader portfolio.

Like macroeconomic stability, prudential regulation and supervision is *a sine qua non* for successful financial opening. Strong regulatory and supervisory policies are important to minimize moral hazard (including corruption, fraud and excessive risk taking) in the banking system, to ensure the viability and health of the banking industry and to make interest rate liberalization more effective. The ultimate objective of prudential regulation and supervision of the banking sector is to achieve stability (and public confidence in such stability) of the financial system, as well as to manage systemic risk and to protect clients. As risks in the financial system increase as a result of more intensified competition, greater market volatility and uncertainty after deregulation and liberalization, the authorities must strengthen prudential regulation and supervision practices, notably with respect to capital requirements and the range of banking supervision. In most developing countries financial institutions are significantly undercapitalized and the regulatory framework often lacks meaningful minimum capital adequacy guidelines. To provide a cushion against unexpected losses for the protection of depositors and to maintain general confidence in the banking system, appropriate capital adequacy requirements should be established. When bank accounting and management information systems are sound, it may be appropriate to adopt the risk-based capital adequacy guidelines formulated by the Basle Committee of Bank Supervisors. Concern over the stability of the banking system may induce the government to impose high capital requirements. However, this may deter entry and foster a rather concentrated banking structure.

It is important that prudential regulations embrace the whole spectrum of risks in the banking industry. Frequently, they just cover credit risk. Other risks such as default liquidity and interest-rate risks should also be supervised and regulated. Effective supervision has to ensure that (i) the supervisors have sufficient autonomy from political interference; (ii) the overall regulatory framework is sound; (iii) the supervisors have adequate resources to hire, train and retain competent personnel as well as to acquire appropriate technology; (iv) the supervisors have sufficient authority to enforce their decisions; and (v) the system of supervision balances off-site supervision and on-site inspection. Among the institutional arrangements needed to achieve these aims are the establishment of 'rules of the game' for commercial banks and other financial institutions, the creation of an early warning system and an intensified as well as standardized communications system between the Central Bank and the other financial institutions.

Improved prudential regulations can also help avoid the problem of non-performing loans, the emergence of interlocking lending among related banks and firms as well as the concentration of loans to specific sectors and firms. In countries with such problems, full interest-rate liberalization should not occur prior to their solution. Successful financial reform also depends on the healthy profitability of the private sector. If the macroeconomic environment is unstable and bank supervision is ineffective, interest-rate liberalization should proceed gradually to avoid possible disruption to long-standing financial contracts that may otherwise be caused by a sudden removal of interest-rate regulations. Given the economies of scale in finance and the temptation to form economic groups based on banks, banking regulations must be devised to limit bank-ownership links, to assure a wide distribution of ownership and control of banks, and to limit loans to any single economic group or sector, especially if it is related to the bank itself.

Prudent regulation is also essential for the development of a healthy capital market. An adequate regulatory environment for securities markets should include systems of corporate disclosure, external auditing and the establishment of credit ratings. Furthermore, regulations on insider trading, price manipulations and other unfair transactions should already be effective before the opening of capital markets.

An adequate information system is an important, but frequently neglected, ingredient for financial system efficiency. Lack of complete and accurate information, the absence of adequate accounting standards and reluctance to make balance sheets and profit-and-loss accounts available to creditors probably constitute the most severe obstacles to financial development in many advanced developing countries. They require institutional reforms that include a strong supporting infrastructure to provide an adequate flow of information, credit appraisal and rating, and legal and accounting systems. Accounting and auditing are fundamental tools not only for managerial decision making but also for lender evaluation of credit risk. Information and disclosure requirements are particularly important for effective securities markets. Publicly available sources of accurate, reliable and honest information is still scarce in most developing countries.

Deregulation, technological advances, financial innovation and the globalization of financial markets imply stronger competition and expose financial institutions to new areas of risk, including foreign exchange risk and position risk in securities trading. In economies with a long history of financial repression, the participating actors, be they banks or managers, borrowers, lenders or public servants, are not trained to deal with these risks. Financial opening has therefore to be accompanied by a further strengthening of bank supervision and surveillance of the financial system. At the same time, banks' capacities to assess new types of risks associated with international financial markets have to be strengthened. While the supervising body should be concerned with the integrity of the financial system as a whole, the banks should receive special attention because they are the major depository of savings and have a central role in the payments and settlements systems.

4.3 Solving the Bad-Loan Problem

The overhang of nonperforming loans in the domestic banking system represents a stumbling block to financial opening, in particular for free entry of foreign banks. In view of the limited number of successful restructuring experiments and because cross-country evidence on cost-effective ways to handle the problem is precarious, not many generalizations on the optimal approach to the bad loan problem can be made. However, some basic principles can be advanced.

The first step for a government committed to solving the bad-loan problem is to determine the precise extent of the damage sustained. The lack of data on nonperforming loans (reflecting the inadequacy of financial statements and accounting methods), the failure of the banks and authorities to recognize the size of the problem and to address it at an early stage exacerbates the cost of rescue schemes. Auditors, who must be independent from the parties (the current bank management, the nonperforming borrowers, the authorities involved in credit allocation) involved in the problem should identify and assess the magnitude of the problem as well as prepare rescue schemes.

In the second step, a choice has to be made whether to liquidate or to recapitalize the ailing financial institution. The decision depends on a country's legislative framework, the size and structure of the national banking system, the amount of loss not backed by the ailing bank's equity and by the weakness (or strength) of government finances. Recapitalization can take various forms. One solution adopted by Chile in the 1980s is for the government to buy up the nonperforming loans by swapping them for government bonds. Another mechanism is to inject of new capital, either by existing or new shareholders or by the public authorities. A third solution is to merge the ailing domestic banks with healthy domestic or foreign corporations. Two recent examples of dealing with the bad loan problem are worth closer scrutiny.

Chile recapitalized its banking system by removing bad loans from the banks' portfolios and then providing a government-backed mechanism for injecting new capital. First, the government identified the damage by means of a special portfolio audit and then purchased the banks' bad loans with long-term government bonds carrying a yield above the banks' cost of funds. With the gradual elimination of problem loans and the positive net income flow from the government bonds, the banks' capital grew over time. Chile's approach placed a considerable burden on the government budget which had to absorb losses on the bad loans and transfer new resources to the banks through interest payments on the government bonds.

An alternative approach was chosen by Malaysia's authorities. Shareholders of ailing banks were required to inject as much capita as possible through a rights issue. The privately injected capital was supplemented by the Central Bank to meet the minimum adequacy requirements. The shares subscribed by the Central Bank were held under a buy-back scheme whereby those shareholders having participated in the rescue operation were allowed to buy back the unsubscribed shares at par plus holding costs. Malaysia's approach meant less government involvement than Chile's and more immediate restructuring of ailing banks (or liquidation if not enough private subscribers could be found).

Financial opening (rather than delay of reform which would preserve financial repression) provides other avenues for solving the nonperforming loan problem in the domestic banking system. Newly entering foreign banks are potential candidates for mergers with and recapitalization of ailing domestic banks. The participation of foreign banks in the consolidation of the domestic banking system can be made part of the entry conditions. There are essentially two options available. The first is the direct merger of the foreign bank with the ailing domestic bank as a precondition for entry. The second option for foreign banks unwilling to participate directly in a rescue operation would be an auction procedure for a limited number of new bank licences. Those with the highest bid would be awarded the licence and the auction proceeds could be earmarked for the rehabilitation of the domestic banking system.

4.4 Phasing out capital controls

The variety of capital flows on which controls are often imposed equips the policymaker with an instrument which is often neglected in economic advice. He can sequence the process of capital account liberalization itself. To develop a watertight blueprint that provides a guarantee against financial crises would be pretentious. Open financial systems always face the risk of crisis, but crisis has often been a forceful catalyst for reform. As this chapter hopes to have made abundantly clear, however, pitfalls with financial opening and openness can and should be avoided by establishing durable macroeconomic stability and tightly enforced prudential regulation and bank supervision.

The instruments available to the policymaker are the various controls which are imposed on different capital flows. Flows must be identified as outflows or inflows, short-term or long-term, bank or nonbank flows. Major capital flows to be distinguished are borrowing and lending, buying and selling of securities, and foreign direct investment. Flows should also be distinguished by whether they are for real investment, financial investment or consumption. Foreign direct investment and trade-related finance, for example, are absolutely necessary for development at the earliest stage. Moreover, they are unlikely to cause trouble for macroeconomic management and financial sector stability. They are early candidates for liberalization, while other capital flows confront the authorities with more complicated issues.

In view of the considerable time needed to establish sound government finances, to lay the ground (and the reputation) for durable macroeconomic stability as well as to implement institutions for prudential regulation and bank supervision, these steps should be undertaken without delay and should precede the dismantling of further capital controls. Fiscal consolidation is a necessary prerequisite for domestic financial liberalization because regular tax revenues obviate the need for government to rely on the implicit taxation of the domestic financial intermediation. The solution of bad loan problems also requires strong government finances.

Even a tight fiscal and monetary stance will not immediately reduce inflation and inflationary expectations. Using the exchange rate regime (a nominal peg, an active crawl, or a pure float) would help speed up the disinflationary process with open capital markets, but the costs of misallocation involved by real overvaluation of the currency would seem too high to make this route advisable. Moreover, only when disinflation has succeeded in reducing nominal interest rates and raising real interest rates can the problems of domestic interest rate deregulation (which are apt to complicate the process of removing capital controls) be avoided. This is part of a strategy of domestic financial liberalization which aims at avoiding sustained interest differentials with world financial centres.

Domestic interest rate deregulation removes both the main incentive for capital flight and the most important obstacle to the development of domestic money markets. Having succeeded in deepening financial markets offering undistorted assets for financial investment, controls on capital outflows can now be dismantled. Deregulating interest rates, reducing minimum reserve requirements and solving the bad loan problem pave the way for the free entry of foreign banks (which can simultaneously help solve the bad loan problem). When and if adequate prudential regulation is in place, the free entry of foreign banks is a realistic strategy for promoting competition in the banking sector.

At this stage of the liberalization process, the major elements should be in place for dismantling controls on short-term capital inflows. With increased bank competition due to free bank entry, with credit market integration from competition, with banks exercising independent credit judgments after the solution of the bad loan problem, with prudential regulation preventing distress borrowing and with lowered interest rates resulting from stabilization, the integration of short-term capital markets should now produce interest rate convergence to world levels. Deepened money markets now allow the authorities to absorb shocks to domestic liquidity in a smoother and less

Debt, Deficits and Exchange Rates

contractive way than before. This is the time to dismantle controls on short-term borrowing for banks and nonbanks and to allow nonresidents to operate freely in the domestic securities markets.

REFERENCES

Branson, William P. (1990), 'Financial Market Integration, Macroeconomic Policy and the EMS' , *Discussion Paper no. 385*, CEPR, London.

Cho, Yoon-Je, and Deena Khatkahte (1989), 'Lessons of Financial Liberalisation in Asia: A Comparative Study', *Discussion Paper no. 50*, World Bank, Washington, D.C.

Corbo, Vittorio and Jaime De Melo (1987), 'Lessons From the Southern Cone Policy Reforms', *The World Bank Research Observer*, vol. 2.2, pp. 111-142.

Diaz-Alejandro, Carlos (1985), 'Good-Bye Financial Repression, Hello Financial Crash', *Journal of Development Economics*, vol. 19 pp. 1-24.

Edwards, Sebastian (1990), 'The Sequencing of Economic Reform: Analytical Issues and Lessons from Latin America', *The World Economy*, vol. 13.1, pp. 1-14.

Fry, Maxwell J. (1988), *Money, Interest and Banking in Economic Development*, Johns Hopkins University Press, Baltimore and London.

Kenen, Peter B. (1988), *Managing Exchange Rates*, RIIA, London.

McKinnon, Ronald (1991), *The Order of Economic Liberalization: Financial Control in the Transition to a Market Economy*, Johns Hopkins University Press, Baltimore and London.

Nam, Sang-Woo (1989), 'The Liberalization of the Korean Financial and Capital Markets, in Korea Development Institute (ed.), *Korea's Macroeconomic and Financial Policies*, Seoul, pp. 133-172.

OECD (1990), *Liberalisation of Capital Movements and Financial Services in the OECD Area*, Paris.

Park, Yung Chul and Hugh Patrick (1992), *Financial Development in East Asia: Experiences of Japan, South Korea, and Taiwan*, Columbia University Press.

Polizatto, Vincent P. (1990), 'Prudential Regulation and Banking Supervision. Building an Institutional Framework for Banks', Working Paper Series no. 320, World Bank, Washington, D.C.

Sheng, Andrew (1989), 'Bank Restructuring in Malaysia, 1985-88', Working Paper Series no. 54, World Bank, Washington.

Williamson, John (1992), 'On Liberalizing the Capital Account', in R. O'Brien and S. Hewin (eds), *Finance and the International Economy:5*, OUP, Oxford.

9. Financial Opening and Capital Flows*

1. Introduction

This chapter[1] focuses on the relationship between financial opening and capital flows. Note at the outset, that higher capital inflows are not the main theoretical benefit of financial opening. The greater benefits seem to stem from increased individual opportunities for cross-border diversification in both risky assets and liabilities. The traditional rationale for opening the capital account in developing countries, however, is that capital inflows will finance increased investment more cheaply, in terms of foregone consumption, than domestic savings. This traditional inflow argument shows lower benefits of financial opening than the risk diversification argument, as it is based only on the difference between capital inflows and outflows (Hanson, 1992). Ignoring the financial benefits from the international diversification of trading in risk is roughly analogous to saying that the benefit from free trade is based on the difference between exports and imports.

Having said that, let us focus on the traditional rationale, financial opening to raise net capital inflows. Capital has the worldwide reputation of being timid like a deer and fast like a hare, but having a memory like an elephant. What can financial opening do to master such a beast? The answer is: nothing much in isolation, and beyond that the answer is not straightforward.

2. Latin American Reform, Capital Controls and Capital Flows

While net capital inflows (including the return of flight capital) into Latin America averaged about $8 billion a year in the second half of the 1980s, the inflows reached $20 billion in 1990 and $40 billion in 1991. Is after all the memory of an elephant not that impressive? An important external factor for the revival of substantial international capital flows to Latin America is the current loose stance of US monetary policy which has widened return differentials in Latin America's favour. But most of the revival is home-

---

*   Originally published in C. Bradford (ed.), *Mobilising International Investment in Latin America*, OECD Development Centre, Paris, 1993.

made.   Balanced budgets, lower inflation, privatization and deregulation, trade liberalization and the restructuring of existing external debt have all contributed to the re-entry of Latin America to the list of viable investment locations for funds available in world financial markets.   *De jure* liberalization of capital movements does not figure prominently in the list of determinants to explain the revival of capital flows.

Even in the absence of *de jure* liberalization, the recent economic reform wave is likely to have raised the *de facto* openness of capital accounts in Latin America.   Estimates of how interest rates are determined in Latin American countries show a small role for domestic factors, but an important one for uncovered interest parity, indicating a large degree of effective openness.   In fact, financial openness in Latin America seems higher than in Korea and Taiwan (Table 9.1).

Table 9.1   Latin America: estimates of financial openness

	Index of openness[1]	Period
Brazil	0.723	1969-87
Guatemala	0.708	1969-87
Uruguay	0.890	1969-87
Memo:		
Korea	0.594	1980-90
Taiwan	0.353	1980-90

[1] Running from zero to one, the parameter rises when a country strengthens its integration with world financial markets.   With the index estimated zero, external factors play no role in the determination of domestic interest rates.   If the index is one, the domestic interest rate is equal to its uncovered parity value, and capital mobility is assumed to be perfect.
Sources: Haque and Montiel (1990); Reisen and Yèches (1991).

The most important channels for evading capital controls are trade-related (Mathieson/Rojas-Suarez, 1992).   One of the most frequently used channels to transfer capital abroad is by over-invoicing import contracts and by under-invoicing exports.   Another trade-related channel for unrecorded capital flows is the leads and lags in the settlement of commercial transactions. With rising export and import shares, such trade-related channels for capital flows will gain more importance in Latin America.   For example, when exports and imports account for 25 per cent of a country's GNP, even a two-month delay in the invoicing of exports and a shortening of import payment terms by one month leads to a capital outflow equal to around 6 per cent of GNP. Such a potential outflow of capital is often more than the country's stock of official foreign exchange holdings (implying the need for currency devaluation).

Notwithstanding the greater scope for circumvention of existing controls in Latin America due to economic reform in the 1980s, capital controls are certainly not completely ineffective. Latin America is not Eastern Europe (Fischer and Reisen, 1992b). It has considerable long-term institutional savings such as held by public social security institutions and private pension funds which are comparatively easy to lock in by way of controls. (That policy may be harmful because undermining cross-border risk diversification means a higher country risk exposure for long-term funds.) And Latin America has the administrative resources to implement foreign exchange regulation because it disposes of a well-developed banking network and of tax and customs authorities, the two administrative pillars of external financial regulation.

Thus, even if the effectiveness of capital controls erodes over time, they can still inhibit or 'tax' certain classes of external financial transactions, limit the access of some individuals or institutions to international financial markets, and discourage the repatriation of capital flight. Consequently, capital controls may well not produce the desired effects of raising funds available for domestic investment. Yet their very existence might generate uncertainty about the possibility of further tightening and thus stem capital inflows and induce outflows beyond the level envisaged by the authorities. In particular, controls on capital outflows reduce the incentive to repatriate capital now by 'taxing' the option of re-exporting capital later (Kenen, 1993).

Such analysis in terms of a two-period framework in which the cost of evading outflow controls is treated as a tax on sending capital abroad may explain why the ending of controls on outflows often leads to the repatriation of domestic capital. This is, however, a result on which it would surely be unwise to rely; presumably the flows so attracted are of a procyclical nature and not the sort of long-term stable investment funds which developing countries are hungry for. What about the reverse case — much more topical for the current situation in Latin America — where policymakers look at the option to dismantle capital outflows to dampen excessive net inflows? Well, as argued above, the possibility that such a move will raise net inflows further rather than slow them down makes the removal of outflow controls an inappropriate instrument for trying to fine-tune the flow of capital (Williamson, 1993)[2].

3. Capital Inflows into Latin America Now and Then

The present episode of important capital inflows into Latin America is not the first this century. The most recent such inflow before the early 1990s occurred during the period from 1978 to 1982 and led to the Latin American debt crisis. Another important episode of capital flows to Latin America was noted in the 1920s. Both periods were dominated by capital inflows from the United States, and in both periods capital inflows were eventually reversed in what turned out to be major crises. Starting in 1929, foreign capital markets dried up, and dollar price deflation led to a marked increase in the real burden of debt servicing. Most countries suspended payments on their external debts and capital controls were introduced for the first time ever. The agony lasted well into the 1940s (Maddison, 1985). In the 1970s, in particular Uruguay, Chile, and Argentina moved towards liberalizing their economies, including their capital accounts. The liberalization episode of the Southern Cone ended with capital flight, generalized loan defaults, banking crises, falling output and massive unemployment. Capital controls were re-introduced.

In order to learn how such a reversal of fortunes (and capital flows) can be avoided in the future, it is interesting to compare features of the present episode of capital inflows with those of the late 1970s (Calvo *et al.*, 1992). There are some similarities in the two episodes: real exchange rate appreciation, booming stock markets, and high domestic-foreign rate of return differentials. Besides these similarities, there are also noteworthy differences. First, government budget deficits and inflation were on the rise in the earlier episode (not in Chile, though), while in the present one inflation rates are declining and government budgets are balanced. A second difference which is related to the first is the nature of external borrowing; while in both episodes most of the capital inflow takes the form of increased net external borrowing, most of this borrowing is now done by the private sector while earlier on it was mostly public; moreover, interest rate risk is now with foreign creditors, while in the earlier period debt was incurred on a floating LIBOR base. Third, the capital inflows observed thus far in 1990-91 are much smaller[3] than in 1978-82 as a percentage of Latin America's GDP. Capital inflows in 1978-82 represented 7 per cent at that time, the capital inflows in 1990-91 are about 4 per cent of GDP. Fourth, while the present inflows are accompanied by approximately equal increases in the current account deficit and in official reserves, the reserve build-up played no great role in the 1978-82 episodes. The current build-up of official foreign exchange reserves points to active intervention by the monetary authorities on the foreign exchange market; since domestic credit aggregates have been largely held under control, these interventions have been sterilized.

In spite of the differences between the two episodes, the sustained rate of return differential and real currency appreciation observed then and now may give rise for concern. To what extent is it possible that the current capital inflows are building another crisis for the future and will again lead to a reversal of capital flows? Recent research at the OECD Development Centre provides a sort of check list to answer that question (Fischer and Reisen, 1992a).

4. How to Avoid Another Debt Crisis

The basic requirement to avoid another reversal of capital flows is fiscal control. First, government finances and tax efforts need to be sufficient to obviate the need for domestic financial repression. Implicit and overt taxation of financial intermediation breeds capital outflows. Second, unless the government has fiscal control, it has to violate the Mundell assignment and use monetary policy for internal balance. To use monetary policy for internal balance requires capital controls to insulate the country from international capital movements. Once the capital account is open, even imperfectly, monetary policy acquires a comparative advantage in dealing with external

Table 9.2　　Latin America: fiscal balances (per cent of GDP)

	1985-90	1991	1992
Financial balance			
Argentina	-9.5	-3.3	-1.8
Brazil	-41.7	-29.6	-36.0
Chile	0.2	1.0	1.6
Mexico	-11.9	-3.5	-1.3
Venezuela	-4.8	1.1	1.0
Primary balance[1]			
Argentina	0.1	2.1	2.4
Brazil	0.6	4.6	1.0
Chile	4.2	6.0	3.0
Mexico	5.1	7.9	6.0
Venezuela	-0.5	6.0	5.0

[1] Excluding interest payments.

Source. J.P. Morgan, *World Financial Markets*, July/August 1992.

balance, while Mundell assigns fiscal policy at maintaining internal balance (Mundell, 1962). Where tax ratios have been raised and government budgets balanced in Latin America, sufficient fiscal control seems to be established to open up capital controls and to avoid disruptive gyrations of capital movements (Table 9.2). Fiscal improvement has gone along with reduced financial repression as is witnessed by the elimination of deposit-rate ceilings in most Latin American countries and lowered inflation rates.

To look at budget balances alone will be insufficient for an assessment about long-term fiscal control. Unsustainable cuts in government spending, temporary privatization receipts and favourable raw material prices may blur the picture. Ideally, we would like to know to what extent Latin America has proceeded in enlarging its tax base. The look at tax ratios, in particular at ratios concerning taxes imposed on income and value-added, may produce some insights. Table 3 shows that even the successful performers in Latin America have tax ratios much below the OECD average (which is about 40 per cent of GDP), and that have tended to decline over the 1980s. In Argentina, price stabilization has reversed the Tanzi effect (according to which high inflation reduces real tax receipts due to collection lags) and thus

Table 9.3   Tax ratios in Latin America

	1982	1991
Argentina	*18.0*	*21.0*
Income	1.8	2.9
Production and sales	10.1	10.4
Chile	*19.5*	*18.2*
Income	5.7	5.4
Production and sales	8.1	10.3
Mexico	*26.9*	*22.8*
Income	8.8	7.4
Production and sales	8.1	10.0
Venezuela	*27.6*	*23.3*
Income	19.8	19.7
Production and sales	1.4	1.0

Source: IDB, ESP 1992 Report; own calculations.

raised real tax receipts. Chile and Mexico seem to have been successful in enlarging the tax base by including agriculture and transportation into value-added taxes. Overall, however, tax collection now does not look very different compared with the early 1980s.

Another requisite to avoid reversal of capital flows is to avoid overvalued currencies. Because overvaluation breeds anticipations of large depreciations, it has been identified as the single most important determinant of bouts of massive capital flight. This was especially the case when capital movements can take place at the official exchange rate, in the absence of dual exchange rates or other forms of controls. In the 1978-82 episode, real exchange rates became overvalued once attempts were made to stabilize inflation expectations by pre-announcing future devaluation rates below current inflation rates. Anchoring inflationary expectations did not work (or with too long a delay): excessive capital inflows exceeded the sterilization capacity of the central bank and loosened fiscal and wage discipline, hence eroding the very foundations on which the nominal anchor approach is built. Subsequently, speculative attacks on unsustainable exchange rates required high interest rates to stem capital flight; high interest rates in turn crowded out productive investment and implied a rapid accumulation of domestic debts, often followed by bankruptcy.

So far, most of Latin America is indeed successful in avoiding overvalued currencies, at least on the wholesale price level (Table 9.4). Real effective exchange rates are between a fifth (Brazil) and a half (Venezuela) below their 1980-82 average. Some real appreciation has occurred in the early 1990s, but it has been a move from levels far below purchasing power parity. Except in Argentina for which no credibility and thus perhaps no alternative to fix the peso to the dollar was left, countries seem not to repeat experiments with extravagant exchange rate regimes such as the *tablita*. The Mexican government has recently softened the peg to the dollar by announcing a gradual widening of the target band for the peso, thus increasing the uncertainty facing speculators. Moreover, it is not budget deficits but the private sector which is crowding in money from abroad. The high share of foreign capital flowing into official reserve accumulation combined with lower money supply growth rates indicates extensive sterilized intervention of central banks. Money and exchange rates have been kept on a flat trend thanks to managed floating. And high official reserves guarantee more power for central banks to counter any speculative attack.

Neither now (1990-92) nor then (1978-82) have capital inflows into Latin America been sufficient to arbitrage away the large return differentials between Latin and North America (Table 9.5). Five explanations have been prominent in explaining sustained interest differentials during the last epi-

*Table 9.4   Latin America — real effective exchange rates
(1980-82 average = 100)*

	1990	1991	1992 September
Argentina	58.9	69.2	67.4
Brazil	118.0	90.7	78.0
Chile	60.0	65.3	68.0
Mexico	69.2	74.4	74.9
Venezuela	52.4	51.7	52.7

Source: J.P. Morgan, *World Financial Markets*, September/October 1992.

sode. First, there was a substantial increase in demand for credit, triggered by an increase in perceived wealth due to overall liberalization and improved private property rights. Second, domestic credit market segmentation prevented interest arbitrage between specialized lending institutions and across sectoral uses of funds: the spread between lending and borrowing rates was not reduced and reflected oligopolistic price behaviour. Third, lack of supervision and interlocking ownership between banks and firms led to the accumulation of bad loans; as a consequence, banks increased interest charges on viable borrowers to compensate for losses. Fourth, nonperforming loans caused further distress borrowing and added to credit demand.

Table 9.5   Latin America: domestic lending rates in dollars[1]

	1990	1991	1992 Latest
Argentina	213.8	11.2	14.8
Brazil	-7.3	2.8	n.a.
Chile	30.4	17.3	20.4
Mexico	34.6	14.8	19.2
Venezuela	8.5	8.2	31.5

[1] Domestic nominal interest rates have been converted into their dollar equivalent by $(1+i)_t e_t/e_{t+1}$, where i is the monthly interest and e the monthly exchange rate. Annual rates are geometric averages of the monthly rate.
Sources: Calvo *et al.* (1992); IMF, *International Financial Statistics.*

Fifth, because of increasingly overvalued currencies, foreign lenders and domestic residents eventually perceived greater exchange risk and demanded higher returns. Whether these factors are also important now in accounting for the size and persistence of rate of return differentials is yet to be determined. To be sure, as long as credit markets are segmented, domestic banking lacks competition and prudential regulation and supervision is not enforced, financial opening is unlikely to generate interest convergence towards world levels.

While it is difficult to establish empirical evidence on microeconomic interest rate determinants, the variety of Mexican debt paper equips us to disentangle country risk, currency risk and expected inflation for that country at least (OECD, 1992). The *tesobono* is indexed to the dollar, so comparing its yield with that of US treasury bills of equal maturity reveals essentially *country risk*. The difference between *tesobono* and *CETES* reveals *currency risk* (although maturities are different). Expected inflation is calculated by comparing inflation-indexed *ajustabono* with CETES. Table 9.6 reveals that most of domestic-foreign interest differentials can still be attributed to expected inflation.

Table 9.6   Risk premia in Mexican interest rates

	Early 1990	March 1992
Country risk	7.5	3.5
Currency risk	36.0	4.5
Expected inflation	31.0	16.0

Source: OECD, 1992.

The present inflow of capital into Latin America is not explained by domestic reform alone. Falling interest rates, a continuing recession, and balance of payments developments in the United States and other industrialized countries have encouraged investors to shift resources to Latin America (Calvo *et al.*, 1992). Since much of these inflows is short-term capital, some countries in the region remain vulnerable to quick reversal in the event of a change in investor sentiment. While OECD countries can spread the costs of such external shocks through time, most Latin American countries do not have this option. They risk losing international creditworthiness, inhibiting consumption smoothing based on foreign borrowing. The sustained interest differentials may thus be due to the fact that investors assign a non-negligible probability to reform collapse in Latin America and the re-imposition of capital controls. If return differentials are indeed so determined, the current run on OECD membership is easily explained. It is a rather costless way to reduce the political risk premium in Latin American interest rates by building investor confidence in the permanence of a policy regime that will respect investors' property rights (Williamson, 1993).

NOTES

1. The author would like to acknowledge helpful comments from Ricardo Ffrench-Davis on a prior draft.
2. When flight capital is surging back, leading to a potentially disruptive expansion in the money supply, allowing banks to use this money to make loans abroad and thus to short-circuit the threat of monetary expansion, may be quite a reliable strategy, though.
3. Though not for all: Mexico during 1978-82 never experienced the 6 per cent deficit on the current account that it had in 1992.

REFERENCES

Calvo, G., L. Leiderman, and C. Reinhart (1992), *Capital Inflows and Real Echange Rate Appreciation in Latin America: The Role of External Factors*, mimeo, IMF, Washington, D.C.

Fischer, B. and H. Reisen (1992a), *Towards Capital Account Convertibility*, OECD Development Centre, Policy Brief no. 4, Paris.

Fischer, B. and H. Reisen (1992b), 'Full Currency Convertibility in Eastern Europe?', *Intereconomics*, (September).

Hanson, J. (1992), *Opening the Capital Account: A Survey of Issues and Results*, Working Paper WPS 901, World Bank, Washington, D.C.

Haque, N. and P. Montiel (1990), *Capital Mobility in Developing Countries — Some Empirical Tests*, IMF Working Paper, WP/90/177, IMF, Washington, D.C.

Kenen, P. (1993), 'Financial Opening and the Exchange Rate Regime', in H. Reisen and B. Fischer (eds), *Financial Opening: Policy Issues and Experiences in Developing Countries*, OECD Development Centre, Paris.

Maddison, A. (1985), *Two Crises: Latin America and Asia 1929-38 and 1973-83*, OECD Development Centre, Paris.

Mathieson, D.J. and L. Rojas-Suarez (1992), *Liberalization of the Capital Account: Experiences and Issues*, IMF Working Paper 92/46, IMF, Washington, D.C.

Mundell, R. (1962), 'The Appropriate Use of Monetary and Fiscal Policy Under Fixed Exchange Rates', *IMF Staff Papers*, vol. 9 (March), pp. 70-77, IMF, Washington, D.C.

OECD (1992), Economic Surveys, Mexico, Paris.

Reisen, H. and H. Yèches (1991), *Time-Varying Estimates on the Openness of the Capital Account in Korea and Taiwan*, OECD Develoment Centre Technical Papers, no. 42, and *Journal of Development Economics* (1993), vol. 40, no. 3.

Williamson, J. (1993), 'A Cost-Benefit Analysis of Capital Account Liberalisation', in H. Reisen and B. Fischer (eds), *Financial Opening: Policy Issues and Experiences in Developing Countries*, OECD Development Centre, Paris.

Part 3

The Case for Exchange Rate Management

The Case for Exchange Rate Management

This third part collects some of the essays that I consider to be my favourite. The essays are variations of a theme: the choice of the "best" exchange rate regime for a small open economy in an interdependent world, with due respect to the country's institutional background. Choosing their preferred exchange rate regime, many economists tend to the extremes: national monetarists opt for purely floating, international monetarists for fixed exchange rates. Somewhere in between are those, including myself, who are deeply convinced of the importance of reliable and competitive (but not immovable) real effective exchange rates for durable economic growth. My conviction owes a lot to East Asia's performance over the past decades and to work by Max Corden, Sebastian Edwards, Peter Kenen and John Williamson.

The essay on New Zealand's economic reform (written with Isabelle Joumard) will demonstrate how a bold, but ill-designed reform can result in macroeconomic disarray which destroys any net benefits from microeconomic liberalization for almost a decade. With financial opening preceding stabilization and labour market reform and with a purely floating New Zealand dollar, post-reform monetary tightening was bound to lead to a Dornbusch-style overshooting of the real exchange rate. The appreciation of the currency forced New Zealand's manufactured industry to exit from world markets causing a quasi-permanent loss of exports, around 20 per cent compared to a situation had the exchange rate shock not happened. The loss in manufactured exports and the missed opportunity to diversify into prospective products calls for a real devaluation of the New Zealand dollar below purchasing power parity if export markets are to be recaptured.

The following essay, written for the Second Monetary Conference of the Landeszentralbank Berlin, has been motivated by what I consider ill-conceived advice. The advice, given by then President of the Deutsche Bundesbank, Karl Otto Pöhl, was that the Asian NICs should peg their currencies to the yen, on the pattern of the European Monetary System. The essay employs a number of suggestive criteria offered by the fruitful theory of optimum currency areas to assess whether the Asian NICs should peg to the yen; the answer is a clear No. The essay also provides a testable yardstick to assess exchange rate policies during the process of catching up, based on Balassa's reformulation of the doctrine of purchasing power parity and on the Summers/Heston data set of comparable real per capita income.

The last essay of this book almost returns to a situation where the book has started. Just like 15 years ago, Latin America is experiencing heavy capital inflows. Is history repeating itself? Not quite. To help avoid another reversal of fortunes (and flows) in Latin America, the essay makes a strong case for sterilized interventions on the foreign exchange and money markets. I was asked to write this essay for *CEPAL Review*, after having given several lectures at the UN Economic Commission for Latin America and the Caribbean. It is argued that capital flows to Latin America in the early 1990s have to be judged as temporary (as opposed to permanent), dismisses pegs and floats as viable exchange rate regimes, and deals with the many objections which economists have raised against sterilized intervention. I finally look for institutional explanations of how a number of Asian countries have been able to reconcile free capital flows, monetary autonomy and stable real effective exchange rates. The Asian sterilization practice holds lessons for open economies with underdeveloped securities markets.

10. Real Exchange Rate Overshooting and Persistent Trade Effects: The Case of New Zealand*

1. Introduction

Although widely ignored, New Zealand's economic reform since the mid-1980s offers important lessons for exchange rate policy and the sequencing of reform. New Zealand's reform has been qualified as the 'most comprehensive economic reform programme undertaken by any OECD country in recent decades (p. 38)' which has 'so far failed to deliver the long-term increases in output and employment which were its ultimate objectives' (OECD, 1991, p. 9). One explanation for New Zealand's low post-reform growth may be the strong anti-tradable bias that reform plus stabilization have induced. In particular, post-reform monetary tightening has led to an overshooting of the real exchange rate which has caused hysteresis in New Zealand's manufactured export volume.

New Zealand's programme of macroeconomic stabilization and economic reform has been ambitious, but in contrast to the order preferred by most economists. Domestic and external financial reform preceded reform in other areas such as labour market and tax reform, and exchange rates have been purely floating (from early 1985 to mid-1988), with no intervention by the Reserve Bank.[1] Government finances (even excluding important privatization receipts) were improved rapidly first through large cuts in subsidies and later through increased tax receipts with greater reliance on indirect taxes. Trade liberalization was asymmetric in speed and scope, a rapid removal of all export subsidies contrasting with the gradual reduction in import protection.[2] Labour reform came last. While wage and price controls were abolished at the end of 1984 and the Labour Relations Act of 1987 intended to encourage decentralized bargaining and union amalgamation, initial reforms had the possibly inadvertent effect of generalizing award minimum wages.

* Originally published in *The World Economy*, vol. 15, no. 3, May 1992, pp. 375-388.

As will be shown in Section 2, with financial opening preceding stabilization and labour-market reform and with a purely floating New Zealand dollar, post reform monetary tightening was bound to lead to a Dornbusch-style overshooting of the real exchange rate. Section 3 will estimate alternative export functions and show that the overshooting has induced hysteresis in New Zealand's manufactured export volume. This finding implies the conclusion (Section 4) that the New Zealand dollar has to devalue below purchasing power parity for some time if export markets are to be recaptured.

2. Real exchange rate overshooting

One explanation for New Zealand's low post-reform growth may be that reform plus stabilization have produced a bias against tradables.[3] Table 10.1 gives a clear indication that the reform shifted resources away from tradables and in particular from manufacturing, and that the contribution of tradable production to national income significantly shrunk. Five years after reform,

Table 10.1   New Zealand: indicators of tradable performance

	1977-84	*1989*
1. Contribution to GDP, in per cent		
— Tradables	33.5	28.2
— Manufacturing	22.8	18.5
2. Contribution to employment, in per cent of labour force		
— Tradables	35.4	28.7
— Manufacturing	24.0	18.0
3. Contribution to investment, in per cent of gross fixed capital formation		
— Tradables	32.6	15.8
— Manufacturing	19.6	10.5
4. Manufactured export share, in per thousand of manufactured exports of total OECD	1.55	1.47

Sources: OECD, *National Accounts*, vol. II (1990); OECD, *Foreign Trade by Commodities*, vols I and 5 (1991); author's calculations.

resources were clearly relocated away from the tradable sector. Both measures, the share of tradable employment in the total labour force and the share of tradable investment in total fixed capital formation, display a strong downward trend for the post-reform period. Even in 1989, after the New Zealand dollar had returned from its high real level, New Zealand's manufactured exports reached a lower market share in the OECD area than in the period before reform. Obviously, the rise in profitability[4] thanks to liberalization and deregulation was not enough to offset the disincentives against tradables linked with New Zealand's reform programme.

The key price to set incentives to produce and consume tradables relative to nontradables in an open economy is the real exchange rate. New Zealand's real exchange rate is displayed in Figure 10.1. The solid line contains quarterly data on the IMF's Real Effective Exchange Rate (line rec of the International Financial Statistics), which is based on domestic and foreign (trade-weighted) consumer prices.[5]

Figure 10.1   Real exchange rate, terms of trade and interest rate differentials

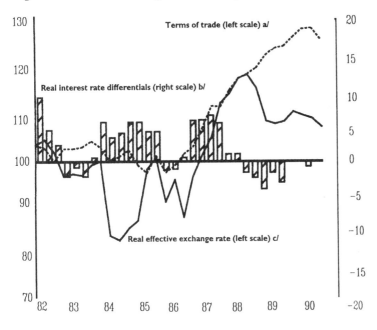

a/ Defined as the ratio of export prices index (1985=100) to unit value of imports (1985=100).
b/ 3 monts Treasury bonds nominal interest rates deflated by the respective consumer price inflation, New Zealand vis. Australia.
c/ Average 1982:3-1984:2 = 100.
Source: Authors' calculation with data from IMF, *International Financial Statistics*.

The 20 per cent devaluation of the New Zealand dollar in 1984:3 was quickly eroded during 1985 when the currency, measured in real effective terms, appreciated back to pre-devaluation levels. The New Zealand dollar softened again in 1986 only to appreciate in turn from late 1986 to mid-1988. By that time, the New Zealand dollar had appreciated in real effective terms by 41 per cent since the capital account had been opened and the exchange rate floated.

The observed post-reform appreciation of the New Zealand dollar, however, does not necessarily imply real exchange rate misalignment. Misalignment can be defined as a sustained departure of the real exchange rate from its long-term sustainable equilibrium level, which is consistent with the simultaneous attainment of external and internal balance (Edwards, 1988).

Among the fundamental determinants, movements in the commodity terms of trade have traditionally closely determined the real effective value

Table 10.2   *Capital market pressure on New Zealand's real exchange rate,*
                 1983-1988

Items	1983	1984	1985	1986	1987	1988
(a) Inflow of capital NZ$, bn.	2.19	5.93	3.52	6.38	1.10	1.35
(b) Net factor payments abroad NZ$, bn.	1.28	1.91	2.69	2.21	2.75	2.73
(c) Acculumation of reserves NZ$, bn.	0.27	2.22	-0.82	3.81	-1.69	-0.41
(d) Net pressure on the real exchange rate [(a) - (b) - (c)]	0.64	1.80	1.65	0.36	0.04	-0.97
(e) Relative index of exchange rate pressure [(d): GDP], Percentages	1.86	4.64	3.69	0.67	0.07	-1.52

(a) Equals the current account deficit, SNA definition, plus change in foreign exchange reserves.
Sources: OECD; own calculations.

of the New Zealand dollar, both under pegged and floating rates (Blundell-Wignall and Gregory, 1990). While the improvement of New Zealand's terms of trade (see Figure 10.1) during the period 1986-88 may have justified real appreciation of the exchange rate, terms of trade are not in line and do not provide much explanation for actual real exchange rate behaviour since the capital account has been opened.

With falling rates of assistance in New Zealand and rising agricultural protectionism abroad, trade policy, has undoubtedly exerted a downward pressure on the equilibrium exchange rate, quite in contrast to the appreciation observed from 1985 on. Higher productivity gains than in the OECD have not necessarily warranted a real appreciation of the exchange rate after 1985, to the extent that they have been evenly distributed across sectors.

To measure the capital market pressure on the real exchange rate, Table 10.2, similar to Harberger (1985), assumes that an increase in net capital inflows will cause the real exchange rate to appreciate (to the extent to which the inflows are spent on nontradables), and that two main forces operate to offset the capital market pressure. First, net factor payments abroad represent a flow of funds in the opposite direction. Second, if the capital inflow is acquired by the central bank and accumulated as foreign currency holdings, there is again no pressure on the real exchange rate (at least, in the shorter term). These two offsetting forces have been taken into account in Table 10.2 by subtracting the relevant flows for each year from the corresponding inflow of capital. The resulting net figure is given in row (d), and is expressed as a percentage of GDP in (e). Obviously, New Zealand did not experience excessive capital inflows after having opened up the capital account.

New Zealand's real exchange rate appreciation has sometimes been attributed to the mix of tight money and loose fiscal policy. However, fiscal policy was considerably tightened, not loose, in 1985 and 1987 (fiscal years) — at a time when the real effective exchange rate appreciated. Contrary to the familiar Mundell-Fleming model, there was a tendency for the currency to appreciate when fiscal policy was tightened. This implied that fiscal policy had a procyclical effect on output (and that tightening deepened the slump). The reduction in aggregate demand implied by fiscal policy did not lead to the depreciation of the New Zealand dollar which in the Mundell-Fleming world is sufficient to restore the initial level of output. In a study featuring time-varying estimates on the determination of New Zealand's short and long-term interest rates, McNelis, Grimes and Wong (1989) find that fiscal variables (both the stock and growth of government debt) did not exert any influence on short-term rates following January 1987. The fiscal impact on long-term rates diminished more gradually, but steadily from mid-

1986 on. At least since early 1987, fiscal policy cannot be blamed for high interest and exchange rates in New Zealand.

We think that after financial opening the New Zealand dollar has been largely affected by monetary policy, rather than by fundamentals. It is now a widely accepted proposition that in the presence of nominal stickiness or inertia in domestic factor and product markets, restrictive monetary policy will lead to substantial overshooting of the nominal and real exchange rate under a floating exchange rate regime. New Zealand's experience during 1985-88 provides a textbook case of Dornbusch-style overshooting. As in Dornbusch (1976), monetary tightening sent New Zealand's interest rates up and created expectations of eventual disinflation and of a future fall in interest rates. Because inflation came slowly, real money balances were first below long-term equilibrium, while real interest differentials and the real exchange rate were above long-term equilibrium. Figure 10.1 gives real interest differentials for three-months treasury bonds in New Zealand minus Australia, the closest asset substitute, and visualizes the close correspondence between real interest differentials and the real exchange rate after financial opening. The New Zealand dollar appreciated until the expectation of future depreciation back toward equilibrium was large enough to offset the interest differential. Figure 10.1 shows also that the appreciation was simultaneous with the increase in the interest rate; this explains why no measurable net capital flow actually took place.

The increase in indirect taxes[6] pronounced real exchange rate overshooting in two ways — directly and indirectly. The direct link goes from higher taxes on goods and services to measured inflation and from there to the real (effective) exchange rate. The indirect link is this: higher indirect taxes widen the asymmetry in the speed of response to monetary tightening between financial markets (including the foreign exchange market) and the labour market; this asymmetry is responsible for exchange rate overshooting. By delaying expectations of disinflation, higher indirect taxes widen the asymmetry by slowing the wage response to monetary tightening. Wage inertia (whence some good prices inertia) stretches out the period of exchange rate overshooting.

Post-reform exchange rate management has meanwhile undergone a profound change in New Zealand. In March 1985, the authorities' 'main consideration leading to the decision to float was the likelihood that floating would *provide more certain price signals* [emphasis added] to market participants during a period of considerable change . . . to be beneficial to those exposed to international trade'. (The Treasury, 1987, p. 212.) Since late 1988, both money and the exchange rate have been successfully kept on a flat trend. This has coincided with the shift of emphasis towards the exchange rate as a guide to monetary policy (Spencer, 1990). Since August 1988, the trade-weighted New Zealand dollar has become the Reserve Bank's principal monetary indicator.

3. Persistent trade effects

Once real exchange rate overvaluation is corrected, exports (and growth) are unlikely to pick up immediately. Binding capacity constraints, lags in delivery, implicit or forward contracts, or regressive expectations can account for a lagged export response to the real exchange rate. New research on hysteresis in international trade, neatly summarized in Krugman (1989), shows that a large enough exchange rate shock can cause structural breaks in a country's export function: 'If you push something hard enough, it will fall over; when you stop pushing it, it won't stand up again'. The structural break is caused by the existence of fixed, sunk market-entry costs which firms incur before engaging into exports, in particular in the case of differentiated manufactured goods. Such entry costs arise through adopting products to foreign health and safety regulations, establishing a brand name (advertising), distribution and service networks and other expenses necessary to penetrate foreign markets. Sunk costs explain why large, temporary exchange rate shocks induce hysteresis in trade prices and quantities, while small exchange rate changes do not. A firm will be willing to break into a market only if it expects to cover its sunk costs, and once these costs are incurred it will hold on to that market even if it covers just its variable costs. The appreciation of the currency thus must be high (or long) enough to induce market exit or to defer market entry.

Hysteresis is likely to be pronounced in countries (such as New Zealand) which are undergoing radical economic change. As price signals in the early reform period (in particular in 1986)[7] have lowered the expected return from investment into tradables, the signals have raised the option value of waiting (Dixit, 1989). Even if investment into tradables turns profitable again, uncertainty will make it rational to wait and see. Investors have an option to postpone investment into tradables and they will wait until the front loading of returns is sufficient to compensate for the risk of relinquishing investments in the nontradable sector.

Earlier studies have found that temporary overvaluation induced hysteresis in traded-good markets. Baldwin (1988) finds evidence that the rising US dollar (before it peaked in 1985) induced hysteresis in US import prices, although not in US import volumes. Bean (1988) shows that the 1978-81 sterling overvaluation had hysteretic effects on British exports. We will now provide evidence for New Zealand. In view of the small domestic market size of New Zealand (as is also the case in most developing countries), we will focus on exports.

Table 10.3 presents some simple, 'conventional' equations for New Zealand's quarterly total and manufactured export volume. Heavy dependence on agriculture and hence strong seasonal variations required seasonal correction of the export volume series. The explanatory variables include a proxy for the foreign (importing) market (all equations), a domestic absorption variable (equations 4 and 5) and the real effective exchange rate, both current (all equations) and lagged (equations 3, 4 and 5). The table shows OLS estimates from 1980:1 to 1990:3, implying roughly five years (twenty quarters) for each pre- and post-reform period. The period includes considerable variation in the exchange rate data, allowing price elasticities to be estimated with much confidence. In fact, the estimated coefficients presented here are similar to those obtained by previous empirical studies on industrial countries (Goldstein and Khan, 1985).

Equation (1) shows OLS estimates for New Zealand's total exports as a function of foreign spending and the current real effective exchange rate. Price and income elasticities have the expected sign and are clearly significant. The high share of agricultural products in New Zealand's export portfolio is reflected in the low significance and parameter value of the exchange rate variable. The price elasticity, but also the foreign income elasticity is considerably higher for manufactured exports, as is evident from equation (2).

The addition of independent variables other than foreign income and current real exchange rates did not add much explanatory power. Equation (3) includes not only foreign demand and current exchange rates, but also the impact of lagged real exchanges rates in determining manufactured export volumes. Estimated lag by lag, past exchange rate numbers produce the correct (negative) sign, but stay all insignificant: when the lag coefficients were constrained to follow some polynomial form, the best fit was yielded with a second-order polynomial where three quarterly lags were significant. Summing up these three lagged real exchange rates and the current exchange rate raised only slightly the estimated exchange rate sensitivity beyond its level found in equation (2). Our finding that lagged exchange rates did not matter much in determining manufactured exports is consistent with the low level of capacity utilization observed in New Zealand. It is also consistent with the absence of regressive expectations.

Table 10.3　　*Alternative export volume[a] equations, 1980:1 - 1990:3 (log-linear time series regressions)*

	Total exports		Manufactured exports		
	(1)	(2)	(3)	(4)	(5)
Constant	-4.00	-9.03	10.41	-16.87	-27.56
	(-2.92)	(-7.22)	(-7.06)	(-4.23)	(-6.29)
Foreign real demand[b]	0.86	1.15	1.26	0.80	1.02
	(8.12)	(11.83)	(10.98)	(2.96)	(4.32)
Domestic real demand[c]				0.93	1.07
				(1.77)	(1.77)
Real exchange rate[d]	-0.26	-0.79	-1.11	-0.73	-0.48
	(-1.24)	(-5.25)	(-5.72)	(-2.67)	(-2.00)
Hysteresis dummy[e]					(-0.15)
					(-3.82)
R^2	0.63	0.77	0.76	0.78	0.85
Durbin-Watson	1.82	1.74	1.78	1.85	2.36

[a] Seasonally adjusted, along the additive moving average technique.
[b] Foreign real demand is defined as trade-weighted GDP plus imports minus exports of the three major importers (Australia, Japan and United Kingdom).
[c] Domestic real demand is New Zealand's GDP minus exports in constant 1985 prices.
[d] Equations (1) and (2) consider only current exchange rates, while equations (3), (4) and (5) report a two-order polynomial sum of the current exchange rate plus three quarterly lags. The exchange rate is the IMF's real effective exchange rate (line rec).
[e] The dummy starts from 1986:1. The procedure to identify the timing of the structural break is described in the text.
Sources: Author's calculations with trade data from OECD, *Monthly Statistics of Foreign Trade* and *Foreign Trade by Commodities*, vol. I; with GDP data from OECD, *Main Economic Indicators*, and with the real effective exchange rate index from IMF, *International Financial Statistics*. Estimation method is OLS, performed on quarterly data with Micro-TSP software. Numbers in parentheses are *t*-statistics. R^2 is the adjusted R^2.

Equation (4) adds to equation (3) the level of domestic demand as a determinant of manufactured exports. The *a priori* assumption that strong internal demand sucks in exportables and that weak demand fosters exports is not confirmed. We find a (weakly) significant positive relationship between domestic demand and exports. This finding suggests that exports did not take up the slack generated by domestic stabilization. Supply-side events (such as market exits) dominated the usual demand-side substitutability between internal and external demand for tradables which usually prevails under full capacity utilization.

The export equations displayed in Table 10.3 would only predict the future well if the overshooting New Zealand dollar had not induced a structural break in these functions. The decline of the New Zealand dollar witnessed since mid-1988 should have stimulated immediately New Zealand's export performance, given the size of estimated price elasticities (around 1) and the absence of significant exchange rate lags in the export equations. We will show now, however, that the strong New Zealand dollar is likely to have done persistent damage to New Zealand's manufactured export position.

A crucial step in the empirical analysis of hysteresis is the determination of the timing of the structural break in the export function. In the Dornbusch (1976) model, like in most other macro models, changes in the monetary-fiscal policy mix result in a perfectly anticipated exchange rate shock. The structural break in New Zealand's export function should therefore have occurred upon announcement of the new policy regime, consistent with Baldwin's 'beachhead' model (1988). In practice, the exact timing of the structural break is difficult to establish *a priori,* given the multitude of monetary and other disturbances and the fact that monetary announcements are less than fully credible. (After decades of high or suppressed inflation, New Zealand's monetary authorities had first to build reputation).

We selected equation (4) for its highest explanatory power (the adjusted R^2) to test for export equation stability over time. Breakpoint and forecast Chow tests (not reported here) for each quarter during 1984:1 and 1989:4 reject at the 99 per cent confidence level and at the 90 per cent level, respectively, the null hypothesis that New Zealand's export function was stable throughout the 1980s. We find that a structural break occurred most likely in 1986: 1.

An iterative dummy procedure supports our findings from the Chow test. We added to equation (4) a dummy (0 before the structural break, 1 after the break) for each quarter during 1984:1 and 1989:4. Starting in 1986:1, the dummy variable yielded the highest coefficient in determining the behaviour of manufactured exports. The estimate is reported in Table 3, equation (5). The results confirm that a highly significant structural break has occurred in 1986:1 The inclusion of the dummy raises considerably the explanatory power (adjusted R^2) of New Zealand's export function. Note also that the inclusion of the hysteresis dummy lowers the responsiveness of manufactured exports to changes in the real exchange rate.

It could be objected that the observed structural break is unrelated to real exchange rates and that the break is due to other causes, notably the removal of export subsidies. Note however, that the most important export subsidies (the export credit assistance facilities) were already removed in September 1984 so that a subsidy-related break in the export functions should have occurred earlier than in 1986: 1.

Figure 10.2   Actual and simulated manufactured exports

a/ Simulation based on equation (4) in Table 10.3, assuming no structural break in the export function.
Source: Authors' calculation (see Table 10.3 for data).

Figure 10.2 compares the actual performance of New Zealand's manufactured export volume with an out-of-sample simulation based on equation (4). The simulation implies the hypothesis that the overshooting New Zealand dollar would not have induced hysteresis in the country's manufactured export equation. The broken line in Figure 10.2 which represents the simulation result indicates that without hysteresis manufactured exports would have been around 20 percent higher than the observed volume (solid line) actually was during 1986:1 and 1990:3.

The failure to price manufactured products competitively on export markets has most likely induced the structural break in New Zealand's export function observed above. To defend their world market share (to avoid exit), firms would have needed to differentiate their prices with respect to their markets. Translated to the country level this would have implied that currency appreciation induced a fall in the export price relative to the domestic price of manufactured goods. In fact, between 1986 and 1988 firms did not make up for real effective appreciation of the New Zealand dollar by reducing relative export prices.[8]

One can envisage a variety of reasons which explain the failure of New Zealand's firms to 'price to the market' since 1986, such as squeezed profit margins due to rising wages and interest rates, the withdrawal of export credit subsidies, the massive privatization programme which involved many export-oriented companies, or net trade diversion effects in the wake of intensifying economic integration with Australia. Whatever is the ultimate cause (or combination of causes) for the structural break, the break implies a lesson for the future equilibrium exchange rate of the New Zealand dollar. To be sure, it is difficult if not impossible to predict the equilibrium level. But to the extent that firms made quasi-permanent decisions to leave export markets when the New Zealand dollar was strong, the dollar must fall below its 1986 level in real effective terms for a while to induce firms back to these export markets. This means that the New Zealand dollar must fall below its purchasing power parity level to achieve this turnaround.

4. Conclusions

By producing a strong anti-tradable bias, New Zealand's economic reform programme has added to the unavoidable stabilization costs in terms of lost output and employment. As the overshooting unwinds, it leaves the country with a persistent loss in manufactured exports and hence a less diversified export base than would have been the case without hysteresis. We draw two major lessons from New Zealand's reform, one for the balance between stabilization and financial opening, and one for exchange rate management under financial opening.

Stabilization and labour market reform should precede financial opening. Stabilizing the economy while some capital controls (notably on borrowing abroad and portfolio flows) are still in place, is the way to avoid burdening of exchange-rate sensitive industries because stabilization then only affects domestic demand. With a clean float of the exchange rate and no capital controls, the effectiveness of monetary policy is enhanced via effecting both domestic demand (tight credit) and foreign demand (strong currency). But the effectiveness of monetary policy comes at an immediate and (as in New Zealand) persistent cost for external competitiveness. Hence a balance between stabilization and financial opening must be found. Policymakers can reduce the overshooting-related cost of purely floating exchange rates and full capital mobility by preceding labour market reform in the sequencing of policies. A backward-looking labour market adds to employment and output cost of stabilization by emphasizing real exchange rate overshooting via widening the asymmetry of response between the labour market and financial markets. Turning the labour market to forward-looking behaviour is to reduce this asymmetry, overshooting and stabilization costs. To achieve this, monetary authorities must quickly establish credibility. Therefore income policy and stabilization must go hand in hand. Such a policy would also dampen the delay in disinflationary expectations generated by tax reforms such as in New Zealand which shift the burden from direct to indirect taxation.

New Zealand's experience also provides a lesson about the appropriate exchange regime for countries which want to open the capital account. While purely floating exchange rates have been shown to enhance the effectiveness of monetary stabilization, they have not helped to reduce economic interdependence. With sticky labour costs and goods prices, the pure float has added to stabilization costs in terms of output and employment losses and intensified the anti-tradable bias of New Zealand's reform programme. The government has realized this and switched to a managed float guided by an (undisclosed) trade-weighted basket of currencies. Indeed, earlier management of exchange rates would have to some extent obviated the importance of an appropriate sequencing of stabilization and reform because it would have helped to stabilize real exchange rate levels. Credible governments without obvious partners to peg their currency to, seem well advised to opt for a managed float under financial opening.

NOTES

1. Within eight months, virtually all controls on financial markets were removed. In July 1984, to combat the foreign exchange crisis, controls on interest rates were abolished, and the currency was devalued by 20 per cent. A month later, administrative controls on credit allocation were ended. The capital account was opened in December 1984 when virtually all controls on foreign exchange transactions were lifted. Finally, all reserve requirement and ratio controls on banks' portfolio went in February 1985. Within months, New Zealand's financial market had moved from being one of the most regulated in the OECD area to one of the most liberal.

2. All existing export credit assistance facilities were withdrawn in September 1984. Import quotas and licensing have been phased out by mid-1988 and replaced by tariffs whose rates remain high by OECD standards.

3. It is a common approximation to treat services as nontradables and the rest as tradables. Within the tradable sector, agriculture and mining are subject to special factors such as weather or terms of trade, so it will make sense to single out manufacturing, too.

4. The OECD (1991) has estimated that rates of return on business capital defined as the difference between value-added and compensation of employees as a percentage of capital stock, increased from ca. 10 to 15 per cent after reform in the late 1980s.

5. We have rescaled the IMF index on the two years preceding New Zealand's financial opening (1982.3-1984.2 = 100), in order to facilitate comparisons of pre- and post-reform levels. Estimates based on other definitions of New Zealand's real exchange rate show the same pattern of behaviour, although the magnitudes of real appreciation since 1985 differ according to the concept chosen (Edwards, 1990). Edwards' estimates — a tradable-nontradable proxy based on New Zealand's consumer prices and on ten trade partners' wholesale prices — produce even higher rates of appreciation than the IMF index used here, as do the *Morgan Guaranty* real exchange rate series. By contrast, a competitiveness index based on relative unit labour costs (corrected by productivity) indicates only slight appreciation after 1985. But, as noted by Edwards, when productivity gains are evenly distributed, as seems to be the case in New Zealand (OECD, 1991), these improvements in productivity will not result in increased incentives to relocate resources towards tradable and, especially, exportables.

6. Tax reform shifted to greater reliance on indirect taxation by introducing a broadly-based goods and services tax (GST), levied at a uniform 10 per cent rate. The GST came into effect on 1st October 1986 and was increased to 12.5 per cent in July 1989. Thus, on two occasions, the GST boosted consumer prices and delayed a fall in households' (and workers') inflation expectations.

7. Following the lifting of the 1983-84 wage/price freeze, wages increased considerably in 1985 and 1986, rising faster than wholesale prices for manufacturing and than export unit prices and thus adding a further squeeze on profits for the affected sectors.

8. The relative export price, defined as the export price as a fraction of the domestic price for manufactured goods, had up to 1986 moved inversely to the real effective exchange rate in New Zealand. By contrast, between 1986 and 1988, the relative export price was positively correlated with the real effective exchange rate.

REFERENCES

Baldwin, R.E. (1988), 'Hysteresis in Import Prices: The Beachhead Effect', *American Economic Review,* 78, 4, 773-785.

Bean, C.R. (1988), 'Sterling Misalignment and British Trade Performance', in R.C. Marston (ed.), *Misalignment of Exchange Rates: Effects on Trade and Industry* (Chicago: Chicago University Press), 39-75.

Blundell-Wignall, A. and R.G. Gregory (1990), 'Exchange Rate Policy in Advanced Commodity Exporting Countries: Australia and New Zealand', in V. Argy and P. de Grauwe (eds), *Choosing on Exchange Rate Regime: The Challenge for Smaller Industrial Countries'* (IMF, Washington, DC) 224-271.

Dixit, A. (1989), 'Intersectoral Capital Reallocation Under Price Uncertainty', *Journal of International Economics*, 26, 3/4, 309-325.

Dornbusch, R. (1976), 'Expectations and Exchange Rate Dynamics', *Journal of Political Economy*, 84,6,1161-1176.

Edwards, S. (1988), *Exchange Rate Misalignment in Developing Countries* (Washington, DC, World Bank Occasional Papers no. 2).

Edwards, S. (1990), *Stabilization and Structural Adjustment in New Zealand: Some Analytical Aspects* (UCLA, mimeo).

Goldstein, M. and M.S. Khan (1985), 'Income and Price Effects in Foreign Trade', in P. Kenen (ed.), *Handbook of International Economics*, 2 (North-Holland: Amsterdam), 1041-1105.

Harberger, A.C. (1985), 'Lessons for Debtor-Country Managers and Policymakers', in G.W. Smith and J.T. Cuddington (eds), *International Debt and the Developing Countries,* (Washington, DC, World Bank), 236-257.

Krugman, P.R. (1989), *Exchange-Rate Instability* (Cambridge, Mass., MIT Press).

McNelis, P., A. Grimes and A. Wong (1989), *Financial Liberalization Down Under: Interest Determination in New Zealand, 1985-1988* (Washington, DC, Georgetown University, mimeo).

New Zealand: The Treasury (1987), *Government Management Brief to the Incoming Government 1987,* 1 (Wellington).

OECD (1991), *Economic Surveys* (New Zealand, Paris, OECD).

Spencer, D. (1990), 'Comment', in V. Argy and P. de Grauwe (eds), op. cit. (Washington, DC, IMF), 277-284.

11. Should the Asian NICs peg to the Yen?*

Once upon a time (up to 1985), the East Asian newly industrialized countries (NICs) — Hong Kong, South Korea, Singapore, and Taiwan — were generally applauded for their exchange rate management. It was then characterized by a strong orientation toward the US dollar and by keeping to a minimum the variation in the real effective exchange rates. In stark contrast to most of Latin America, exchange rate policies of East Asian NICs avoided discrimination against export industries, they never allowed substantial black market premiums to develop, and they generally supported the successful attainment of external and internal balance.

Beginning in the first half of 1985 and especially after the September 1985 Plaza Agreement among the industrialized countries, there has been a growing discrepancy between the real exchange rate movements of the East Asian NICs and Japan (see Figure 11.1). This was caused by the sharp depreciation of the US dollar against key currencies (such as the yen and deutsche mark) since 1985. On the other hand, the East Asian NICs maintained either a de facto peg to the US dollar or appreciated significantly less against the US dollar than the yen did, leading to a depreciation of the currencies of the NICs in real effective terms. This was the end of the applause for them. Since then, Korea and Taiwan, in particular, have been blamed with (1) preventing the global adjustment process toward financeable trade balances, (2) reaping windfall profits behind the shield of the yen appreciation, (3) exercising exchange rate protection, and (4) keeping the capital account too closed.

These criticisms, however, can hardly be substantiated, except for Taiwan. Exchange rate protection is characterized by the preferential treatment the tradable sector receives in relation to the nontradable sector through maintaining an undervalued exchange rate or effectively preventing its appreciation. If the subsequent shift toward the tradable sector is accompanied by a

* Originally published as a comment in E.M. Claassen (ed.), *Exchange Rate Policies in Developing and Post-Socialist Countries*, International Center for Economic Growth, ICS Press, San Francisco, CA, 1991

Figure 11.1   Index of real effective exchange rates for Japan and the East Asian NICs, 1985-1990

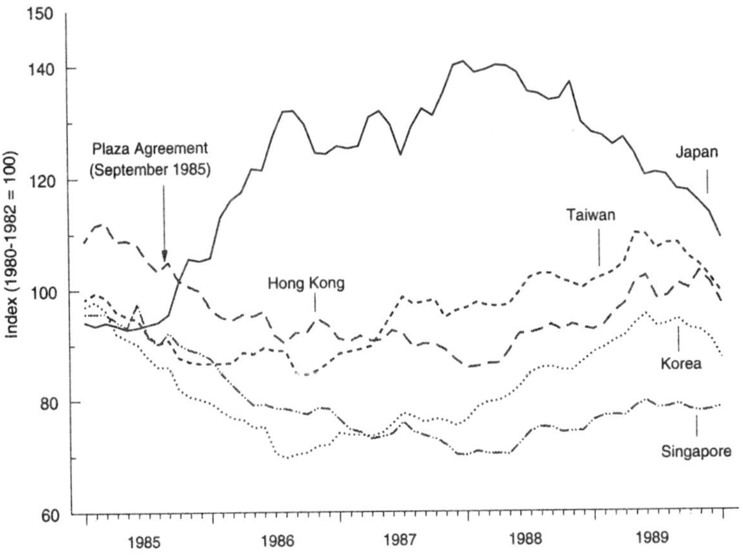

Note: A rise of the index denotes appreciation. Calculated on six-month averages.
Source: Morgan Guaranty Bank, *World Financial Markets.*

decrease in absorption in order to balance supply and demand in the nontradable sector, a current account surplus and higher stocks of foreign reserves will be the logical consequence. Table 11.1 reveals, however, that Korea's foreign reserves remained remarkably stable in terms of imports throughout the 1980s. Since 1986, Korea has been using its current account surplus to pay off part of its massive foreign debt, benefiting from favourable external conditions, such as lower interest rates and raw material prices. Neither Korea nor Hong Kong and Singapore are traditional surplus countries. The current accounts of Hong Kong and Singapore fluctuated between -US$ 1.5 billion and +US$2 billion during the 1990s, while Korea's current account has switched back to deficit in early 1990.

The monetary focus on exchange rates provides little explanation for the recent surpluses of the east Asian NICs and no explanation for the global imbalances. Current account imbalances have been associated with disparities between national savings and investment rates, largely determined by

Table 11.1   Economic characteristics of the East Asian NICs, 1980-1988

Economic indicator	Period	Japan	Hong Kong	Korea	Singapore	Taiwan
GDP per capita (current US dollars)	1988	23,190	9,550	3,725	8,860	5,600
Relative, PPP-adjusted (United States = 100)	1985	69.6	70.4	23.3	69.7	27.5
Consumer prices (annual inflation rate)	1985-88	0.5	5.0	4.3	0.2	0.8
Unemployment (% of labour force)	1985-88	2.7	2.3	3.4	4.2	2.3
Share in NIC exports (%)	1985-88					
United States			38.2	37.6	20.4	43.8
European community			20.9	12.6	11.9	11.8
Japan			4.2	15.5	6.6	12.8
Share in NIC imports (%)	1985-88					
United States			7.7	18.3	14.7	24.0
European community			11.0	9.0	11.8	11.4
Japan			19.4	29.7	20.0	31.5
Foreign reserves (months of imports)	1980-84	2.2	n.a	2.8	4.6	4.3
	1985-88	4.1	n.a.	1.5	5.4	20.2

n.a. = not available.
Sources: Hong Kong: *Monthly Digest of Statistics*; Korea: Economic Planning Board, *Major Statistics of Korean Economy*; Singapore: *Yearbook of Statistics*, and Ministry of Trade and Industry, *Economic Survey of Singapore*; Taiwan: Council of Economic Planning and Development, *Taiwan Statistical Data Book*; Japan: International Monetary Fund, *Direction of Trade Statistics Yearbook*; Organisation for Economic Co-operation and Development; *Economic Survey of Japan*, various issues.

intertemporal optimization within the private sectors and by changed government savings (with little evidence for "Ricardian equivalence"). While investment ratios have been quite stable since 1985 in the East Asian NICs,
variations in savings ratios were closely related to deviations from potential
gross national product (GDP) growth. But the current accounts of these
countries reflect not only the internal but also the external savings-invest-
ment balances, in particular that of the United States. Global current account imbalances are likely to persist as long as the United States fails to
raise its savings and to resolve its deficits.

Even if the link between global imbalances and exchange rate policies of
the East Asian NICs is not a matter for serious concern, there are other
important new developments that warrant a new look at optimal exchange
regimes in East Asia. While the growing trade and production integration
among the East Asian NICs and Japan has turned the earlier de facto peg to
the US dollar into a destabilizing policy, the same pitfalls would hold for a
peg to the yen. I will argue that fixed nominal rates have also become obsolete for other reasons, namely, the growing capital mobility caused by financial liberalization and the need for long term appreciation of real exchange
rates in the process of catching up. Assuming that the East Asian NICs will
be subject to both foreign monetary and real domestic shocks, I will make
the case for a managed float as the best policy response. In a departure from
the entrenched short-termism in the exchange rate literature, the chapter will
emphasize the longer view for countries in a rapid industrializing process.

Exchange Rate Policies for Catching Up

Governments of countries that have experienced a sustained period of export-led growth (such as Korea and Taiwan now, and Germany in the 1960s)
are likely to eagerly avoid any real appreciation of their exchange rate. They
may ignore that real appreciation will come at any rate, with rising wages
and prices in the nontradable sector if nominal appreciation is delayed.

When a country "catches up" with initially richer countries, its goods
become more expensive because productivity in the tradable sector rises
more than in the nontradable sector (where the lack of external competition
introduces slack). The prices of nontradables (such as housing) therefore
rise faster than those of tradable goods, reflecting the increasing scarcity of
the former. Comparing productivity growth between the tradable sectors of
the country that is catching up and a rich country, the former will exceed the
latter. Also, assuming equal inflation of tradables worldwide, real wages
will hence rise faster in the country that is catching up than they will in the
rich country. With lower productivity growth in the nontradable sector in

both countries and dependent on their weight in the purchasing power parity (PPP) basket, general prices will rise faster in a country such as Korea than in Japan or the United States, in order to balance the impact of higher money wages on the nontradable sector.

Figure 11.2   Deviations from purchasing power parity (PPP) in Germany 1953-1979, and in Korea, 1968-1987

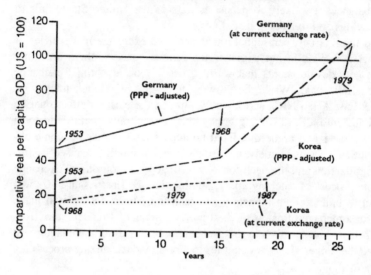

Sources: Robert Summers and Alan Heston, "Improved International Comparisons of Real Product and Its Composition: 1950-1980", *Review of Income and Wealth* 30 (June 1984): 207-62; and Angus Maddison, *The World Economy in the 20th Century*, OECD Development Centre Studies (Paris: OECD, 1989).

Figure 11.2 presents real per capita income levels (relative to the United States) for Germany (1953-1979) and for Korea (1968-1987). Since nontradables tend to be cheaper in poorer countries, a purchasing power parity adjustment is essential to make meaningful international comparisons of income levels. By comparing PPP-adjusted real income with real income in current dollars, I implicitly derive the deviations from PPP at different years. In a smooth path (not drawn here), comparative real per capita GDP in dollars should deviate negatively from PPP-adjusted income at the beginning of the catching-up process. With PPP-adjusted income approaching the benchmark country level (100), the negative deviation should gradually become smaller and disappear when the developing country has reached the benchmark country.

Figure 11.2 clearly suggests that Korea has stayed a "cheap"country in PPP terms, although it experienced *relative* growth with a move of real per capita income from a sixth to a third of that of the United States. Should a country such as Korea cease to stay cheap in PPP terms, and should a gradual appreciation be brought about by an upward float? The German experience may provide some answers, as recalled by Herbert Giersch (1984):

'Sooner or later the country will — like West Germany at the end of the 1960s — discover that it has an oversized export sector. An adjustment process will gather momentum either in the form of a domestic cost push — higher wages and costs at the given exchange rate — or in the form of a currency revaluation at constant prices. This adjustment process amounts to an improvement in the country's terms of trade. All rents from superior design and quality, from reliability and punctuality which were formerly used for promoting volumes will then be collected in the form of higher export prices. This improvement in the terms of trade goes along with an upward deviation from the previous real exchange rate, most likely also with an overshooting compared to long-run PPP.'

In fact, Germany's exchange rate adjustment was repeatedly delayed during 1968 and 1973 (when the Bretton Woods system was abandoned). Wages and profits "exploded" and announced the end of wage restraint in Germany, leading to an upsurge of strikes and fierce distribution fights and, finally, to persistent unemployment caused by low capital profitability and capital shortage. Hence, Korea today resembles the German situation in the 1970s. In the judgment of the former president of the Deutsche Bundesbank, Ottmar Emminger (1976), the delayed revaluation of the deutsche mark bears an important responsibility for the subsequent German "stagflation." Thus, instead of pegging nominal exchange rates and accommodating the inevitable real appreciation through rising wages and rising prices of nontradables, a nominal upward float is suggested by historical evidence as the only operational policy to attain external and internal balance during a rapid industrialization. Also Singapore's failed wage experiment in the early 1980s suggests that industrial upgrading is achieved with smaller risks when nominal rate flexibility quickly accommodates relative productivity growth while wages lag behind.

The Case Against Premature Asian Monetary Integration

In search of alternatives to the past dollar peg of the East Asian NICS, those calling for closer monetary cooperation among Asian countries have been becoming louder (for a more extensive discussion, see Reisen and van Trotsenburg, 1988). There are essentially two proposals: a kind of Asian monetary system around Japan on the pattern of the European Monetary System (EMS), or joint independent floating by the East Asian NICs (excluding Japan). A point in favour of closer monetary ties to the yen is that it would strengthen the yen as an international currency and thus would help to counter inflationary pressures on Japan and the NICS, if they were to emerge again from dependence on the US dollar. In this way, the Asian region could restore the independence of collective monetary control. The problem, of course, is that monetary policy would no longer be decided by the NICs but in Japan.

In a static view and thus ignoring different income levels, the East Asian NICs and Japan share some common characteristics that qualify them to be appropriate candidates for a joint currency area (see Table 11.1). Inflation differentials have narrowed during the 1980s below the margins among EMS countries, and low inflation accompanied low unemployment and high income growth. Also, important for expected long-term price trends and tax liabilities, all East Asian countries (with the notable exception of the Philippines) are characterized now by a low debt burden and the absence of noninterest budget deficits that would risk being monetized eventually. Hence, low inflation differentials would be likely to obviate the need for frequent nominal exchange rate adjustment within the proposed Asian monetary system.

In a dynamic setting, the outlook is different. As has been argued in the preceding section, the further economic development of the East Asian NICs (relative to Japan) not only requires trend flexibility in *real* exchange rates but also in *nominal* rates, if inflationary pressures are to be avoided. Countries with divergent rates of productivity growth cannot have the same inflation rate under fixed exchange rates, hence the proposed Asian monetary system would experience considerable inflation differentials — a clear invitation for speculative attacks against the system. Figure 11.3 demonstrates that, although productivity growth is still high in Japan, it has been largely exceeded by Korea's long-term productivity trend.

Figure 11.3   *Index of productivity growth in manufacturing in Japan and Korea, 1970-1988*

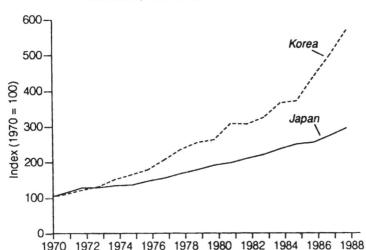

Sources: B. Balassa and J. Williamson, *Adjusting to Success: Balance of Payments Policy in the East Asian NICs* (Washington, D.C.: Institute for International Economics, 1989); Economic Planning Board, *Monthly Statistics of Korea* (1989); US Department of Labor *Monthly Labor Review* (February 1990).

The intention of the Korean and Taiwanese governments to proceed with external financial liberalization adds a second important case for nominal exchange rate flexibility. Maintaining effective domestic monetary control is difficult when the authorities simultaneously peg the domestic currency and permit free international capital flows. A case in point is again the German experience in the 1960s and early 1970s, where changes in the domestic credit component of the money supply generated offsetting movements in foreign exchange assets through balance of payments imbalances, rendering stabilization policy 'self-defeating' (Emminger, 1976). While sterilization of international capital flows is always possible in a technical sense, the sustainability of such a policy depends on the cost of reducing central bank domestic credit and on the scope and persistence of the inflows (Mathieson, 1988).

A clear case against premature Asian monetary integration is based on the small integration of trade among the Asian economies, as Park and Park (1991) rightly emphasize. Let us assume that any exchange rate arrangement between small middle-income countries and a large industrial (reserve-currency) country is bound to become asymmetrical. Japan would keep monetary independence and the four East Asian NICs would peg their currencies to the yen. By pegging to a single currency, floating rates among key currencies destabilize the effective exchange rates and increase the macroeconomic effects of external shocks for the East Asian NICS, as theoretical and empirical evidence on the optimal peg has abundantly shown (Black, 1976). With a peg to the yen, the NICs would find themselves forced to revalue their currencies against non-yen currencies if the yen appreciated sharply in the foreign exchange market. By pegging to a trade-weighted basket instead, the NICs can reduce the effect on their international trade of large swings in the values of the individual currencies in the basket.

Fluctuations in the value of the currency to which a particular currency is pegged would matter little as long as most foreign exchange transactions in trade and services (including foreign debt service) were denominated in the pegged currency. That is clearly not the case for the East Asian NICs with respect to the yen, nor will it be true in the foreseeable future. To be sure, there has recently been rapid integration of trade and foreign direct investment among the five countries. Japan is shifting assembly and low technology production to the East Asian region at a rapid pace. The NICs are narrowing or even reversing their chronic trade deficits with Japan in standardized products, such as textiles, steel, and television sets. But even if Korea, Taiwan, and Japan would quickly abolish existing trade restrictions, there would still be a long way to go before intraregional trade replaced the existing dominance of the US, European, and raw-commodity-producing trade partners. Trade integration among the Asian economies is weak, even when compared with that existing among European economies before the European Economic Community (EEC) was founded.

Moreover, similar production structures, considerable supply diversification, and proven adjustment flexibility reduce the need for swings in the real exchange rates only among Korea, Taiwan, and Japan. The other countries are still commodity-dependent (Malaysia and Indonesia), or are dependent on these countries (Singapore), or form a special political case (Hong Kong). The different structure of these countries fails to protect them from divergent swings in real exchange rates in response to external shocks. Hence, there is little scope for monetary integration in East Asia, with or without Japan.

The Case for a Managed Float Under Stochastic Shocks

Park and Park (1991) focus on fluctuations among key currencies, such as the US dollar and the yen, as the likely major disturbance to the economies of the East Asian NICS. If their concern is correct, it adds another case for nominal exchange rate flexibility, since fluctuations among third currencies act like a monetary shock on the affected economies. Fischer (1976) has demonstrated that when exogenous shocks are monetary, the variance of steady-state consumption is lower under a flexible exchange rate system than under a fixed rate system. On the other hand, when the exogenous shocks are real, the fixed rate system is preferred, relying on borrowing and lending as the most efficient buffer for the domestic economy. The use of an appropriate basket peg would then also stabilize the real effective exchange rate.

However, the recent upsurge of labour unrest in Korea may suggest that wage disturbances will become important, too. Pursuit of PPP-oriented exchange rate policies, implicitly placing a high cost on the variability of real exchange rates, will generate macroeconomic costs when wage disturbances are predominant-that is, increased instability of domestic prices and potentially increased instability of output (Dornbusch, 1982). With monetary accommodation of higher wage costs, by contrast, output is stabilized directly and indirectly by dampening the costs of imported intermediate goods.

A third source of disturbance is varying levels of protectionism by the Organisation for Economic Cooperation and Development (OECD). It will consequently be difficult (if not impossible) for the authorities in the East Asian NICs to observe and identify separately monetary and real disturbances. The optimal exchange rate regime will thus involve a system of managed floating with a degree of intervention that allows the external economy of the East Asian NICs to serve as the most efficient buffer for the domestic economy (Frenkel and Aizenman, 1982).

REFERENCES

Balassa, Bela and John Williamson (1989), *Adjusting to Success: Balance of Payments Policy in the East Asian NICs*, Institute for International Economics, Washington, D.C.

Black, Stanley (1976), 'Exchange Rate Policies for Less Developed Countries in a World of Floating Rates', *Princeton Essays in International Finance*, no. 119, Princeton, N.J.

Dornbusch, Rudiger (1982), 'PPP Exchange Rate Rules and Macroeconomic Stability", *Journal of Political Economy*, vol. 90, no. 1, pp. 158-165.

Emminger, Otmar (1976), 'Deutsche Geld-und Währungspolitik im Spannungsfeld Zwischen Innerem und äusserem Gleichgewicht (1948-1975)', in Deutsche Bundesbank (ed.), *Währung und Wirtschaft in Deutschland 1876-1975*, Frankfurt, pp. 485-554.

Fischer, Stanley (1976), 'Stability and Exchange Rate System in a Monetarist Model of the Balance of Payments', in R. Aliber (ed.), *The Political Economy of Monetary Reform*, Allanhel, Osmum and Co., Montclair, N.J., pp. 59-73.

Frenkel, Jacob and Joshua Aizenmann (1982), 'Aspects of the Optimal Management of Exchange Rates', *Journal of International Economics*, vol. 13, no. 3/4, pp. 231-256.

Giersch, Herbert (1984), 'Real Exchange Rates and Economic Development', *Kiel Working Papers*, no. 218, Kiel Institute of World Economics.

Maddison, Angus (1989), *The World Economy in the 20th Country*, OECD Development Centre Studies, Paris.

Mathieson, Donald (1988), 'Exchange Rate Arrangements and Monetary Policy' in Hang Sheng Cheng (ed.), *Monetary Policy in Pacific Basin Countries*, Kluwer Academic Publishers, Boston, Mass., pp. 43-80.

Park, Yung Chul and Won-Am Park (1991), 'Exchange Rate Policies for the East Asian Newly Industrialized Countries', in E.M. Claassen (ed.), *Exchange Rate Policies in Developing and Post-Socialist Countries*, International Center for Economic Growth, ICS Press, San Francisco, CA.

Reisen, Helmut and Axel van Trotsenburg (1988), 'Should the Asian NICs Peg to the Yen?', *Intereconomics* (July/August), pp. 172-77.

Summers, Robert and Alan Heston (1984), 'Improved International Comparisons of Real Product and Its Composition: 1950-1980', *Review of Income and Wealth*, vol. 30 (June), pp. 207-262.

12. The Case for Sterilized Intervention in Latin America

1. The Policy Setting

Much of Latin America has enjoyed a substantial revival of foreign capital inflows since 1990. While the region received about $8 billion per annum on average in the late 1980s, capital inflows rose to $24 billion in 1990, $40 billion in 1991, and $57 billion in 1992. To be sure, after a decade of foreign capital shortage, it is nice to be rediscovered as a viable investment location for funds available in world financial markets; even more so when foreign investors are prepared to pay higher prices for a country's domestic assets; it is all the nicer if the underlying capital inflows can be sustained.

An optimistic interpretation of the origins and permanence of the current investment flows to Latin America would exclude any major role for policy intervention. Such interpretation would hold the revival of flows as home-made: balanced budgets, lower inflation, privatization and deregulation, trade liberalization and the restructuring of external debt have all contributed to the re-entry of Latin America to the list of viable investment locations. There would be little reason to expect an early reversal of the capital flow which Latin America is now enjoying.

Yet, the present episode of important capital inflows is not the first this century. The most recent such inflow before the early 1990s occurred during the period from 1978 and 1982 and led to the Latin American debt crisis (Calvo, Leiderman, Reinhart, 1993). Another important episode of capital flows was noted in the 1920s (Maddison, 1985). Both periods were dominated by capital inflows from the United States, and in both periods capital inflows were eventually reversed in what turned out to be major crises. Such a reversal cannot be excluded this time since much of the current inflows seem to chase the high interest differentials which exist between North and South America. Temporary flows may give rise to policy intervention as their sudden reversal can trigger a domestic financial crisis and as 'hot money' results in undesired appreciation of the real exchange rate and to misallocation of resources.

By comparing Argentina and Mexico with Chile, this policy brief builds a case for sterilized intervention on foreign exchange markets in Latin America. To bring inflation down to the US level, both Argentina and Mexico have tightened their monetary links to the US dollar; Chile, instead, has stressed the existence of a trade-off between a domestic inflation target and a real exchange rate target. This policy brief will support Chile's policy, backed by several observations. First, it measures the temperature of capital flows to the three countries and finds them rather hot than cool. Second, it examines past disinflation performance and the outlook for future inflation in order to assess costs and benefits of exchange-rate based disinflation; it finds incomes policy too strained and anticipated rates of inflation still too high in Argentina and Mexico to warrant a case for a dollar peg. Third, the policy brief examines real exchange rate behaviour, both over the 1990s and from a global purchasing power parity (PPP) perspective, finding Argentina's currency grossly, Mexico's slightly and Chile's not at all overvalued. Fourth, arguing that fiscal restraint is neither reliable nor feasible to reduce overvaluation, the case is made for sterilized intervention by dealing with some objections which have been raised against that policy.

2. The 1990 Inflows: Cool or Hot?

A reversal of fortunes (and flows) is less likely this time than it was in the past, according to many observers. Some hold that the flows are not hot money at all but lukewarm to cool — money to stay, such as foreign direct investment (FDI) and that the share of cool money will go on rising. Nunnenkamp (1993), for example, argues that the structure of capital flows to Latin America resembles closely to those of East Asia and that the reversibility of capital inflows is linked to country-specific policy performance. In this view, capital flows are unlikely to be reversed as long as economic reform is maintained. In fact, the precarious database on capital flows makes it difficult to judge the "temperature" of the money Latin America is now receiving.

For industrialized countries, Turner (1991) has recently examined the volatility of different capital-account items in order to arrive at a distinction between permanent versus temporary, and autonomous versus accommodating flows. For the period 1975-89, those capital flows that were most highly correlated with financing requirements were classified as most accommodating. The most accommodating types of capital flows corresponded closely to the most temporary flows, proxied by the standardized variability (coefficient of variation) over the period 1975-88. Turner finally ranked four capital-account items from the most autonomous and permanent to the most accommodating and temporary (volatile) flows:

– long-term bank lending;

– foreign direct investment;

– portfolio investment;

– short-term bank flows.

There should be no cause for concern and policy intervention when net inflows mainly consist of long-term bank lending and foreign direct investment. Ever since the debt crisis, however, long-term bank lending has been an unimportant source of foreign finance for Latin America. Foreign direct investment, the second component of 'cool' capital inflows, has actually declined as a fraction of net capital inflows, down to 27 per cent in 1992 from 30 per cent in 1991 and 40 per cent in 1990 (Jaspersen and Ginarte, 1993).

Private portfolio investment flows are on the rise to become the most important source of foreign finance in advanced developing countries. According to AMEX Bank Review estimates, from 1989 to June 1992, Latin America received the bulk of private portfolio flows, $31.6 bn, while Asia received only $13.3 bn over that period. Latin American countries are more open (with the exception of Chile) than the Asian markets and therefore dominate portfolio flows, accounting for over half of the International Fin-

Table 12.1   Portfolio flows to Latin America, $ bn

	1990	1991	1992
New bond issues	1.0	4.6	8.2
Equities	-	4.4	4.5
Borrowing facilities[a]	-	4.7	6.4
	1.0	13.7	19.1

[a] Includes note issuance facilities, multiple-component facilities and other facilities underwritten by banks (for Mexico only), as well as Euro-commercial paper programmes and other non-underwritten syndicated borrowing.
Source: OECD, *Financial Market Trends*, no. 55, June 1993.

ance Corporation's (IFC) investable index, compared with just a third of the global IFC index.

The breakdown of portfolio flows reported by the OECD does not permit any judgement on their reversibility (Table 12.1). More (and across sources, consistent) data would be needed, in particular data about the sources of investment (Gooptu, 1993). Institutional investors (such as pension funds and life insurance companies) can be taken as a more risk-averse group interested in participating in long-term, high-yield investment. Euro-bond houses will be driven by portfolio diversification motives, exploiting higher mean returns and low correlation of returns between emerging and established financial markets. While this group of investors will become more important for Latin America in the future, they did not seem to provide the bulk of portfolio investment in the early 1990s. Most of the portfolio investment has come from more speculative sources in the expectation of short-term returns, notably from domestic residents with overseas holdings, private foreign investors and from managed funds (country funds and mutual funds).

There are several reasons to consider the current **rate** of capital inflows as temporary, rather than permanent. First, a large part of inflows has been in response to privatization which in countries such as Chile and Mexico is by and large now completed (Oks and van Wijnbergen, 1993). Second, part of the increased capital inflows consisted of previous flight capital which can only be repatriated once. Third, the sharp drop in US short-term interest rates has been an important stimulus to relocate assets from North to South America (Calvo, Leiderman, Reinhart, 1993). The drop reduced external debt service on floating-rate debt, improving the solvency of Latin American debtors; and not only did it raise the incentive for repatriation of funds held in the United States, but also for increased borrowing on US capital markets by Latin America. Likewise, a future cyclical swing in the United States back to higher activity levels and asset returns will be associated with decreased or reversed capital flows to Latin America. Fourth, some countries — notably Mexico, Argentina and Peru — are heavily dependent on short-term capital inflows vulnerable to quick reversal in the event of change in investor sentiment. Note that the structure and maturity of capital inflows depend on the exchange rate regime (Schweickert, 1993). As long as a peg to, say, the US dollar is credible it allows investors to exploit nominal domestic-foreign interest differentials in short-term interest rates; the peg is apt to raise the "hot money" share in capital inflows. The recent surge in capital flows to Latin America can thus be interpreted as the result of both cyclical and portfolio stock-adjustment phenomena, unlikely to be sustained. Last but not least, the sustainability of capital flows to Latin America will greatly depend on future export performance. Since the Latin American debt crisis, exports have become an important indicator of creditworthiness; ratios of debt stocks and debt service to exports are now routinely used in quantifying country risk.

Table 12.2 suggests for Argentina, Chile and Mexico that portfolio (and debt) flows have risen faster than FDI flows (the relatively high share of FDI flows in Argentina reflects the ongoing privatization process). In all three countries, government budgets are balanced and inflation has fallen. Thus, most of the foreign inflows have originated in private sector decisions. Chile differs, however, in other respects.

3. Disinflation

Chile's authorities have stressed the existence of a trade-off between a domestic inflation target and a real exchange rate target. To lock the disinflation process in, the Banco Central was made independent in 1990 with a law establishing its responsibility for monetary stability. To avoid rapid exchange rate appreciation, the authorities discouraged net inflows with a variety of measures, including a tax on short-term foreign borrowing. Chile's exchange rate is allowed to fluctuate within a band around a passive crawling basket peg set daily by the Banco Central. The width of the band was 5 per cent in June 1989 and increased to 10 per cent in January 1992. During 1990-92, the actual exchange rate has often been at the lower limit, causing the central bank to intervene. The rise in the central bank's net foreign assets corresponds almost one-to-one to the country's net capital inflows, with the current account in the balance of payments in small surplus (Table 12.2). Chile has sterilized 80-90 per cent of the inflows during 1990-92.

Both Argentina and Mexico have tightened their monetary links to the dollar much more closely than Chile did. Since April 1991, the Argentine peso has been fixed to the dollar and, under the "Convertibility Law", the central bank cannot issue money unless backed by foreign reserves. Mexico has had an active crawling peg with the dollar since 1989, with a pre-announced devaluation falling short of inflation differentials with the United States. The daily slide of the Mexican peso was first reduced in several steps, but in October 1992 the authorities doubled the maximum annual rate of devaluation to 4.6 per cent. Both countries have seen quickly rising current-account deficits, reaching 6.5 per cent of GDP in Mexico in 1992, and 4 per cent of GDP in Argentina. Nevertheless, foreign exchange reserves have risen although at a declining rate. In Mexico, much of the rise in the central bank's net foreign assets has been sterilized. To the extent that foreign investors purchased privatized government enterprises, there has

Table 12.2   Net capital inflows and monetary policy (annual averages, $bn)

	Argentina			Chile			Mexico		
	90	91	92	90	91	92	90	91	92
Net inflows	0.8	5.8	4.8	3.3	0.9	2.2	8.5	20.4	22.7
. cool (FDI)	2.0	2.5	2.5	0.2	0.6	0.6	2.6	4.8	6.2
. warm to hot	-1.2	3.3	2.3	3.1	0.3	1.6	5.9	15.6	16.5
Monetary authorities									
. rise in for. reserves	3.1	2.0	3.0	3.5	1.9	3.4	3.4	7.8	1.4
. rise in mon. base	4.0	1.1	4.4	0.3	0.4	0.4	1.9	2.5	1.6
. sterilisation	-0.9	0.9	-1.4	3.2	1.5	3.0	1.5	5.3	-0.2
Memo:									
CPI inflation (fourth quarter)	1,631	92.3	17.6	28.7	18.2	13.2	29.6	19.5	13.2
REER appreciation									
. CPI	21.5	23.9	4.7	-5.3	1.4	3.6	1.8	9.3	7.1
. WPI	-2.2	-3.7	-12.2	-6.0	5.6	3.0	0.0	10.3	9.4

Source: IDB; IFS Tapes; ECLAC; own calculation.

been an automatic sterilization of capital flows insofar as the government utilized the proceeds from sales to retire its debt towards the central bank.

Whether exchange-rate based disinflation such as practised in Argentina and Mexico can succeed depends on a) how quickly inflation can be brought down to the rich-country level and b) the cost implied by the loss of international competitiveness. Chile's authorities are still traumatized by the failure of exchange-rate based disinflation in their own country during 1978-82 when backward wage indexation hampered inflation from converging quickly to world levels (Edwards, 1992). More generally, inflation will persist unless wage inflation becomes forward-looking (by breaking backward looking indexation or by introducing an incomes policy) or unless exchange rate depreciation falls below the past rate of inflation (Dornbusch and Fischer, 1991). Table 12.3 takes a closer look at the disinflation process.

Table 12.3   Disinflation^a (annual percentage points)

	CPI $(\pi-\pi_{-1})$	Wages $(\dot{w}-\pi_{-1})$	Peso/US Dollar Exchange Rate $(\dot{e}-\pi_{-1})$	Growth (GDP, real)
Argentina				
91	-1,260	-1,268	-1,248	7.3
92	-66.3	-72.4	-80.1	6.0
Chile				
91	-8.6	+0.4	-16.2	5.8
92	-6.0	+2.7	-16.6	9.5
Mexico				
91	-11.1	-1.8	-25.6	3.6
92	-6.9	-7.1	-10.5	2.7

^{a} Accumulated inflation during year of observation.
Source: CEDEAL, Situacion Latinoamericana; own calculations.

Unlike in Chile today and a decade ago, wage disinflation has greatly contributed in both Argentina and Mexico to dampen the rise in consumer prices. While in Chile backward looking wage indexation has been replaced by bilateral bargaining between unions and employers, the country faces a labour-shortage problem these days. Argentina and Mexico, by contrast, suffer from un(der)employment which has helped wage disinflation. It is unlikely that it will do so in the future. High rates of growth have pushed Argentina towards an accelerating-inflation level of output, while incomes policy in Mexico after several years of **real wage cuts** and ahead of the 1994 election is unlikely to deliver further wage disinflation.

It is noteworthy that Mexico's stabilization performance does not look better than Chile's, in spite of Mexico's modest growth performance and exchange rate peg. To shed some further light on inflation expectations in Mexico, we can interpret interest differentials of government paper newly issued in late 1989 (*ajustabonos* and *tesobonos*) and in late 1990 (*CETES* with a maturity of 364 days).

Figure 12.1   Risk premium in Mexican interest rates

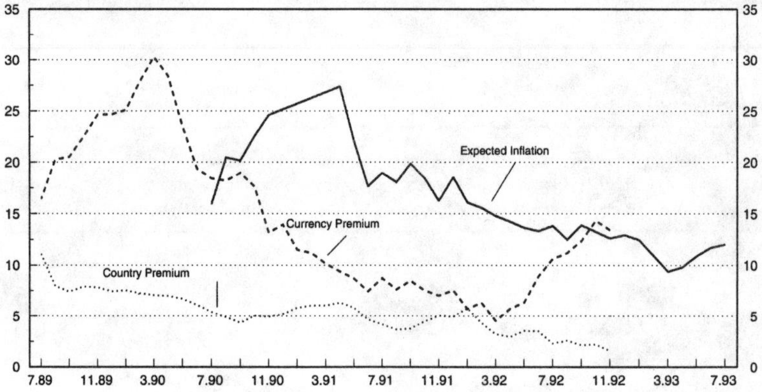

Notes: Country premium: *Tesobono* minus US Treasury Bond.
Currency premium: *CETES* minus *Tesobono*.
Expected inflation: *CETES* minus *Ajustabono*, 12 months ahead.

The variety of Mexican debt paper equips us to disentangle country risk, currency risk and expected inflation. The *tesobono* is indexed to the dollar, so comparing its yield with that of US treasury bills of equal maturity reveals essentially *country risk*. The difference between *tesobono* and *CETES*

reveals *currency risk* (although maturities are different). Anticipated inflation if calculated by comparing inflation-indexed *ajustabono* with *CETES*.
Figure 12.1 reveals that most of domestic-foreign interest differentials can
still be attributed to expected inflation, while the country premium is now
negligible. Between July 89 and March 90, both the currency premium and
expected inflation continued to rise. Subsequently, there was a continuous
and rapid fall of perceived currency risk and of anticipated inflation. While
the drop in *CETES* rates in March and April 1990 is to be attributed to the
Brady deal, the period from May 1990 on (when the daily slide was reduced
to 80 cents) can really tell us by how much the peg reduced inflation expectations. Not very much. Inflation expectations fell by 6 percentage points
(to 9 per cent in March 92 from 15 per cent in May 90). The currency premium, however, tumbled from 23 to 5 percentage points during the same
period. Since March 1992 when doubts about the conclusion of NAFTA
started to materialize, both expected inflation and the currency premium
have risen again.

Figure 12.2   CETES, term structure, (364 days minus 28 days)

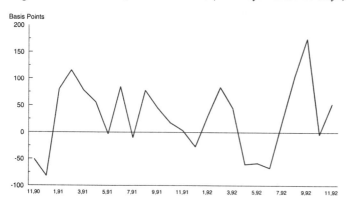

A significant reduction of inflation expectations failed also to show up in the term structure of CETES rates (Figure 12.2). The expectation hypothesis of the term structure holds that the yield curve has a negative slope when short-term interest rates (and inflation) are expected to fall below today's level. That only happened during two short periods: end 1990 and mid-1992. Reputation gains from slowing the active crawl proved to be modest and short-lived.

4. Competitiveness

While inflation has come down to comparable rates in all three countries, there is a striking contrast in the movement of their real effective exchange rates (REER). Cumulative appreciation over 1990-92 based on CPI indices has been next to nil in Chile, 19.2 per cent in Mexico, and 57.6 per cent in Argentina. The numbers in Table 12.2 are based on CEPAL (1992) data because they distinguish between indices based on wholesale prices, and consumer prices; moreover, the CEPAL indices are based on new trade weightings (1986-90), while the often-cited Morgan indices are outdated. Mexico has appreciated in REER terms on the wholesale price, as well as on a consumer price basis; the respective indices are almost back to levels attained during the period which preceded the debt crisis. Argentina's real exchange rate has clearly appreciated during the past years when measured by consumer prices; on the wholesale price level, by contrast, the currency has depreciated in real effective terms since 1989. Chile has seen some real effective appreciation since 1990, but current exchange rate levels remain far below the level attained during the last episode of heavy capital inflows.

Exchange-rate based disinflation as well as trading agreements have better chances to succeed when they are started with an initially undervalued currency. First, inflationary inertia is unlikely to be deleted entirely and immediately by anchoring the currency; some real exchange rate appreciation during the transition to (or below) US inflation levels is thus inevitable. Second, while it is sure that the entrant to a rich-country club will receive a credibility bonus during the honeymoon, there is considerable uncertainty about the effect of such entry on the equilibrium real exchange rate (Krugman, 1990). It is thus wise for the policymaker to err on the side of undervaluation since the cost of a few years' inflation needed to eliminate initial undervaluation would be lower than that needed to correct initial overvaluation.

Whether Argentina and Mexico started the dollar peg from a "considerable" level of currency undervaluation is open to dispute. Negative financial transfers during the 1980s (when new money fell short of debt service payments) had required a deviation of the exchange rate below levels set by purchasing power parity.

To find out whether currencies were initially undervalued in PPP terms we should not look at the Big Mac index, for there is a better indicator available from the UN Income Comparison Project (ICP). Figure 12.3 reveals a close cross-country correlation between PPP-adjusted real per capita GDP (relative to the US income level) and the deviation of the currency below PPP, since services tend to be cheaper in poorer countries. A country's deviation from the nonlinear OLS fit is taken as a yardstick to measure its position in world competition which excludes Africa and Eastern Europe). The underlying data are taken from the World Development Report 1991 which conveniently provides 1990 data.

Figure 12.3   Deviations from PPP, 1990

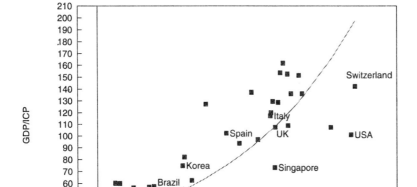

The figures show that not all Latin American debtors were "cheap" countries in PPP terms when the current episode of capital inflows started in 1990. Argentina and Brazil (who did not service foreign debt anyway) were 25 per cent and 30 per cent above the US income level as determined by their comparative per capita income (as indicated by the bold line in Figure 12.3). While Brazil has meanwhile returned to that level, Argentina has further moved to the right and to above. Mexico is now as slightly overvalued as it was undervalued in 1990 (around 10 per cent). Chile (and Colombia), by contrast, have remained very "cheap" in PPP terms by international standards. Their deviation from PPP is comparable to the some Asian competitors whom the US Treasury has not yet "negotiated" into appreciation.

The overvaluation (in PPP terms) in Argentina and, less so, in Mexico should be no cause for concern if justified by fundamental determinants. However, depressed terms of trade and sizeable import liberalization have rather called for a real **depreciation** in recent years. To the extent that thorough economic reform has raised productivity growth, this may in principle warrant some real appreciation in the exchange rate. Competitiveness will be maintained by way of lower unit costs. But it is to be doubted that productivity growth can be kept sufficiently high to compensate for still-existing differentials in inflation rates against major OECD trade partners. Sustaining a corresponding lead in productivity growth requires high investment levels. If a new surge in foreign debt dynamics is to be avoided, high investment levels require a rise in national savings, still relatively low in Latin America. This rise must originate in the private sector (the defusing bubble in stock markets may help) where the public sector balance has shifted into surplus.

For real exchange rates such analysis implies that the appreciation observed in the early 1990s will eventually give way to a depreciation. The temporary appreciation would be no problem with perfect capital markets: export firms could borrow and invest when the domestic currency is overpriced to be prepared for the time when the return of the real exchange rate to long-run equilibrium has increased their external competitiveness. But capital markets are far from perfect. The temporary appreciation is likely to cause overinvestment in services and underinvestment for exportable production. In fact, only in Chile and Mexico have the present capital inflows been used to finance increases in investment. For Mexico, however, Oks and Wijnbergen (1993) collect evidence that the real peso appreciation has tilted the balance of investment towards nontradables; fixed capital formation in manufacturing, by contrast, has declined.

In principle, Argentina and Mexico could bring the desired real depreciation about by still more fiscal restraint; but several factors make such a route both unmanageable and unreliable. First, fiscal policy is already very tight in both countries while social needs and human capital formation have badly suffered from spending cuts. Second, both countries — like the rest of the region — meet structural problems in enlarging their tax bases, with tax ratios far below OECD average. Fiscal rigidities thus prevent the use of fiscal instruments for short-term targets. Third, with increasing financial openness and a falling country-risk premium on public debt paper, interest rates and exchange rates will be less responsive to variations in the fiscal stance.

While temporary appreciation of the real exchange rate is apt to induce resources into consumption and the service sector, Latin America needs a stable, reliable and competitive level of real exchange rates if it wants to follow East Asia's path of export-led growth. Productivity growth has been faster in trade-oriented than in inward-oriented economies. Learning by doing implies that such productivity growth is a function of accumulated experiences. Hence active trade promotion (implying a competitive exchange rate) is called for to capture these dynamic gains from trade. Examining cross-country determinants of long-term (1960-85) real growth rates, De Long and Summers (1991) have found that it is necessary to be outward-oriented **and** to have a high machinery investment share in order to achieve rapid growth. Moreover, their results imply a social return to machinery investment of at least 30 per cent per year **if** exchange rate overvaluation is avoided. Using the residuals from a pooled regression on twelve developing countries during 1965-85 that explained real exchange rate movements in terms of a set of fundamentals, Edwards (1988) established an index of misalignment. Both pooled and time-series regressions showed a strong negative relationship between the average growth of real GDP and the degree of real exchange rate misalignment. The index significantly explained 27 per cent of the shortfall in GDP growth.

5. The Case for Sterilized Intervention

The rediscovery of Latin America for global asset portfolios amounts, after years of credit constraint, to an effective financial opening of the region. The resulting capital inflows cause the domestic currency to appreciate in real terms, unless there is sterilized intervention on the foreign exchange market. The nominal exchange rate appreciates when it is flexible; the domestic price level rises when the nominal rate is pegged. With either fully floating or pegged exchange rates, the real appreciation of the exchange rate resides in the failure of the monetary authorities to supply the mix of assets which domestic and foreign investors are now demanding. The authorities do nothing in the floating-rate case; they issue money in exchange for foreign assets in the pegged-rate case. They should issue bonds instead, by engaging in sterilized intervention (Kenen, 1993). To the extent that reform and stabilization cause investors to increase their demand for both domestic money and domestic bonds, the optimal response will be a higher money supply and a fractional sterilization (Frankel, 1993). Many economists are dismissive of sterilized intervention, however.

First, while there is agreement among economists that nonsterilized intervention (just as any other monetary policy) can affect nominal exchange rates, the effectiveness of sterilized intervention is much more controversial. Changing the composition of central bank assets without changing their aggregate size, it is often argued, cannot be an effective policy to influence the relative price between two monies. Such agnosticism ignores two channels through which sterilized intervention can influence exchange rates:

a) the **information** channel; Kenen (1987) suggests that intervention signals may effectively "change the market's confidence in its own projections. . . when expectations are heterogeneous and especially when a bubble appears to be building" (p. 198). Here, the monetary authority is assumed to have more information about relevant fundamentals than the market and can convey that information. However, if the information revealed involves own future policy intentions, then sterilized intervention should not be considered an independent tool for central banks.

b) the **portfolio-balance** channel; in the case of capital inflows, the corresponding rise in the central bank's net foreign assets will be sterilized by a rising supply of domestic-currency bonds. If domestic and foreign bonds are imperfect substitutes (due to currency or sovereign risk), investors will require a higher expected return on domestic bonds to hold their larger outstanding stock; the currency will tend to depreciate. Casual observation (Cumby and Obstfeld, 1983 on Mexico; Edwards and Khan, 1985, on Colombia) suggests that the portfolio-balance channel can be exploited by Latin America's monetary authorities. Uncovered interest parity does not hold, and there exists a stable relationship between domestic government debt and the domestic-foreign interest differential.

For OECD countries, recent empirical evidence shows that sterilized intervention operations do affect exchange rates. While the Jurgensen report (1983) only found small and transitory effects for the period 1973-81, studies of intervention policies in the 1980s suggest that more recent operations have been more effective (Dominguez and Frankel, 1990). A recent study, using daily data on official intervention operations of 16 central banks participating in the procedure, shows that co-ordinated interventions since the Plaza agreement proved in practice to be both effective and repeatedly strong enough to reverse the market direction of exchange rates (Catte, Galli, and Rebecchini, 1992). The improved empirical support for the efficacy of sterilized intervention may be explained by the fact that the US, Japanese and German authorities avoided intervening at cross-purposes over the 1980s, in contrast to the preceding decade. Efficacy also requires a certain degree of exchange rate flexibility to create sufficient investor awareness that the exchange rate is variable (Frankel, 1993).

A second objection to sterilized intervention, particularly raised in the Latin American context (Calvo, Leiderman, and Reinhart, 1993), stems from the alleged fiscal costs. This objection is based on two arguments: (a) To dampen the appreciation, the central bank typically has to swap low-yield foreign exchange for high-yield domestic bonds; the accumulated interest differential can become an important fiscal (or quasi-fiscal) burden. (b) Sterilized intervention deprives the government of a reduction in its debt-service burden by preventing the decline in the domestic interest rate that normally accompanies a capital inflow. Both arguments are unlikely to hold in present value terms if the capital inflow and exchange rate appreciation are correctly assessed as temporary:

–   With risk premiums in domestic interest rates sufficiently small, the short-term fiscal losses derived from swapping low-yield foreign exchange for high-yield domestic bonds should be partly offset by a subsequent capital gain derived from the appreciation of foreign exchange reserves. The central bank, like Friedman's (1953) stabilizing speculator, should make money by buying dollars when they are cheap (in peso terms) and by selling dollars when they are dear. Moreover, the evidence for developing countries has shown a shortfall of domestic-foreign return differentials to compensate for depreciation losses (Frankel, 1989). This would imply that the authorities derive a net fiscal gain from engaging in sterilized intervention of temporary capital inflows. Note that sterilized intervention may raise interest rates when the disturbance is not external (as assumed here), but due to higher domestic money demand or an improvement in the trade balance which require monetary or fiscal expansion (Frankel, 1993).

–   While it is true that sterilized intervention prevents a decline in interest rates that normally accompanies a capital inflow, it does not follow that alternative exchange rate regimes would compare favourably in the longer run. Sterilized intervention aims at dampening real exchange rate overshooting. This implies less real appreciation of the exchange rate first, and less real depreciation back to the equilibrium rate later. Interest parity requires a corresponding move in real interest rates: with sterilized intervention, the lower real appreciation entails a comparatively higher level of real interest rates which is then offset by a comparatively lower interest rate level when the currency depreciates. But what really matters for public debt dynamics in the long run, is the real GDP growth relative to real interest rates (Reisen, 1989). The Asian example suggests that sterilized intervention can succeed in keeping monetary aggregates on target, hence keeping inflationary expectations down, that it simultaneously dampens real exchange rate variability, hence keeping foreign exchange risk in check, and that low inflation and reliable exchange rates are good for long-run growth.

Third, developing countries may experience practical problems with sterilized intervention due to underdeveloped domestic securities markets (Fischer and Reisen, 1992). Lack of government debt paper (which is often the case in Asian countries) forces central banks to issue obligations of their own, swelling central bank liabilities relative to the monetary base. Putting pressure on the refinancing schedule of central bank liabilities, sterilized intervention can endanger future control of the monetary base. Such pressure on the monetary base can be attenuated to some degree by carrying intervention in the foreign exchange market from the spot to the forward market. Finally, with shallow domestic securities markets, sterilized intervention in developing countries can exert a contractionary supply effect which is felt much quicker than in the typical OECD country: the sectoral distribution of the domestic credit squeeze is sharper; working capital costs for unpreferred borrowers in the informal credit markets rise faster; and the sale of government bonds tends to crowd out the shallow corporate bond market. But these are second-order objections to a first-best policy response. Some Asian examples will demonstrate that there are always ways to solve these practical problems.

6. Generalized Forms of Sterilized Intervention: Some Asian Examples

The Asian sterilization practice holds lessons for open economies with underdeveloped securities markets. In fact, the monetary authorities in Singapore, Indonesia and Taiwan have dealt with massive capital flows without losing price stability and external competitiveness. Moreover, they have not been helped by capital controls to target simultaneously money supply and exchange rates. But they do not shy away from (sometimes mandated) transactions to manipulate the flow of liquidity into the banking system in response to external capital flows. They often swap government excess savings (originating, say, in social security funds or public enterprises) held with banks into (and out of) government bonds. This practice can be considered as a generalized form of sterilized intervention. It should be noted that the approach relies on the existence of public-sector savings and hence on "fiscal complicity". Moreover, Frankel (1993) suggests that Asia retained the ability to sterilize with open capital markets because domestic financial liberalization has been delayed.

Singapore and its neighbour countries, Malaysia and Indonesia, have been largely (though not continuously) successful in reconciling exchange rate stability at competitive levels (Figure 12.4) and a fair amount of monetary independence with an open capital account. In Singapore, any remaining capital controls had been abolished by June 1978, motivated by Singapore's

Figure 12.4   Real effective exchange rates: Indonesia, Malaysia, and
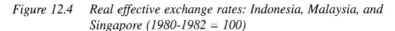
Singapore (1980-1982 = 100)

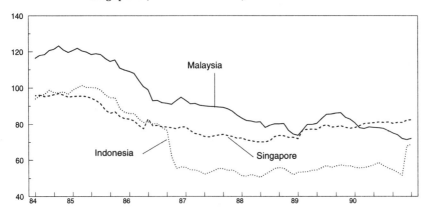

Source: JP. Morgan, *World Financial Markets.*

aspiration to strengthen its role as an international financial centre. And Singapore's financial centre has traditionally been to Indonesia and Malaysia what the informal curb market is to so many developing countries. Hence, capital controls could not have been effective. The Indonesian and Malaysian authorities simply had to cope with open capital accounts. All three countries have nevertheless managed to shelter their monetary base from increases in foreign exchange reserves and to slow down an incipient appreciation of their currencies.

Singapore has been extremely successful in reconciling financial openness with stable money supply growth, very low inflation and remarkably stable real effective exchange rates. Singapore's authorities did not only have to cope with the usual constraints imposed on stabilization policies by financial openness. By choosing the US dollar (in addition to the Singapore dollar) as a vehicle for the development of an international financial centre, the authorities had also to cope with the risk of currency substitution in favour of the US dollar (or, alternatively, with the "internationalization" of the Singapore dollar).

The division of the Singaporean banking system into a domestic banking sector operating in Singapore dollars and an off-shore sector transacting in US dollars has provided the monetary authorities with a separation fence against speculative capital movements. Since the establishment of full convertibility in 1978, however, the height of the separation fence has been lowered, notably with residents' access to loans and deposits in the US dollar market. A major explanation for Singapore's achievements in targeting money **and** exchange rates does thus not seem to lie in the insulation of its domestic financial sector, but can be found in its exchange rate management and sterilization policies (Claassen, 1992).

Since 1975, Singapore has chosen a multi-currency peg to stabilize the effective (trade-weighted) exchange rate. Official foreign exchange reserves were four times higher than the monetary base in 1990, pointing to considerable sterilization activity in the past. As a result of heavy sterilized intervention, strong net capital inflows in 1984/85 and 1989/90 neither resulted in a rise of the monetary base nor of the real effective exchange rate.

Central to the understanding of Singapore's sterilized intervention policies are the combined effects of a public-sector budget surplus and portfolio allocations of the Central Provident Fund, a mighty social pension fund, for the management of domestic liquidity. Until recently, employers and employees had to contribute each 25 per cent of wages to the Fund, a very high proportion which explains to a large degree the high level of Singapore's domestic savings. Currently, the combined rate stands at 40 per cent (17.5 per cent for employers, 22.5 for employees). For prudential reasons, the Central Provident Fund's portfolio consists mostly of government bonds. With the government budget mostly in surplus and with a high level of forced private savings, private sector liquidity is always tight. Consequently, while sterilized intervention may be usually characterized by, say, the central bank's purchase of foreign exchange in exchange for central bank liabilities (a rise in the monetary base) and a **subsequent** contraction of central bank credit to the domestic sector, the order is exactly reversed in Singapore. Money and foreign exchange market intervention regulate money supply instead of reacting to changes of the money supply (Moreno, 1989). Figure 12.5 illustrates the specific monetary-fiscal policy mix on which sterilized intervention has been based in Singapore: quasi-permanent budget surpluses as well as government deposits and other central bank liabilities (mostly to the Central Provident Fund) have consistently tended to contract the money supply. Nonsterilized intervention on the foreign exchange market has offset the liquidity drain. Fine-tuned exchange market intervention served to adjust the money supply to satisfy the government's exchange rate target.

Figure 12.5   Sources of monetary base: Singapore

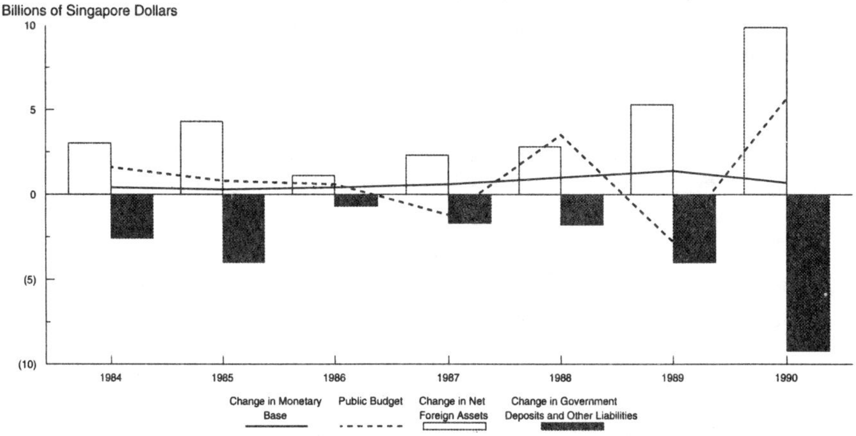

Source: IMF, *International Financial Statistics.*

We turn to **Malaysia** now which shares with Singapore a common monetary history (and an excellent track record of low inflation and Central Bank credibility), due to their Currency Board established in 1897 and ended in 1967. Government revenue is still quite dependent of oil and other raw materials, and thus tends to rise and fall with the movements in foreign exchange reserves. Since Malaysia has experienced permanent budget deficits over the past two decades (in contrast to Singapore), higher raw material prices raise government revenues and lower Central Bank credit to the government, thus tending to stabilize the monetary base.

Since 1983 on a basket peg, the Malaysian ringgit is increasingly determined by asset markets, but the Central Bank is an active intervener on the foreign exchange and monetary markets. For foreign exchange management, the public oil company has been an important instrument (earning up to one fifth of the country's foreign exchange earnings). For the management of domestic liquidity, the Employee Provident Fund has played an important role, though less so than in Singapore. The Fund is the country's biggest saver and holds 20 per cent of total domestic financial assets. Usual intervention practice is directly on the foreign exchange market, and often the sterilization is only done subsequently. The well-developed swap market was used extensively in the past. Meanwhile, open market operations have become increasingly important, thanks to an active policy to foster direct securities markets (credit rating for private debt paper, broad supply of government securities, share issue price regulation for the stock market).

From 1989 on, however, the policy of targeting interest rates and exchange rates simultaneously became increasingly unsustainable. Strong domestic credit demand, growing FDI and short-term capital inflows which were incompletely sterilized produced an inflationary rise in the monetary base. Rescue measures were implemented without much hesitation. The legal reserve ratio of the banking system was significantly raised to dampen the rise in the volume of currency outside the banking system. To drain excess liquidity before entering the banking system, the monetary authorities resorted to quantity-oriented measures in 1990, in particular the central management of government deposits which were withdrawn from the banking system and transferred on a special account at the Central Bank.

Indonesia has quite successfully defied all orthodoxy established in the development literature on the sequencing of reform. The capital account was opened first (1971), trade was gradually liberalized in the early 1980s, interest rates were freed in 1983 and institutional aspects of the financial system were deregulated in 1988. Indonesia, a resource-rich but low-income country, did not encounter the usual difficulties in targeting money and exchange rates until quite recently. The government controlled a large share of foreign exchange earnings from oil and gas exports which could be used to counteract movements in the private capital account of the country. On the other hand, the Indonesian private sector lacked creditworthiness in offshore markets.

Figure 12.4 displays the remarkable stability of Indonesia's real effective exchange rate from end 1986 on. According to textbook economics, the peg of the Indonesian rupiah (even if it is not a nominal peg to a single currency, but a peg to a trade-weighted basket of currencies) would deprive the monetary authorities of all power to influence domestic economic conditions with open capital markets. Monetary tools could only be assigned the role of preserving external balance (say, keep foreign exchange reserves stable), while internal balance (with absolutely flexible labour markets, this can only be low inflation) would be assigned to fiscal policy. In practice, however, the central bank has retained considerable power on monetary control, in joint action with the government.

Monetary independence in spite of an open capital account stems largely from two different sources, a) the risk premium (or credit rationing) of private Indonesian offshore debt and b) the use of public enterprises' deposits in commercial banks for monetary management. Indonesia's capital account is still dominated by concessional long-term capital flows, and foreign exchange reserves by the trade balance. This reflects the fact that the Indonesian private sector until recently had almost no access to commercial foreign lending. Now, things have started to change with short-term flows gaining importance in the capital account. Indonesian companies tried to escape monetary tightening at home by borrowing offshore to avoid rising domestic interest rates.

The internationalization of the big Indonesian companies and falling liquidity constraints in the wake of the 1988 deregulation of the banking system have strengthened the potential of "hot money" movements. The two jump devaluations of the rupiah in 1983 and 1986, each around 30 per cent against the US dollar, underline the potential return to speculation in foreign exchange. Meanwhile, the central bank is only building up its reputation to defend the stability of the currency. Unlike most central banks in OECD countries, however, it cannot spread the costs of external shocks and financial crises through time. A fragile international credit standing inhibits consumption smoothing based on commercial foreign borrowing. Domestic securities markets are too small to absorb shocks through variations in domestic liquidity. Therefore, instead of using indirect money tools, the monetary authorities resorted twice recently to direct credit rationing by way of mandated transactions.

Early 1991, rumours of an imminent devaluation started spreading because of falling oil prices in the wake of the Persian Gulf War. Official exchange reserves started to decline slightly. End February 1991, state enterprises were instructed to convert bank deposits into holdings of Bank Indonesia certificates (SBI); actual conversions totalled 42 per cent of outstanding money supply (M_1) and equivalent to about 7.5 per cent of GNP. At the same time, to ease the immediate liquidity impact of this move, the central bank acquired an equivalent amount in money market instruments (SBPUs), resulting in a net withdrawal of liquidity. These mandated transactions were similar to those taken in mid-1987, when state-owned enterprises were ordered to withdraw rupiah from government banks for the purchase of SBI, equivalent to about 5 per cent of the 1987 money supply (M_1). In both cases, the relocation of government-owned deposits served to defend the currency and to contain inflationary pressures. Strong interest rate hikes had to be accepted, but they were short-lived and thus failed to cause a recession. The pragmatic use of credit-rationing measures also helped strengthen SBIs and SBPUs as instruments of monetary control. Banks that lost their deposits were in turn partially compensated through the sale of SBPUs to the central bank. Since the SBPUs are of shorter maturity than the 12-months SBIs, the central bank has gained better control of the domestic component of base money through the timing of SBPU repurchases.

Taiwan's foreign exchange reserves grew from a level of around 10 billion US dollars in 1981 to more than 80 billion US dollars ten years later. Most of that rise occurred during 1985 and 1987. To smoothen the inevitable appreciation of the New Taiwan dollar (which rose by almost 40 per cent against the US dollar over that period), the central bank engaged in frequent sterilization policies. An amount equivalent to 65 per cent of the increase in the central bank's net foreign assets was sterilized by forcing commercial banks to buy treasury bills and certificate of deposits issued by the central bank. The remainder was sterilized by using Taiwan's postal savings system. Part of postal savings are redeposited with the central bank, and part with the domestic banking system. To contract the net domestic assets component of base money, it sufficed to order a rise in the redeposit share held with the central bank. It has been quite an achievement of Taiwan's monetary authorities to sterilize the country's excess savings (running up to 20 per cent of GDP a year) and to keep monetary aggregates, inflation and exchange rate appreciation in check.

The Asian evidence establishes clearly that sterilized intervention is an effective instrument to target money and exchange rates, even absent capital controls. Many economists tend to explain the effectiveness of sterilized intervention with foreign exchange risk and expectations thereof alone. Such explanations do not only ignore the dualism between formal and informal sectors and the informational imperfections which give rise to curb markets whose assets have a low degree of international tradability. They also ignore the art of central banking in South-East Asia which consists in the pragmatic use of public institutions such as social security funds, state banks and public enterprises as a monetary instrument. The use of public-sector savings or of mandatory private savings has to make up for the lack of developed domestic money markets on which in most industrial countries open-market operations are effected. Such a policy, however, requires public-sector savings and thus fiscal discipline. Where tax ratios have been raised and government budgets been balanced in Latin America, the fundamental requirement to repeat the Asian example of sterilized intervention is now fulfilled.

REFERENCES

Calvo, G., L. Leiderman and C. Reinhart (1993), "Capital Inflows and Real Exchange Rate Appreciation in Latin America: The Role of External Factors", *IMF Staff Papers*, vol. 40, no. 1, pp. 108-151.

Catte, P., G. Galli and S. Rebecchini (1992), "Exchange Markets Can Be Managed!", *International Economic Insights,* September/October, pp. 17-21.

Claassen, E.M. (1992), "Financial Liberalization and Its Impact on Domestic Stabilization Policies: Singapore and Malaysia", *Weltwirtschaftliches Archiv,* 128.1, pp. 136-167.

Cumby, R. and M. Obstfeld (1983), "Capital Mobility and the Scope for Sterilization: Mexico in the 1970s", in: P. Aspe, R. Dornbusch and M. Obstfeld (eds), *Financial Policies and the World Capital Market: The Problem of Latin American Countries,* Chicago: Chicago University Press, pp. 245-269.

Delong, B. and L. H. Summers (1991), "Equipment Investment and Economic Growth", *Quarterly Journal of Economics,* 56.2., pp. 445-502.

Dominguez, K. and J. Frankel (1990), "Does Foreign Exchange Intervention Matter? Disentangling the Portfolio and Expectations Effects for the Mark", Cambridge, Mass.: *NBER Working Paper* no. 3299.

Dornbusch, R. and S. Fischer (1991), *Moderate Inflation,* NBER Working Paper no. 3896 (November).

Edwards, S. (1988), *Exchange Rate Misalignment in Developing Countries,* Washington, D.C.: World Bank, Occasional Papers no. 2.

Edwards, S. and M. Khan (1985), "Interest Rate Determination in Developing Countries: A Conceptual Framework", *IMF Staff Papers,* 32.3, pp. 377-403.

Fischer, B. and H. Reisen (1992), "Policies towards Capital Account Convertibility", Paris: OECD Development Centre, *Policy Brief* no. 4.

Frankel, J. (1989), "Quantifying International Capital Mobility in the 1980s", Cambridge, Mass.: *NBER Working Papers* no. 2856.

Frankel, J. (1993), *Sterilization of Money Inflows: Difficult (Calvo) or Easy (Reisen)?,* Washington, D.C.: International Monetary Fund, mimeo.

Friedman, M. (1953), "The Case for Flexible Exchange Rates", in M. Friedman, *Essays in Positive Economics,* Chicago: Chicago University Press, pp. 157-203.

Gooptu, S. (1993), *Portfolio Investment Flows to Emerging Markets*, Washington, D.C.: The World Bank, WPS 1117.

Jaspersen, F. and J. Ginarte (1993), "External Resource Flows to Latin America: Recent Developments and Prospects", in: C. Bradford (ed.), *Mobilising International Investment for Latin America*, Paris: OECD Development Centre.

Jurgenson, P. (1983), Report of the Working Group on Exchange Market Intervention, G7 Report.

Kenen, P. (1987), "Exchange Rate Management: What Role for Intervention?", *American Economic Review*, 77.2., pp. 194-199.

Kenen, P. (1993), "Financial Opening and the Exchange Rate Regime", in: H. Reisen and B. Fischer, *Financial Opening: Policy Issues and Experiences in Developing Countries*, Paris: OECD, pp. 237-262.

Krugman, P. (1990), "Macroeconomic Adjustment and Entry into the EC: A Note", in: C. Bliss and J. Braga de Macedo (eds.) *Unity with Diversity in the European Economy: The Community's Southern Frontier*, Cambridge, Cambridge University Press, pp. 131-140.

Maddison, A. (1985), *Two Crises: Latin America and Asia, 1929-38 and 1973-83*, Paris: OECD Development Centre.

Moreno, R. (1989), "Exchange Rates and Monetary Policy in Singapore and Hong Kong", *Hong Kong Economic Papers*, 19, pp. 21-42.

Nunnenkamp, P. (1993), *The Return of Foreign Capital to Latin America*, Kiel: Institut für Weltwirtschaft, Kiel Working Paper no. 574.

Oks, D. and S. Van Wijnbergen (1993), "Mexico After the Debt Crisis: Is Growth Sustainable?", in: C. Bradford (ed.), *Mobilising International Investment in Latin America*, Paris: OECD Development Centre.

Reisen, H. (1989), "Public Debt, External Competitiveness, and Fiscal Discipline in Developing Countries", *Princeton Studies in International Finance*, no. 66.

Reisen, H. (1993), "South-East Asia and the Impossible Trinity", *International Economic Insights*, May/June, pp. 21-23.

Schweickert, R. (1993), *Lessons from Exchange Rate Based Disinflation in Argentina*, Kiel: Institut für Weltwirtschaft, Kiel Working Paper no. 567.

Index